Dharma Talks

Dharma Talks

The Best of Pali Meditations

Tseten Thokmey
(Alexander Duncan)

CHRONIKER PRESS △ TORONTO

Alexander Duncan (Tseten Thokmey) (b. 1954) is the author of *Buddhist Self-Ordination: A Dharma Strategy for the West, Khatas, Dharma Notes, Fundamental View: Ten Talks on the Pali Canon,* and *Conversations with the Buddha: A Reader's Guide to the Digha Nikaya.* He holds an Honours B.A. in English from York University. His blog, palisuttas.com, is read in 138 countries. He lives in Toronto with his dharma cat, Zenji.

First Edition (previously *Dharma Notes,* fourth edition)

Printed in the United States of America

ISBN: 978-1-10-593846-7 (paper)
ISBN: 978-1-365-86655-5 (cloth)

chronikerpress.com

For Dave

OBSIDIAN

I experience the slick of my brain,
Geometric structures,
Ecstasy,
Consciousness.
Immediately
I realize my wounds.
Perfectly brilliant,
Either slips back.
Ecstatic perhaps, my brain
A serpent,
I see the body experienced.
The serpent knows.
Clarity touches.
Vivid.
Smooth.
I can't, disappearing along
Evolution, slowly coated
By facts, backgrounds, anything.
I recognize and state the fact.
The room is raised in feet.
The sensation of my arm happens.
The goddess,
Psychotic, primitive, superior, anything,
Simultaneously OM, paradoxically
Appears in my vision.
Without a future, everything slips.
My mane-shaped existence
Contemplates chanting.

Contents

Preface

THIS BOOK ORIGINATED in a series of online blog posts located at www.palisuttas.com. This blog is now read in 138 countries. Originally intended to present a synopsis of the major *suttas* of the Pali Canon, very quickly it became something much more extensive and comprehensive, including dharma talks on my research that I was invited to present to the members of the Buddha Center, original poetry, and original experimental translations of the chapters of the Tao Te Ching. The synopses of the *suttas* of the Pali Canon became a series of talks on the Digha Nikaya, which has been published separately by Chroniker Press as *Conversations with the Buddha: A Reader's Guide to the Digha Nikaya.* My Tao Te Ching translations will soon be published by Chroniker Press as *The Right Way of Laozi.*

Dharma Talks were originally conceived of as a collection of occasional articles, including speculations about a variety of topics of Buddhist interest, entitled *Dharma Notes.* However, over time the book has become more of a digest of my general dharma talks that I presented to the members of the Buddha Center and the Riverview Dharma Centre, which were generally one hour in duration (approximately five thousand words, the same as the Tao Te Ching). Although the number of chapters is the same, none of the original chapters has been retained from *Dharma Notes.* This is an entirely new book with a new title.

Alexander Duncan (Tseten Thokmey)
February 3, 2017
Toronto, Ontario

1
Buddhist Hermeneutics and the Problem of Tradition

BUDDHIST HERMENEUTICS – FROM the Greek *hermeneutikos,* 'of or for interpreting,' commonly but erroneously associated with the Greek god Hermes, the messenger of the Gods – is still in its infancy in the West, as the Dharma Transmission to the West, now in its 108th year, continues to take hold and grow. The most common Buddhist hermeneutic, especially among both traditional and modern Theravadins, is *historicism,* i.e., the belief that the meaning of the Buddhist message is identical with the words uttered by the historical Buddha. Although this hermeneutic may seem to many to be straightforward and self-evident, critical evaluation reveals it to involve numerous problems and ambiguities, including:

- Objective identification of the actual historical words of the Buddha (the *Buddhavacana*);
- Determination of the correct meanings of the words and the doctrines that they imply;
- Resolution of apparent contradictions;
- Resolution of apparent nonsense, including the problem of what nonsense actually is in the context of cultural relativism (i.e., what may be nonsense to you may not be nonsense to me and vice versa, and what may be nonsense to us may not have been nonsense 2,500 years ago); and

- The question of whether the *Buddhavacana* is comprehensive, complete, and exclusive, even if it is accurate and true.

These problems occur against a religious backdrop that tends to hold, influenced by the Buddhist doctrine of the "degenerate age," that "later = false," thus disparaging later texts as inherently non-historical and dubious, even within the Pali canonical tradition itself. This kind of necrotizing fasciitis threatens to devolve into nihilism. The latter also represents a decisive break with orthodox Theravada, even though many people who criticize the Pali Canon in this way often hold themselves out to be Theravadin.

The orthodox Theravada, which still has numerous adherents, both in Asia and the West, holds that the Pali texts of the Pali Canon, including the Vinaya, Suttas, and Abhidhamma, all incorporate the exact words used by Siddhattha Gotama, in the language spoken by the Buddha, remembered pre-eminently by Ananda, who was graced with the gift of photographic memory, and verified by the arhants of the First Buddhist Council and their successors who were perfect and infallible in their understanding of the dharma. Thus, the collective text of the Pali Canon is the literal *Buddhavacana*, handed down without error for 2,500 years. We in the West are of course familiar with such thinking among Jews and Christians (the Bible is the literally inspired Word of Yahweh or the direct inspiration of the Sophia) and Muslims (the Quran is the literal Word of Allah, dictated to Mohammed by the angel Gabriel and preserved through an impeccable process of collation, after which all deviant texts were destroyed).

However, even if we accept the orthodox premise, the problem of hermeneutics is not yet solved. There is still the problem of interpreting the meaning of the language of the infallibly revealed scriptures and doctrines and the questions as to whether these meanings are complete and comprehensive, and whether the texts themselves exhaust all possible meanings, therefore illegitimizing any subsequent interpretation.

A lot of academic and scholarly effort has been put into the Pali Canon in the past hundred years, thanks to the pioneering efforts of F. Max Muller, Rhys Davids, and others. Although there are extremists who deny any legitimacy to the Pali Canon, the general consensus today is that the Pali Canon, especially the Four Great Nikayas, so-called (the Digha, Majjhima, Samyutta, and Anguttara), represent the historically oldest strata of Buddhist scriptures, and are probably substantially similar to the books that were compiled in the first century BCE, three hundred years after the death of the Buddha, even though we have few texts actually dating from that period due to the perishable nature of the writing materials that were used. This has led some denialists to reject the Pali Canon tradition entirely as the invention of "Western Orientalists."[1] It might even be true that these texts are substantially similar to the texts as they appeared in the mid-third century BCE, about 150 years after the Buddha's death. (For comparison, this corresponds to the Christian literature between 180 and 380 CE, none of which is canonical.)

On the other hand, the Pali Canon has the virtues of repetition and size, so that it is possible to identify recurrent themes in the texts that were *presumably* emphasized in the original teachings. However, even here there is controversy. The important Polish Buddhologist, Stanislaw Schayer, undeservedly little known in the West, opined that the exceptional, contrary, and idiosyncratic material that was left in the Pali Canon may be even more significant than the stock doctrines precisely because they were left in the Canon by its reactionary redactors. By emphasizing *these* teachings, Schayer arrives at a proto-Mahayanist view that contradicts the mainstream view that still regards the Theravada as the most historically authentic school. Based on the current consensus of the dates of the Buddha, called the "median chronology," which places his "passing on" (*parinibbana*) about 400 BCE, these texts were passed down orally for about three hundred years before being committed to writing, although some parts of some texts may have been written down as early as the third century BCE. The Four Nikayas consist of several thousand *suttas,* or 'discourses,' mostly attributed to the Buddha, purportedly delivered over the course of forty-five years after his Enlightenment experience. These include the places, names of the interlocutors, and some-

---

1. Tenzin Peljor (personal communication).

times evidential information concerning the relative dates of the discourses. However this information is highly dubious given two passages in the Vinaya that describe a process of arbitrarily assigning places to *suttas* for which places were not known, and discrepancies of places and people involved in discourses that are very similar or even identical (of course, it is also possible that the Buddha gave the same or similar discourses in different places, especially during the last years of his teaching career). On the other hand, the doctrinal significance of such differences is negligible.

In English translation, the Four Nikayas constitute about six thousand pages, or two million words. This corresponds to roughly 250 hours of speech, about five hours for each year that the Buddha reportedly taught. The *suttas* represent the Buddha as engaged in a virtually continuous process of communication with monastics, lay followers, and interested visitors based on a dialogic question-and-answer process, with intermittent wandering and retreats. Clearly, if this is true, five hours per year does not come close to what the Buddha must actually have said, even allowing for repetitions, which also occur in the Pali *suttas* themselves, so these cancel out. Even if we cautiously assume that the Buddha spoke for two hours per day, two days per week, his actual speech must have been nearly fifty times this. Thus, it seems that the view of the Dharmaguptaka, a sect of the "Hinayana" (c 232 BCE), that the "original teachings of the Buddha had been lost," is justified, *at least in part.* It has also been pointed out that many of the passages in the Pali Canon pertaining to the major doctrines are merely lists; the doctrines themselves are not explained in any detail. Thus, a great range of interpretations is still possible.

Most scholars today do not believe that the Pali language in which the Pali Canon is preserved is the actual language of the historical Buddha. Rather, Pali appears to have been an artificial language hybridizing several prakrit dialects constructed post facto in order to address the increasing linguistic and geographic diversity of the Buddhist community (*sangha*) that emerged in Western India during the third century BCE. On the other hand, it seems likely that Pali was similar to the language or languages that the Buddha spoke. Thanks to the herculean efforts of the Pali Text Society, especially the *Pali-English Dictionary* (1921–1925), Pali is fairly well understood, though more comparative and historical studies of the vocabulary as used all through the Canon need to be done and are now possible using computer analysis. Pali and Sanskrit also draw on a common set of etymological roots in Vedic proto-Sanskrit, the study of which greatly facilitates interpretation and translation. Peter Masefield has complained, however, that Pali translators are insufficiently attentive to the technical philosophical meanings of the words.

The state of knowledge in this area has been nicely summarized by Bhikkus Sujato and Brahmali in their monograph on this topic entitled "The Authenticity of the Early Buddhist Texts," published by Chroniker Press. Rhys Davids and Pande (*Studies in the Origins of Buddhism*) have also made significant contributions. Sujato and Brahmali appear to adhere to the revisionist Theravadin sect sometimes called "Modern Theravada," a.k.a Progressive Theravada, Early Buddhism, or Original Buddhism. The main conclusion of this study that is relevant to the present discussion is that the Early Buddhist Texts (EBTs), which they identify generally with the Four Great Nikayas and some other texts including the Vinaya disciplinary code (*patimokkha*), parts of the Sutta Nipata, Udana, Itivuttaka, Dhammapada, Theragatha, and Therigatha, are "authentic." Their general argument is that the description of the political geography, social conditions, economic conditions and trade, and religious context accurately correspond to the period during which the Buddha lived and taught; that oral textual transmission is both reliable and dateable; that the remarkable vision and consistency of the Canon, including peculiarities that can only be explained historically, is evidence of a unitary founder who was a real historical person; that archaeological research supports the antiquity and accuracy of the Pali Canon and the reality of the Buddha; and that a comparison of later and earlier strata of the Canon shows an ideological development typical of other religions.

The whole tenor of Sujato and Brahmali's argument consists of general assertions of this kind, such specific passages as they adduce having little or no doctrinal significance. However, even if we grant the veracity of this argument, it comes nowhere near proving their main thesis, their "theory of authenticity" (TOA), i.e., "that texts that purport of be the words of the historical Buddha and his immediate disciples were in fact spoken by them" (p. 9). Although their language largely finesses this point, if their argument is that the words contained in these texts accurately preserve the actual words of the historical Buddha, and not merely the general situation,[2] this conclusion is far too specific to be supported by the evidence that they adduce. Perhaps it would be fair to say, then, that the Pali Canon preserves an overview *or outline* of the *major doctrines* of the historical Buddha *as interpreted by his successors* and preserved as they were perceived and understood roughly 150 to three hundred years after the Buddha's death. I believe Bhikku Bodhi has made the point more correctly when he states that the Pali Canon *may* include passages that *resemble* certain statements originally made by the Buddha. The problem then is how to identify and extract the true utterances of the Buddha, such as they are, from the mass of material in which they are embedded, or if this is even possible.

Some Pali linguists would like to suggest that the strict application of a scientific methodology of Pali linguistics to the Pali Canon in combination with other critical methods could identify such passages. However, in practice one finds that such academics tend to find what they want to find, merely constructing an explanatory framework that justifies post facto their own particular ideological and cultural view. One can of course "connect the dots" to justify

---

2. In fact three forms of the TOA are identifiable: (1) the strong form: where the Pali Canon quotes the historical Buddha, it does so accurately, with little or no variation from his actual diction and syntax (the orthodox Theravadin view); (2) the semi-strong form: where the Pali Canon quotes the Buddha, it does so using diction and syntax that broadly resembles the actual diction and syntax of the historical Buddha; (3) the weak form: the general situations described in the Pali Canon accurately portray the life and times of the Buddha, including his general ideas; some actual sayings of the Buddha probably survive in the Canon, and it is possible to trace a kind of chronological development in the Canon. The weak form of the TOA necessarily allows for a broad range of alternative doctrinal formulations. At best, the evidence for the TOA supports the weak form.

any particular theory in retrospect, simply rejecting passages as "late" or using other criteria that do not conform to one's preferred interpretation, based on the fallacy already alluded to that "late = false." (Academics frequently fall into this hole.) Let us look at this hermeneutical doctrine in detail.

The assertion that "late = false" is based on two premises: (1) that everything that is true about the Buddha's teachings was said by the Buddha himself, and perhaps his immediate disciples, and (2) that no doctrinal development is possible or permissible. That is to say, that the Buddha's teachings are comprehensive, complete, and exclusive. Therefore, all that is necessary is to identify the "original teachings." However, I have already shown that it is extremely improbable that the Pali Canon preserves *all* of the original teachings of the Buddha or that it is even possible to identify the *actual* words of the Buddha. What we have is a composite of what the Buddha said and did, what his immediate disciples understood him to mean and do, and what their successors understood them all to mean, all inextricably interwoven together into an aggregate of texts, some earlier, some later, some a mixture of earlier and later, and some of indeterminate earliness or lateness, and all embedded in a particular cultural matrix. Moreover, it is clear that the Pali tradition moved gradually over time after the Buddha's death, first from northeast to western India, and then south to Sri Lanka (c 250 BCE), thus exposing it to a variety of cultural influences. If one's objective were to identify *actually and objectively* the *precise* technical language used by the historical Buddha, on which alone precise hermeneutical interpretations could be based, I would submit that this state of affairs is so complex and so ineffable that it is, practically speaking, impossible to sort out in an analytical or reductionist way, leaving us with a non-exclusive "headline" theory *at best*.

Moreover, even if we accept that we can identify in broad outline perhaps even *most* of the original teachings of the historical Buddha, does this mean (1) that we have actually understood what the Buddha meant by those teachings, or (2) that those meanings are incapable of further understanding through a process of progressive examination, refinement, elucidation, and realization? With respect to the first point, the whole tenor of this discussion so far has been focused on the person of the historical Buddha. This bias corresponds to the use of the English word, "Buddhism," literally "the doctrine of the one who understands." However, if we accept the Pali text, the actual word used by the Buddha to refer to his philosophy is *Dharma-Vinaya,* literally "truth and training," which might be interpreted as training in the truth, i.e., more or less what we might mean by "education" or "praxis of being." Elsewhere he also refers to his followers as "sons of the Shakyan," referring to Shakya, the Buddha's home country. It is quite clear, however, that the Buddha's object of concern was not himself, but rather the *dharma* or truth itself, in its most general and universal meaning, i.e., the truth of being or reality, which he discussed and debated with his contemporaries, not merely as personal opinions, but rather as an objective reality that can be discussed, known, understood, and realized both by individuals and collectively through a critical process that includes both reason and realization.

The Buddha did not merely discuss the dharma with his disciples. If we accept the Buddha as the Buddha, then we accept him as the supreme expositor of this truth, at least when and where he lived, but there is no suggestion in the Pali texts themselves that the Buddha's realization was personal, exclusive, or arbitrary in any sense. He also discussed it with other *samanas,* with whom he shared the desire to comprehend and realize this truth, even though they were *not Buddhists.* Therefore, this truth is *objective.* His doing so implies that he believed that it was possible for him and them to come to a shared understanding of the dharma. His primary purpose was not merely conversion or persuasion, but shared understanding, although of course by declaring himself "Buddha" he was also implying that he had attained realization. Here we depart decisively from mere academic scholarship, which is only concerned with establishing "the facts of the matter," generally in superficial rationalist, historicist, and social contexts. As Buddhists, our primary focus is (or should be) not merely to understand the *Buddha,* but also, through understanding the Buddha, to understand the *dharma.* Thus, we have dharmic and nondharmic scholarship. While the latter may have utility to us, as Buddhists, only the former is of fundamental or ultimate concern. This raises many additional and subtle questions and concerns that go far beyond mere academic or profane scholarship.

Can we understand the dharma entirely and exclusively by understanding the person of the Buddha? Even the Buddha is ultimately merely an historically and culturally contingent construct. Is the dharma something that is fixed or frozen in time, identical with the original words of the Buddha that we seek to discover in the Pali Canon? Is the dharma even "historical"? Is the Buddha the sole authority for understanding the dharma? If the dharma can be understood by his successors, and the Buddha's teaching career makes no sense otherwise, then there must be successors who are also authorities, perhaps even buddhas themselves, whose utterances are therefore also relevant to understanding Buddhism, perhaps even more relevant than the Pali Canon, given its opacity. If the Buddha has successors, then he probably had predecessors. There is no suggestion in the Pali Canon that the Buddha claimed to be unique. Rather, again, if we accept the relevant texts, the Buddha stated that he was merely rediscovering an ancient truth, known to but long forgotten by the brahmans and perhaps others too. This provides additional contexts for understanding the dharma that go far beyond the contingencies of place, time, and the historical and cultural circumstances of the Buddha. Ultimately, dharma is the truth of reality itself. Therefore, it cannot be separated from any other form of knowing. As the truth of reality, it must be universal and implicit in all. Since reality is boundless and indeterminate, it seems extremely improbable that the Pali Canon encodes or could encode the totality of dharma. Therefore, how can we restrict ourselves to it as anything other than a provisional foundation for further elaborations and exegeses, potentially even limitless in extent?

2

The Pali Canon Phenomenon

"Start with the universe." Bucky Fuller

The Pali Canon is the term used to describe a set of texts published in Pali between 1871 and 1956. There are five editions of the Pali Canon extant, including the first Burmese Edition (1900, 38 vols.) Pali Text Society Edition (1877–1927, 57 vols.); Thai Edition (1925–1928, 45 vols.); the Sixth Buddhist Council Edition (1954–1956, 40 vols.); and the Sinhalese Edition (1957–1993, 58 vols.). The Sixth Buddhist Council Edition, called the Chattha Sangayana, is available online at www.tipitaka.org. Thanks to the efforts of the Pali Text Society and others, almost all of the Pali Canon is now available in English translations ranging from fair to good, both in print and online. A new, truly critical edition of the Pali Canon is in the early stages of preparation in Wat Phra Dhammakaya, north of Bangkok. When finished, it will supersede through incorporation all of the previous versions of the Pali Canon. The Pali Canon will be truly restored to its theoretical singularity. But will that event constitute the manifestation of the *ekayana* – true, universal dharma? It was not lost on the redactors of the Sixth Buddhist Council Edition that their project would culminate in 1956, which according to their calendar marked the 2500th year of the Buddhist era. In fact, 2100 is closer to the year 2500 BE.

A modern critical edition of the Pali Canon did not exist prior to 1900, about 2,300 years after the death of the Siddattha Gotama, the Buddha. Nevertheless, very few if any scholars doubt the antiquity of the modern text, based on the demonstrable antiquity of the Pali language and comparative study of texts similar or identical to texts in the Pali Canon in other ancient canons, especially the Chinese canon, and other traditions, especially the Sarvastivadin tradition, an almost complete collection of which was discovered recently in Afghanistan. The Pali Canon is a text of the Sthavirivada school, from which the Theravada derives. It is, therefore, a sectarian collection though it includes a substantial number of pre-sectarian texts too.

There is no reason to contest the traditional statement that the original Pali Canon was written down on palm leaves at the end of the first century before the common era, almost three hundred years after the death of the Buddha about 400 BCE. This latest consensus date came out of the Gottingen symposium, the results of which were published in *The Dating of the Historical Buddha* by the Gottingen Academy of Sciences in 1991 and 1992. Only the first two of a projected three volumes have been published. The range of dates for the death of the Buddha that is now increasingly given is between 410 and 370 BCE, supplanting the older date of 487 to 483 BCE, which in turn supplanted still older dates, going back to as far as 2420 BCE! This is a good thing for the Pali Canon. According to the Theravadin view, the Buddha died in 545 BCE and the Pali Canon was first written down in 29 BCE, 516 years after the death of the Buddha. The new date means that the Pali Canon may have been written down as early as 341 years after the death of the Buddha. This should increase our confidence in the veracity of the Canon by as much as a third.

The interval between the death of the Buddha and the approximate final form of the Pali Canon may even be smaller than this. Many scholars accept the view that the Canon achieved its approximate final form prior to the reign of Ashoka, who is nowhere alluded to, which would put the Canon prior to Ashoka's conversion to Buddhism about 263 BCE, a mere 107 years after the death of the Buddha, just about the time of the Great Schism. For comparison, the Buddha predicted the future rise and fall of the city of Pataliputra (modern Patna) in the last year of his life, according to the Pali Canon. The Buddha's prophecy refers to the rise of the Mauryan empire in 321 BCE. Barring actual prescience, these considerations broadly place the date of the Pali Canon between 321 BCE and 263 BCE, 49 to 147 years after the death of the Buddha. The Great Schism occurred during the Second Buddhist Council when the elder Sthaviras, the ancestors of the Theravadins, split off from the majority Mahasamghikas over a disagreement on Vinaya, about 100 to 110 years after the Buddha's death. I am vastly oversimplifying because the Pali Canon is not a singular text but a collection of texts, some parts of which are certainly older and some parts of which are certainly more recent than the range of dates I have suggested.

It is clear from internal evidence that the Canon was edited, revised, and copied over hundreds of years. Thus, it is a heterogeneous cocktail of a text, riven by differences of details but characterized by a broad underlying uniformity, the product of a process of such intense intellectual energy that we can only infer. In the early days, changes or elucidations were probably made to clarify differences of doctrine, whereas as time passed the nature of the changes probably became more editorial in character. Thus, the Canon would have gradually congealed into stasis over time. The Canon itself indicates the conservatism and seriousness with which the task of preserving the dharma teachings was taken, as it still is today. To regard it as something that just "appeared" more or less spontaneously and effortlessly is surely a mistake. We must believe that there is an ontological veracity at the core of the Canon. Nevertheless, while the Pali Canon can be said to derive from this core nothing in the Pali Canon can be simplistically identified with it. A range of interpretations is always possible. The best approach seems to be to keep an open mind.

The Pali Canon is an aggregate of texts, some earlier, and some later. Rhys Davids classified the chronology of the Pali Canon in approximate strata, in which the earliest identifiable texts of the Pali Canon are the Parayanavagga and the Atthakavagga, the final two chapters of the Suttanipata. We find these texts in the Khuddaka Nikaya surprisingly, since the latter is generally associated with later matter. The third early text is the Pattimokkha, the

rules of the sangha, although the Pali Canon alludes to a Pattimokkha of only 150 rules, compared with the 227 rules of the Pali
Vinaya. This causes us to classify the Vinaya as a post-*sutta* text.
The famous Rhinoceros or Khaggavisana Sutta, also in the Sutta-
nipata, may be included here. These four texts, to which we can
add the Five Precepts (Pansil), are as close as we can come to the
words of the historical Buddha in the Pali Canon as it exists today.

The Atthakavagga addresses such basic concerns as desire, attachment, philosophy, mindfulness, detachment, the nature of
Buddhahood (referred to as the *Muni,* or 'Sage,' similar to the Tao
Te Ching, and *Bhagavat,* 'Lord'), and the path. The *suttas* emphasize the importance of independence and disdain philosophizing
and seeking salvation through others. We must save ourselves.
The Buddha opposes the doctrine of self-purification through the
cultivation of inward peace to the doctrine that one is purified by
the practice of philosophizing based on speculation and argument. Even at this early date, we see the Buddha celebrated and
even worshipped as a descendent of the Sun, a *Muni,* an *Isi,* and
a *Sambuddha* ('perfectly or self-enlightened'). The Buddha is said
to have been reborn from the Tusita ('joyful, contented') heaven,
associated with the bodhisattva doctrine. The Buddha is described
as having the thirty-two marks of a great man and as having the
psychic power of telepathy. The realm of the deities (devas), including earthbound devas and Mara, are also referred to. The path
is described as both gradual and instantaneous. The Buddha prohibits some of the same superstitious practices, especially prog-
nostication, that he criticizes in the first *sutta* of the Digha Nikaya, the Net of Confusion (Brahmajala Sutta). As observed by
Mrs. C.A.F. Rhys Davids, asceticism is deemphasized. Pain is observed, but not cultivated. The liberated person is free from attachment *and revulsion* and sees happiness everywhere. They are
friendly and tolerant to all, much like the sage of Laozi. These
texts, especially the Parayanavagga, introduce the same question
and answer format that structures almost all of the *suttas,* suggesting that this may have been the major teaching method used
by the historical Buddha.

Yet even these texts cannot be identified with the historical person of Siddhattha Gotama. For one thing, the Buddha is already partly divinized. They are rather interpretations of the teachings of the Buddha by the immediate successors of those arhants that convened the First Buddhist Council under Mahakassapa. By definition, we do not know who was not present at that meeting, or whose potential contributions were forgotten. Ananda's significant contribution was only saved by his attaining the state of arhantship on the night before the council was set to meet. I have discussed these documents in "The Oldest Buddhist Scripture." Rather than get into dogmatic minutiae here, here I want to discuss the general implications of these discoveries for our understanding of the Pali Canon and its place in the context of the Dharma Transmission to the West, the *ekayana,* and the whole Buddhist oeuvre, from a holistic perspective.

While on this topic of chronology I would like to address a common concern that one finds cropping up constantly in discussions of what Buddhism says and means, or should say and mean, and that is the statement that because a text is "later" than another text the later text can be disregarded. (This is precisely opposite of the Quranic precept that the later suras have greater and indeed definitive veracity, as we see with regard to the prohibition of alcohol for example.) This bias seems to be based on the notion that through the application of a reductive method one can ultimately identify a hypothesized "Q" text that is therefore identical with the actual historical teaching of Siddattha Gotama (this is also based on the hidden axiom that Buddhism is restricted by or to the historical teachings of Siddhattha Gotama). Thus, one goes from the non-essential to the essential by a process of elimination. Unfortunately, as with the stock market or psychic prophecies, no objective methodology on how to do this has been described and no new canon proposed based on the application of the method.

This historicist/reductionist/"academicist"/fundamentalist approach to the Pali Canon is really missing the point. Even if we were able to identify the exact words of the Buddha, and thus create a revised, "corrected" Canon, in which only historically reliable material appears – based on the assumption that the dharma itself is historical and nothing else – the twin problems of 'meaning and praxis' (*dharma-vinaya*) would not disappear. Even during the Buddha's own lifetime, these problems intruded. Even if we were able to apply an absolutely rigorous method to this "Q" text to identify with certainty what each and every word of the historically corrected Pali Canon meant in the context of the meanings of the words in other, similar sentences and in the context of the Buddha's cultural milieu, we cannot avoid the syntactic and semantic uniqueness of the sentences in which he used these words without denying the significance of the Buddhist project and we cannot identify what these sentences meant to the Buddha in his own interiority. We cannot identify the Buddha's "authorial intent." We can only know the Buddha's mind through knowing our own Buddha mind.

Even so, such an analysis inevitably ignores what these sentences imply and what they might mean to us, both collectively and as individuals. Even in the Pali Canon, the Buddha is represented as giving different teachings and techniques to different individuals based on their personal needs and stages of spiritual development. Thus, to infer any perfectly consistent system from a historical reconstruction of the "original" teachings of the Buddha, himself merely one of many historically and samsarically contingent beings, is inherently paradoxical since the second half of the equation, the individual subjects themselves, are absent. Moreover, the axiom of impermanence (*anicca*), itself militates against any such possibility. As Kierkegaard notes, there is no repetition. While dharma itself may be supermundane, every samsaric expression of dharma is necessarily relative and contingent. There is no ultimate manifestation of dharma anywhere but there are expressions more or less perfect based on their completeness (it does not follow however that these are all equal). The fundamentalist project is at its root self-contradictory and thus invariably degenerates into religious fascism and ultimately nihilism, as we clearly saw in the person of Devadatta, who also wanted to impose a maximally rigorous "Buddhism."

Not all of the Pali Canon purports to represent the 'words of the Buddha' (*Buddhavacana*). It is clear from the compilation of the

Canon that the "canonicity" of the Canon does not inhere only in its being identical with the words of Siddattha Gotama. There are also *suttas* and poems uttered by others, rules, formulas, precepts, catechisms, summaries, stories, commentaries, analyses, histories, and the expositions of the the Abhidhamma, the third major section of the Pali Canon, which codifies the *suttas* and was supposed to have been taught by the Buddha to his mother in Tavatimsa, the Heaven of the Thirty-Three Gods.

The Buddha was not mainly or even at all concerned with his own person. The goal of his renunciation was not personal; it was universal. His purpose in leaving home was very specific, and it only had to do with Siddhattha insofar as he was one of many. His purpose was to discover the dharma or reason underlying the universal suffering of living and sentient beings and its cure. The Buddha had already clarified that this is what he wanted to do himself to some extent. It is in the course of this quest or search that Siddhattha Gotama discovers the praxis and thus became a Buddha. It is the praxis, not the theory, which made Siddhattha a Buddha. Theory also precedes praxis.

Thus, our concern in trying to identify the words of the Buddha, insofar as we can do that, is not to find out about the Buddha himself but to find out about the dharma that he sought and taught, the most generalized meaning or interpretation of which is "natural law" or simply "truth," especially the First Noble Truth of Suffering, and the praxis. These are not two things but one thing, since wisdom implies praxis and praxis implies wisdom. Thus, the Buddha said that we should make the dharma, not the Buddha or the sangha, our refuge and our teacher, and reason and experience our criteria of evaluation, not teachers or texts, including, presumably, the Buddha and the Pali Canon. The Buddha deemphasized himself, and said that he was merely one of a series (the lineage of buddhas) and part of a group (the sangha). This does not, however, negate the fact of the Buddha's primogeniture. This ontological fact alone proves that the path that leads to Buddhahood, the path of the bodhisattva so-called, is not the same as the path that leads to arhantship, the path of the sravaka so-called, regardless of what another text may or may not say. However, it is clear from the Pali Canon that the fundamental difference between buddhas and arhants was recognized in the earliest *suttas*.

The main part of the Pali Canon that quotes the Buddha or his close disciples includes the *suttas* or 'discourses' of the Digha Nikaya, Majjhima Nikaya, Samyutta Nikaya, Anguttara Nikaya, and Khuddaka Nikaya. In the Khuddaka Nikaya, only the Khuddakapatha (five *suttas*), Itivuttaka (112 *suttas*), and Suttanipata (71 *suttas*) include actual *suttas*. Thus, there are approximately 5,572 *suttas* in total.

Digha Nikaya: 34 *suttas* (521 pages)
Majjhima Nikaya: 152 " (1,151 ")
Samyutta Nikaya: 2,889 " (1,888 ")
Anguttara Nikaya: 2,308 " (1,588 ")
Khuddakapatha: 188 "
Vinaya: 1 (1,214 ")

The *suttas* vary greatly in length, from 1,214 pages to one and a half pages. In English translation, they may be about 6,644 pages in total. This is about 3,322,000 words. As a lecturer, I use a rule of thumb of about 5,000 words per hour. Thus, all of the texts of the Pali Canon attributed to the Buddha, disregarding duplications of material, represents about 664 hours of speech. Since we know that the Buddha taught for forty-five years, we can say that the Pali Canon presents about fifteen hours of speech for each year that the Buddha taught – less than twenty minutes per week. Yet the Pali Canon itself represents the Buddha as engaged in almost continuous dialogue with visitors and Buddhist monastics on a wide variety of topics as well as a legislator of Vinaya. (Interestingly, Bucky Fuller said that he could summarize the essential meaning of his life's work is just about fifteen hours.) It is obvious that the Pali Canon itself is only a small fraction of what the Buddha himself must have actually said. The Pali Canon says even less about praxis. Many practices are referred to but not explained, let alone described. This may indicate that the redactors of the Pali Canon were forgetting the practices or perhaps these were considered too sacrosanct to commit to writing. The Buddha alludes to something similar, when he says that the wisdom of the Buddha, "vast as the leaves of simsapa trees in a simsapa forest," vastly exceeds what he actually says. Elsewhere the Buddha is presented as being reluctant to discuss speculative matters, warning his followers against becoming mere intellectuals and debaters, while emphasizing the pre-eminent importance of wisdom and meditation. The Pali Canon also represents the Buddha as hesitating to teach the dharma for fear he would not be understood.

This view of "lateness" derives from the Buddhist identification of time with entropy, which is identical with the axiom of *anicca* or impermanence. Thus, everything decays into its elements and loses its identity over time. "Even the dharma will be forgotten" is a familiar refrain in the Pali Canon. From this fear, the fundamentalists gain their motivation. Preserving the dharma from its own demise becomes a sort of *bodhicitta*. However, even in the context of the Buddhist world-view this axiom is inadequate because it is incomplete. Time is both entropic and negentropic. There is devolution but there is also evolution. Living systems demonstrate this and so do information systems. As Bucky Fuller famously observed, information systems grow and expand, like a brain. As long as there is memory, there is progress. Thus, it is as absurd to say that a later school is ipso facto degenerate and therefore false due to the passage of time, even if not a single sentence of the teachings of that school is identical with a sentence spoken by the historical Siddhattha Gotama, as it is to say that the history of Western philosophy has no meaning or value in relation to the pre-Socratics or that quantum physics is inferior to Einsteinian relativity, which is inferior to Newtonian physics, etc. This is an extreme view that turns out upon analysis to be incorrect. Thus, the fundamentalist project is false in its essence. In the Pali Canon, we read that the dharma wheel cannot be stopped and that it never stops rolling. However, in such a kinetic system it is clear that the *older* schools will be the ones most likely to become corrupted, whereas the newer schools will represent a mixture of error and insight, devolution and evolution, depending on their conditions. Thus, the quality of the manifestations of dharma changes over time as a function of changing conditions.

We cannot infer anything evidential from the non-appearance of a doctrine or concept in the earliest versus the later texts simply because the survival or non-survival of the early texts is certainly fortuitous and therefore arbitrary. We can assume I think that a significant number of early texts were incorporated into later texts of the corpus, and there is evidence in the Pali Canon of *suttas* being spliced into other *suttas*. Thus, old wine may appear in new bottles! Nor can we assume that the Pali Canon corpus itself is complete and therefore exclusive for the reasons already stated. While we might infer some meaning from the presence of a doctrine in the earliest texts of the Pali Canon – there is a functional difference between the foundation and the attic of a house - no negative connotation can be inferred concerning the truth or falsehood of a later doctrine or text, any more than any "implication" can be stated to be inferior to an "axiom." Axioms and implications have the same relationship to each other as causes and effects. For this reason when the Buddha refers to testing a new text or doctrine by reference to the established corpus he does not mean that it must be identical but rather that it must be continuous. Any other interpretation violates the axiom of impermanence (*anicca*).

The Buddha repeatedly implies that the application of reason to problems of religion can arrive at true conclusions "on the basis of truth," even though he admitted that ultimate meaning and emancipation itself are beyond verbalization, linguistic categories, and rationality itself. Thus the Buddha discouraged empty speculation and cautioned his followers against dogmatism and sectarianism, referring each one to the authority of their own conscience, since enlightenment, like death, is experienced by and for oneself alone. The fruits of enlightenment may be shared but in itself, it is not a collective phenomenon. It is however false to infer from this fact that wisdom is unimportant and that all that matters is practice, since the Buddha emphasized the salvific primacy of wisdom both in his statements and in his behavior, where he spent the better part of forty-five years teaching and instructing others.

Praxis without wisdom is unintelligible (as is wisdom without praxis). The Buddha made no distinction between Buddhists and non-Buddhists, rich and poor, lay and monastic, and men and women, instructing everyone who came to him openly and without prejudice, giving to each one what they needed at that time to take the next step in their spiritual progress. It is only later after the Buddha's death that the predominantly male monastics began to make and enforce such discriminations. After the Buddha's death, his successors established an increasingly dogmatic, authoritarian, and hierarchical system that included systemic discrimination against women, dogmatic disputatiousness, and arguments about the practice and enforcement of the rules, culminating in the Great Schism of the Second Buddhist Council, about a hundred years later. This was followed by the disintegration into the Eighteen Schools, including disputes focused especially on the spiritual perfection and infallibility of arhants in relation to the Buddha.

Many scholars seem willing to accept the texts cited plus the Four Great Nikayas (Digha, Majjhima, Anguttara, Samyutta) as the foundation of "mainstream Buddhism," but even these texts demonstrate a significant ideological development as well as internal doctrinal differences, especially in the matter of the spiritual status of men and women, which I have discussed at length in "The Status of Women in Ancient India and the Pali Tradition." Those who advocate the notion that later texts are necessarily and inherently corrupt fail to consider that development may also imply an original potential implication that may very well originate in the person of the Buddha himself, just as a tree originates in an original and originating "seed," even if the appearance of the mature form differs greatly from the germ, yet who says that the tree is not implicit in the seed or inferior to the seed or, even more absurdly, not the seed?

To take just one example, the Pali Canon includes a collection of Jatakas or "birth histories" attributed to the Buddha. According to the Pali Canon, the Buddha remembered many if not all of his past lives during his Enlightenment experience, and all through the course of his subsequent life, he would identify people, places, and events in his present life as Siddhattha Gotama with people, places, and events that he remembered from past lives. The Jatakas are generally dated to the fourth century BCE. Scholars recognize that many of the stories in the Jatakas come from other languages and media, including vernacular oral traditions that predate the Pali compositions and are also found in Hinduism. Therefore, many academic Buddhologists and "modern" religionists might be inclined to reject the doctrine of rebirth itself based on the historical implausibility of the Jataka tales, but does this inference follow logically from the premise? The fact that the conservative redactors of the Pali Canon included the Jatakas in the Pali Canon, along with many accounts of supernatural powers, characters, and events in the *suttas,* are also relevant facts. Similar considerations apply to the Mahayana literature. Questions of history and questions of meaning and value are not coterminous.

Another example: psychic powers. We need not believe that the Buddha actually levitated, teleported, and bilocated to accept that the Buddha demonstrated psychic powers on occasion, along with the vast host of other holy beings, both human and non-human, yet the evidence for the reality of some sort of psychic power is growing, and such powers as well as profound and powerfully transformative charisma and wisdom are commonly attributed to and demonstrated by so-called exceptional individuals all through the human experience. This is the universal testimony of human history and Buddhism is not an exception to this. This is not surprising since the Buddha did not claim any originality for himself.

A fascinating aspect of this association is the UFO phenomenon, wherein many of these powers are experienced both in the UFO contact experience itself and in its aftermath. The UFO phenomenon is fully evident in the Pali Canon (I have discussed this connection at length in "Buddhism and the UFO Phenomenon"), in accord with the historical hypothesis of Jacques Vallee in his book, *Passport to Magonia.* In view of the demonstrated physicality of at least some UFO appearances, we should not arbitrarily reject the possibility of such powers, although the Buddha himself said that the development of such powers is not the main point of his teachings. Psychic powers and the UFO phenomenon itself also manifest in the context of the psychedelic experience and visionary phenomena, which are also attested to in the Pali Canon.

One of the advantages of the Pali texts in relation to the founding texts of Christianity is the sheer abundance of material – three hundred pages or so of primary Christian scripture compared with about forty volumes of material in the Pali tradition. Moreover, the Pali material is highly repetitive. One may hypothesize in such a situation that the tropes of the original and originating Buddhist texts were extensive and significant enough to (a) be preserved and (b) generate complex associations of meaning that led to meaningful implications that can then be refined by applying logical criteria to them. Quite simply, we know a lot more about Shakespeare because he wrote thirty-seven plays than we would know if he only wrote {pick any single play at random}. The project is then to identify the large tropes in the Canon, collate them with each other, and submit them to criticism, to arrive at the truth of dharma.

This is precisely contrary to the fundamentalist project that tries to reduce the Pali Canon to a hypothesized set of original sentences, denies the value or legitimacy of any sentences outside that set or that any unstated implications do or could exist, and identifies through intensive comparative analysis the meanings and connotations of the words and sentences as they were spoken by the Buddha in a given semantic context, approximating as far as possible to "authorial intent." That such a project is impossible in principle is proved by the axiom of impermanence (*anicca*). There are no "permanent truths." The truth is the middle way between dogmatic fundamentalist extremism on the one hand and subjectivism on the other. Mahayana and Hinayana need and correct each other. Without Mahayana Hinayana degenerates into arid literalism, whereas without Hinayana Mahayana degenerates into a flight of fantasy. The *ekayana* and the Dharma Transmission to the West include them both. We find this point of view most highly developed in the schools of Tibetan Buddhism, Chan, and esoteric Buddhism, and least developed in the Theravada sect, whose orthodox adherents still uphold the view, now thoroughly discredited, that the Pali Canon represents the verbatim utterance of the Buddha, in the language spoken by the Buddha, recalled by the photographic memory of Ananda, and handed down for several hundred years by a perfect or nearly perfect process of group recitation till it was written down on palm leaves and meticulously preserved for 1900 years and finally printed in Burma. The scorpion of self-purification has arisen in the heart of Theravada Buddhism in the form of so-called progressive or "modern" Theravada, as it has in Islam. It ends in historical nihilism, whereas the sutras state that after 2,500 years in the new age now dawning the dharma of the future will be personal, intimate, and esoteric.

Conclusions

The Pali Canon is a sectarian collection of sectarian and pre-sectarian materials, indiscriminately worked and reworked over centuries to form a composite textual aggregate.

The core suttas of the Pali Canon were probably established by the mid-third century BCE, approximately a century and half after the death of the Buddha circa 400 BCE.

The early and later Buddhist texts represent a complementary process of preserving and clarifying the original teachings of Siddattha Gotama, in the context of the universal dharma that he sought in relation to his special concern: the problem of universal suffering and its cure.

The Pali Canon only represents a fraction of what the Buddha said, and what the Buddha said only represents a fraction of the dharma. The original teachings of Siddhattha Gotama and the dharma are not conterminous or coextensive.

Dharma can only be ultimately understood by each individual for themselves through the exercise of reason and experience.

Devolution and development in time co-occur. The dharma itself is unconditional and omni-evolutionary, yet its samsaric manifestations appear, develop, decay, and disappear and are always subject to error, flux, and change.

Every expression of dharma is conditional and relative to what each individual needs at that moment. Universal dharma can only be inferred from this by a process of collation and abstraction and can never be perfectly arrived at. Largely it is intuitive and symbolic and ultimately transrational.

*Fundamentalism, organizationalism and authoritarianism all contradict the axiom of impermanence (*anicca*), since there are no permanent forms, and are thus adharmic. They are all contrary to authentic spiritual progress and are decadent, corrupt, reactionary, and devolutionary. After 2500 years all historical Buddhist schools are more or less in the same boat. The whole system is stagnant. This is the* mappo.

What is needed is a radical comprehensive reformation. This is the Dharma Transmission to the West.

Potentially all non-self-contradictory tropes in the Pali Canon are ultimately relatable to an original and originating trope. The task is to identify the recurrent patterns and recognizing them as deriving from an original axiom, essentially expressed, identifying their implications and ultimately their praxis.

"Original Buddhism" is the set of primary axioms.

The complete set of primary axioms must explicate all subsequent implications.

Tropes that contradict the known prejudices of the conservative male monastic organizationalists who compiled the Pali Canon may have been too well known and too entrenched to be expurgated, like similar passages in the Christian New Testament, thus highlighting their interest and integrity. Anything that contradicts the status quo is unlikely to have been invented.

The Buddhavacana *includes dharma teachings not spoken by the Buddha. Thus, the denial of canonicity to Mahayana sutras is inconsistent. The latter may represent symbolic and visionary expressions of authentic implications of the axioms of the dharma and thus constitute authentic dharma realizations without being historically factual or spoken by the Buddha at all. Because dharma is unconditional potentiality the continuity of authentic dharma traditions, lineages, canons,* suttas, *sutras, and* termas *is infinitely extensive and diverse. Dharma is an open, not a closed, system.*

Spiritual development and enlightenment imply the experience of altered states of consciousness, visionary states, meditative states, dream states, radical metaphysical and philosophical intuitions and insights, powerful affective states, and influential charismatic states, similar to all other spiritual practices and traditions. Buddhism is continuous with Aryan/Indian tradition and exists in the universal context of shamanism and the perennial philosophy, the prehistorical ground of all human spirituality.

By collating all Buddhist expressions and resolving their complexities and contradictions into a coherent system of axiomatic generalizations one arrives at dharma. This is the hermeneutical method of the ekayana. *This is the project of the Dharma Transmisison to the West, which will achieve its apotheosis on all planes in the historical manifestation of Shambhala, the dharma teleology.*

3
Gotama's Quest

PART 1
Conception to Enlightenment

The Shakyan Republic

GOTAMA, AS HE is consistently called all through the Pali Canon, referring to his family or clan name, was born in Lumbini, in what is now Nepal, about 25 km from the Indian border, in the traditional territory of the Shakyan tribe. *Shakya* means 'capable, able.' The Shakyan region was an independent tribal confederacy, with its capital in Kapilavastu, but it was politically subject to Kosala, its powerful neighbour to the west, and some Buddhist texts refer to the Buddha as Kosalan. The Shakyans were notorious for their pride and love of independence. Kosala waged a war of genocide against the Shakyans toward the end of the Buddha's life. Chinese pilgrims visiting the site centuries later described it as desolate. The Magadhan Empire subsequently annexed Kosala itself. The language of the Pali Canon is sometimes described as Magadhan.

Gotama's family were members of the prestigious Ikshsvaku dynasty, a.k.a. the Suryavamsa or Solar Dynasty.

Manu, the first human being and legislator of mankind, was an ancestor of the Solar Dynasty, much as Moses was an ancestor to the Hebrews. In the Buddhist view, Maha Sammata founded this dynasty in prehistoric times. The texts say that the original government of the world was democratic (since there were no rulers yet), and Gotama's father was an elected chieftain in a sort of aristocratic proto-democracy, not dissimilar from the Greece of Socrates, who was a contemporary of the Buddha. After regarding Suddhodana as a monarch or an oligarch, scholars now see him as an elected chieftain. At the time of the Buddha, the fragile values of quasi-democracy coexisted with a world of aggressive hereditary monarchs and military dictators hungry to tax the new wealth of mercantilism, frequent wars of annexation, widespread lawlessness and brigandage, and terrible punishments for crimes, including mutilation, blinding, impaling, strangling, and beheading. Trade was extensive but travel was dangerous. At the time of Gotama, Brahmanism, which came from the west, had still not deeply penetrated northeast India, and the *samana* counterculture was widespread. Shakya itself did not have a caste system, although in countries where the caste system was established the Buddha is always identified as a member of the kshatriya (Pali *khattiya*) or military caste that also constituted the political class.

The father of Gotama was Suddhodana. Suddhodana's father was Sihahanu. Sihahanu's father was Jayasena. Suddhodana was known for his prowess in warfare and swordplay. He was also known to be a just and righteous ruler.

The mother of Suddhodana was Kaccana. She was a member of the Koliyan clan. The Koliyans ruled the region to the east of the Rohini River, whereas the Shakyans governed the west side.

The mother of Gotama was Maya. Her father, Suppabuddha, was the king of Devadaha (modern Butwal), located approximately 40 km northeast of Kapilavastu "as the crow flies." Maya was Suddhodana's cousin. Suddhodana had another wife, Pajapati, Maya's younger sister, who raised Gotama after Maya's death. Both Maya and Pajapati were the daughters of Suppabuddha.

The Shakyans and the Koliyans were both vassal states of the Kosala kingdom to the west. The Shakyans and Koliyans had intermarried between themselves since ancient times in order to maintain the purity of their bloodlines, and were the two most prominent families in the region.

According to the dominant tradition, Suddhodana and Maya lived together chastely for twenty years, at which time Maya became pregnant and gave birth to Gotama.

The Conception of the Buddha

Maya was the daughter of Suddhodana's uncle and, therefore, his cousin. Kapilavastu (probably present-day Tiraulakot), Lumbini (present-day Rumindei), where the Buddha was born, and Devadaha, are all located in the Rupandehi district of Nepal. Lumbini is 24 km southeast from the site of Kapilavastu and 32 km southwest from Devadaha.

The third-century BCE brick-palace complex located at Tiraulakot is believed to be based on an original wood structure, and is 1,300 × 1,700 m square (about 546 acres). This accords well with the statement of the Chinese pilgrim Xuangang, who stated that the royal precinct of the city was 14 or 15 li in circumference (about 400 or 500 acres). An alternative site is Piprahwa, across the border in India, which seems to be less favoured by scholars.[3]

Interestingly, Kapilavastu is named after its founder, the philosopher Kapila who lived two hundred years earlier and is regarded as the founder of Samkhya. Like Kapila, the Buddha emphasized meditation as a technique for removing suffering, regarded the Vedic gods as subject to limitations and conditions, and opposed Brahmanic ritual and doctrines.

In accordance with the custom of the time, still practised in Nepal, Maya left her husband's house late in her pregnancy to deliver at the house of her parents in Devadaha. Although Maya was travelling by carriage, an entourage accompanied her, so it seems unlikely that she made better time than average walking speed. Assuming she covered 20 km per day, the trip would have taken roughly five days, or the better part of a week, but she never got to Devadaha.

Stopping in Lumbini, merely two days into her trip according to our estimate, it appears that Maya was overcome by the exertion,

---

3. Some have suggested that the second site is the location where the Shakyans resettled after the attempted genocide of the Shakyans by the Kosalans.

and in the heat of the afternoon, she went into labour in a park of *sal* trees. Therefore, Gotama was born prematurely, despite the claim of the texts that Maya's gestation period was exactly ten lunar months. Alternatively, Hajime Nakamura has suggested that Maya travelled back to Lumbini for a ritual purification in the baths there, but the texts clearly imply that Maya stopped at Lumbini en route to Devadaha. The texts also state that the *sal* trees came into bloom about this time, which suggests the month of March or April, not mid-May as popularly believed. Exhausted, Maya returned to Kapilavastu with her newborn son, Siddhartha. Assuming a due date in March, Gotama's conception may be placed in June (the Indian month of Jyeshtha, associated with high summer, the time of traditional midsummer, a solar holiday that places his conception about the time of the summer solstice).

It is said that when she conceived, Queen Maya experienced a dream in which four spiritual beings transported her to Lake Anotta, a mythical Himalayan lake, where she was ritually bathed and then impregnated through her side by a great white elephant.

This lake is now associated with Lake Manasarovar at the foot of Mount Kailash, located in mid-western Tibet just over the border from Nepal, north-west of Kapilavastu. This dream was held to portend the birth of a great being.

The Birth of the Buddha

When Gotama was born, Asita, a wandering hermit ascetic, predicted that Gotama would become a Buddha. Five days after the birth, at Gotama's naming ceremony, seven brahmans predicted that Gotama would become either a universal ruler or a universal teacher. However, Kondanna, the youngest brahman there, alone predicted that Gotama would become a Buddha. These predictions appear to have been based on a combination of physiognomy and astrology. According to later tradition, Gotama was then given the name Siddhattha, 'wish-fulfilled' or 'he who accomplishes the goal.' Two days later, Maya died.

A great man is supposed to manifest thirty-two significant bodily signs. Although some authors emphasize the supernatural character of these signs, most of them are not difficult to visualize. The bodily signs include flat feet; long slender fingers; pliant hands and feet; fine webs on the toes and fingers (which in extreme cases exists as a medical condition known as syndactyly); large heels; arched insteps; athletic thighs; long arms; a small penis; dark, curly hair; soft, smooth, golden skin; rounded soles, palms, shoulders, and crown; a large, ample, muscular torso; erect and upright posture; full, round shoulders; white, even, close teeth; a large jaw; ample saliva; a long and broad tongue; a deep and resonant voice; deep blue eyes; long, thick eyelashes; a tuft of white hair between the eyebrows; and a large cranium.

Clairvoyants may also discern wheels on the soles of the feet, a ten-foot aura, and forty teeth – eight more than what is usual for humans, but interestingly the maximum number for mammals. Despite these unusual characteristics, Gotama is described as not exceptional, though handsome, in appearance. There is a story in which a wandering ascetic met the Buddha in a barn one night. They spent the night talking together, but only in the morning did the ascetic realize with whom he was speaking. Although this is widely interpreted to mean that the physical appearance of the Buddha was not exceptional, it was night. Of course, in their enthusiasm the redactors of the Pali Canon generally exaggerate the wealth and power of the Buddha's family, the beauty of the Buddha and his male monastics, and the size of the sangha. The Buddha was probably refined, slightly androgynous, and thoughtful in appearance. Given his military upbringing and later self-mortifications, he was probably physically fit and strong.

The Buddha's Youth and Marriage

Suddhodana wanted his son to become a world ruler and not a spiritual man, so from birth Gotama was raised in an atmosphere of opulence, as well as receiving the education proper to a member of the military caste. Gotama's education appears in his interest in politics and his broad knowledge of social history and international matters.

As a young child, Gotama experienced a taste of realization while he was sitting under a rose-apple tree beside a field where

his father was performing a ceremonial plowing. This early experience of meditation was crucial in his realization of Enlightenment
two decades later, as we shall see.

Gotama was extremely hedonistic, and lived for the four
months of the rainy season in the female quarters, entertained by
female musicians. This behavior was somewhat contrary to Indian
norms, which valued chastity and manliness, leading to the accusation of effeminacy later on.

Subsequently he was married at the age of 16 (some sources say
19) to his cousin, Yasodhara (a.k.a. Bimba, Bimbadevi, Bhaddakac-
ca, Bhaddakaccana, or Rahulamata), the daughter of Suppabuddha and Pamita, the sister of the Buddha's father. Yasodhara
was the same age as Gotama. Gotama may have had two other
wives too. The Tibetan Vinaya mentions Gopa and Mrigaja.[4]

Although the popular view is that Gotama abandoned his station, family, wife, and child spontaneously shortly after the birth
of his son, Rahula ('fetter'), in disgust for a night of carousing, Rahula's name itself suggests that Gotama's decision was the result
of a process of reflection. The Sarvastivadins have an alternative
explanation of the meaning of the name Rahula, which is 'eclipse,'
but since Rahu, the eclipse deity, is also an ill omen, the implication is similar. The texts also refer to the bodhisattva's progressive
realization of the principles of interconnectedness (*paticcasamuppada*), including the five aggregates of the self; impermanence
(*anicca*); and suffering (*dukkha*) before his renunciation. Gotama
must have informed his parents about these feelings, because
a *sutta* says that they wept and tried to convince him to stay.
Therefore, he left home against his parent's wishes, a violation of
Vedic norms, which frowned upon renunciation by the young in
any case.[5]

---

4. The *Buddhacarita* (see n. 5) mentions "wives" (5:41).

5. The *Buddhacarita* (Acts of the Buddha), the first full biography of the Buddha, a post-canonical Sanskrit poem written in the early second century, about
150 years after the Pali Canon was committed to writing (its author, the Maha-
sanghiika ascetic Asvaghosa, lived from 80 to 150 CE), but clearly incorporating
earlier traditions, states explicitly that Gotama did not renounce the home life
for some time after the birth of Rahula (2:54) and asked his father for permission
to leave the home life, which he refused (5:28).

The Renunciation

The mainstream tradition has it that Gotama left his home at the age of 29, after thirteen years of marriage, but there is some support in the *suttas* for the view that he was still a youth, "a boy in the first phase of life,"[6] which would make him about nineteen years of age according to the Vedic theory of the four stages of life. This tradition is preserved by the Nichiren tradition. According to this view, he attained Enlightenment at the age of thirty. However, most texts state that he attained Enlightenment at the age of thirty-five. (Asians, however, count life as beginning at conception, not birth, and give their age accordingly, so allowance must also be made for this difference.)

The immediate cause of Gotama's renunciation was his realization of the universality of sickness and death. The Buddha says that this realization destroyed the vanity of his youth. Inquiring into the causes of this condition, the Buddha realized that we are all born into a dangerous and violent world. We compete to survive, and in the process we cause suffering and we suffer ourselves. This suffering is inherent in life itself and cannot be escaped. "Life eats life" is the original Vedic insight. Even if we succeed in realizing a life of relative happiness, we all grow old, suffer, and die. Nothing is permanent. Consequently, Gotama formulated the desire to attain "the unborn, unaging, unfailing, deathless, sorrowless, undefined cessation of bondage," and became increasingly dissatisfied with the household life so that he named his only son Rahula, 'fetter.'

When Gotama left home, he abandoned his station, family, wife, and young child for a life of homeless wandering. He gave up his patrimony and possessions, shaved his hair, and exchanged his fine clothes for the ochre rags of a *samana*.

At first, he lived in a cave on the eastern slope of the hill of Pandava, near Rajagaha in Magadha, and begged for his food on the streets of the city. This was the life of a *samana*, a homeless ascetic. By this time – roughly 450 BCE – the *samana* counterculture was already a century old. In a time of social fragmentation

---

6. DN 4:6.

and spiritual and philosophical inquiry, the *samanas* were an established institution of northeast India. While not universally embraced, they were tolerated and often sought out, much as they are today in India and Nepal, for their insight, even in matters of secular policy such as war.

Gotama's Search

Gotama's quest, traditionally stated to have taken six years, passed through three distinct stages before resulting in the Enlightenment that he sought. He meditated alone in the forest, overcoming the emotion of fear. He studied meditation with two meditation masters, Alara Kalama and Uddaka Ramaputta. Finally, he spent an extended period with the Group of Five, practicing austerities. When that almost killed him, he was abandoned by his companions and settled down in the forest to meditate, once more alone.

Alara Kalama

Alara (Arada) Kalama was a brahman hermit-saint who lived and taught a kind of proto-Samkhya yogic meditation near Rajagaha. After mastering the doctrine, Gotama proceeded to practice, and attained the plane of nothingness, the second highest plane of samsara. This was the highest state of consciousness that Alara had attained. Alara offered to accept Gotama as an equal partner, but Gotama was dissatisfied with this state and left Alara.

Uddaka Ramaputta

Next Gotama studied under Uddaka Ramaputta, a Jain hermit, reputed saint, and yogic meditation teacher. Uddaka was the son or disciple of Ramaputta. Under Uddaka, Gotama attained the plane of neither perception nor non-perception, which Uddaka himself had not yet attained (the Salayatanasamyutta states that he falsely claimed this attainment). Uddaka offered to make Gotama the head of his sangha, but Gotama was dissatisfied with this attainment and left Uddaka.

Note that by moving from a Brahman to a Jain teacher Gotama was clearly moving away from Brahmanism, from an *astika* (orthodox) to a *nastika* (heterodox) philosophical orientation.

The Group of Five

When Gotama left his home at Kapilavastu, Kondanna, the youngest brahman, who alone had predicted that Gotama would become a Buddha, also renounced the household life, accompanied by four others – Bhaddiya, Vappa, Mahanama, and Assaji.

After he left Uddaka, Gotama travelled to Uruvela (now known as Bodh Gaya) where he joined the group of five in the practices of extreme asceticism, including living and sleeping in charnel grounds, exposing the body to the elements, intense meditation, controlling and holding the breath, and near-starvation. A stock description of the practices of ascetics found frequently all through the Pali Canon includes nakedness or rough clothing; rejecting conventions; licking one's hands; not coming or stopping when asked; not accepting gifts or invitations; avoiding spiritual "pollution," especially anything associated with the householder life, especially women and sex; eating next to no food; no meat; no alcohol; eating grass and dung; living only on windfalls; pulling out the hairs of one's head and beard; standing or squatting continuously; sleeping on spikes; and frequent bathing [sic].

After several years of these practices, Gotama was on the verge of dying:

> ...my body reached a state of extreme emaciation. Because of eating so little my limbs became like the jointed segments of vine stems or bamboo stems. Because of eating so little my backside became like a camel's hoof. Because of eating so little the projections on my spine stood forth like corded beads. Because of eating so little my ribs jutted out as gaunt as the crazy rafters of an old roofless barn. Because of eating so little the gleam of my eyes sank far down in their sockets, looking like a gleam of water that has sunk far down in a deep well. Because of eating so little my scalp shriveled and withered as a green bitter gourd shrivels and withers in the wind and sun. Because of eating so little my belly skin adhered to my backbone; thus if I touched my belly skin I encountered my backbone, and if I touched my backbone I

encountered my belly skin. Because of eating so little, if I tried to ease my body by rubbing my limbs with my hands, the hair, rotted at its roots, fell from my body as I rubbed.[7]

One day, while sitting beneath a pipal (some sources say banyan) tree by the river Neranjara, near Uruvela, a girl, named Sujata, from Senani, the village across the river, came to offer some rice gruel to the tree spirit as thanks for answering her prayers for a husband and a son. Gotama accepted her offering, followed by a bath in the river. When his companions saw him thus eating, drinking, and consorting with a girl, they abandoned him, declaring that he had returned to the effeminate life of his youth.

PART 2

Enlightenment to Parinirvana

Enlightenment

Having now rejected the meditations on nothingness and neither perception nor non-perception and the painful and self-destructive austerities of the Group of Five, Gotama cast his mind about for what to do. He recalled an experience he had had as a child sitting under a rose-apple tree watching his father engage in a ceremonial ploughing. He recalled the sensation of bliss that he experienced then, and reflected whether this pleasure might be the key to success? It appears from the texts that Gotama had previously rejected this experience because it was pleasurable, but now he reasoned that the pleasure of meditation is not unwholesome. He realized that the pursuit of bliss is incompatible with bodily torment and emaciation, and resolved to regain his health.

Ironically, Gotama has come full circle – from a life of hedonism through a life of pain he now reconsiders his attitude to pleasure in a new light. Therefore, he took some boiled rice and bread. The texts present this process as virtually instantaneous, but after years of deprivation and abstinence, it is clear that this must have

---

7. MN 12:52.

taken some time. Thus, he lived alone for some period beside the river Neranjara, meditating and begging for alms in Senani.

The night before his Enlightenment, Gotama had five dreams: in which the earth was his couch and the Himalayas his pillow; a creeper grew out of his navel and stood touching the clouds; white grubs with black heads crawled up his legs from his feet to his knees and covered them; four birds of different colours flew to him from the four quarters and, landing at his feet, became white; finally, arising, he walked upon a huge mountain of dirt without being defiled. According to the texts, these dreams imply that he would become a World Teacher, teaching the Noble Eightfold Path, with many lay disciples [sic], that all the castes would become as one, and that he would live in the world without being defiled by it.

The next day, Gotama meditated as usual and attained the fourth jhana state, characterized by perfect equanimity with neither pleasure nor pain. Then, during the first third of the night, he realized the truth of past lives. During the second third of the night, he experienced the "divine eye" and realized the truth of karmic causality. Finally, during the third third of the night – for this night he did not sleep – Gotama realized perfect freedom from the three taints – sensual desire, being, and ignorance. At dawn, traditionally about 5 a.m., Gotama realized his Enlightenment, and became a Buddha. According to tradition, this occurred during the night of the Full Moon in late April or May (Indian month of Vaisakha). Many scholars now think this occurred about 445 BCE.

According to the texts, the Buddha, as we will now call him, remained in a state of transcendent ecstasy for a full week, insentient to the world, seated cross-legged and motionless under the Bodhi tree. During the final night of the seven, the Buddha meditated on the doctrine of interdependent origination (*paticcasamuppada*) in forward, reverse, and forward and reverse order, and thus emerged from his trance. He remained near the Bodhi tree for another six weeks, for a total of seven weeks or forty-nine days.

First Sermons

After attaining Enlightenment, the Buddha hesitated to teach, fearing that he would not be understood. However, Sahampati, a Great Brahma, appeared to the Buddha and entreated him to teach for the salvation of the world and so that Sahampati himself might earn merit. The Buddha reflected that the dust of worldliness obscured the sight of some people less than others, and that he would teach for their benefit, knowing that the dharma would be lost on most people and, once articulated, fall into degeneration like all things.

The Buddha's first thought was to teach Alara Kalama and Uddaka Ramaputta, his first teachers, but when he learned of their deaths he resolved to travel to the Deer Park in Isipatana, outside Benares. En route, he met a wandering ascetic on the road, named Upaka. Upaka was an *ajivika,* a heterodox philosophy characterized by a strict fatalism in which past karma could not be destroyed. Future karma was also fixed, but might be accelerated by ascetic practices similar to those practiced by the Jains, and thus could be used to achieve a state of emancipation. Like the Jains, some Ajivikas went about naked. They were also anti-caste and "a-theistic," but some worshipped Shiva and Vishnu. Voluntary suicide was also practiced. The *ajivikas* reached the height of their popularity during the second century CE, but went into decline and by the thirteenth century had almost completely disappeared. Upaka, impressed by the Buddha's physical appearance, asked the Buddha which teacher or teaching he followed. When the Buddha told him that he was self-enlightened, Upaka replied, "Would that it were so,"[8] and passed on. Therefore, the Buddha's first opportunity to convert a hearer had failed.

When the Buddha arrived at Benares, the Group of Five looked at him askance, but there was something about him that caused them to think twice, and they allowed him to sit with them. At first, they were suspicious but, as he spoke, the dawn of realization arose in their minds and in their hearts and they were converted. Kondanna was the first to attain arhantship, after meditat-

---

8. Mahavagga I:14(9) (V IV); MN 26:25, 85:49.

ing for only five days – two days less than the seven days that is usually prescribed as the minimum requirement.

The first sermons of the Buddha included "Setting Rolling the Wheel of Dharma"[9] and "The Discourse on the Not-self Characteristic."[10] In "Setting Rolling the Wheel of Dharma," the Buddha declares the doctrine of the Middle Way, which he identifies with the Noble Eightfold Path. He then declares the Four Noble Truths and the three phases of penetration – *knowing, abandoning,* and *realizing,* including *maintaining* the realization of them.

In "The Discourse on the Not-self Characteristic," the Buddha declares the doctrines of non-self-identity (*anatta*), impermanence (*anicca*), and dispassion or detachment, which arises spontaneously because of the realization of the first two principles. Because of hearing the last discourse, all of the members of the Group of Five became liberated arhants.

The Creation of the Sangha

The first person outside of the Group of Five to accept the new teaching was an ordinary merchant's son named Yasa. Yasa experienced a spiritual awakening in the middle of the night and, overcome by disgust for the householder life, he left his home near Isipatana. He came upon the Buddha in Deer Park, who, having awoken early (insomniacal?), appears to have been practising walking meditation in the open. Yasa was distraught. The Buddha taught him dharma. Although he had a wife, Yasa must have been young, as his father the merchant came looking for him. Yasa became the first person outside the Group of Five to join the sangha. In addition, he became the personal attendant of the Buddha, and his father became the first householder to accept the dharma. Subsequently, both the merchant's and Yasa's wife also converted, becoming the first female followers of the Buddha.

This story appears in the Vinaya, and contradicts the story in the *suttas,* now regarded as invented by many scholars, in which Ananda persuades the Buddha to ordain his mother's sister and

---

9. SN 56:11.
10. Ibid, 22:59.

his stepmother, Pajapati, against his better judgment. The dharma spread, starting with four prominent merchant families in Benares, friends of Yasa. At that time there was no ordination formula. The Buddha simply said to the candidate, "Come, the dharma is well proclaimed. Lead the holy life for the complete ending of suffering." Also through Yasa, fifty more followers joined the sangha, until the number of monastics totalled sixty-one. Interestingly, the Vinaya seems to regard everyone who joined the sangha at that time as an arhant. Having taught them the dharma, the Buddha sent them out to wander and bring the good news of the dharma to all those able to receive it. The Buddha himself went to a place called Senanigama in Uruvela.

Soon so many were seeking ordination that it became burdensome for the Buddha to receive all of the candidates himself, and he authorized the monastics to admit applicants to the sangha by the simple formula of Taking Refuge in the Dharma (later elaborated into the Triple Jewel, consisting of Buddha, Dharma, and Sangha, or, in the Tibetan tradition, Buddha, Dharma, Sangha, and Lama). Thus, the Buddha established the sangha as a decentralized order of monastics, quite unlike the hierarchical system that we find in most Buddhist organizations today.

The Fire Sermon

Sometime after his Enlightenment, the Buddha travelled to Gayasisa (near Gaya), where he addressed the monastics in the famous "Fire Sermon."[11] The Buddha famously declares that "all is burning" with the cravings of desirous attachment. This is a disease for which he prescribes "delivery from the taints by not clinging" as the cure. Thence he travelled to Rajagaha, the capital city of Magadha, where the First Buddhist Council would be held forty-odd years later.

Here King Bimbisara honours the Buddha and presents the sangha with the gift of the Bamboo Grove, a place described as close to the city and accessible, but lonely, quiet, and hard to find, for the Buddha and his monks to spend the rainy season retreat

---

11. Mahavagga I:21 (V IV); SN 35:28.

together. However, the Buddha was not popular everywhere. Some people complained that the Buddha was promoting childlessness and widowhood and obliterating the clans. Most of the time the monastics lived in woods, at the foot of trees, under overhanging rocks, in ravines, hillside caves, charnel grounds, jungle thickets, in the open, or on heaps of straw.

Seven years after Gotama's renunciation, about a year after the Enlightenment, the Buddha's father, Suddodhana, heard of his son's success and sent messengers inviting him to return to Kapilavastu. Many of these messengers joined the sangha. According to tradition, he converted his father to the dharma, who died as an arhant some four years later. The Buddha also converted his half-brother, Nanda, on the same day that he was to be married. The texts say that the Buddha lured him away and that Nanada joined the sangha more out of regard for the Buddha than personal inclination, and continued to cling to luxury even as a monastic.

This was also the famous occasion on which Pajapati sent Rahula to the Buddha to ask him for his patrimony. This is often misinterpreted to refer to the crown of kingship, but this interpretation is not feasible since the Shakyans elected their chief (and the chief elected subsequent to Suddhodana does not appear to have been related to the Gotamas). The Buddha, however, directed Sariputta to ordain Rahula as a novice monk. Presumably, Rahula's ordination preceded the rule that a novice must be fifteen years old.[12]

The Buddha returned to Kapilavastu four years later, when his father was dying. It appears that his father was at least 80 when he died. It was also at this time that the Buddha formally established the order of nuns, the *bhikkunisangha*, although it is clear from other texts, already cited, that female monastics were admitted to the sangha from the beginning. This has led most scholars to doubt the intrinsically unlikely story that the Buddha did not want to establish a female monastic order and had to be persuaded to do so by Ananda, responding to the entreaty of Pajapati, who made the Buddha admit that women were equally capable of attaining nirvana as men. Scholars also doubt the miso-

---

12. Alternatively, Rahula might have been eight when the Buddha left home at 29.

gynistic diatribes that mar the texts of the Pali Canon as the inventors of anonymous male redactors.

The Life of the Sangha

The sangha expanded, including monastics who never knew the Buddha, as monastics ordained new monastics in an ever-expanding circle. Of course, such expansion also meant that not all monastics were worthy. There were many reasons that one might want to join the sangha. However, through the practices of dharma talk, *uposatha,* and the rains retreat, the sangha retained its coherence for at least a hundred years after the Buddha's passing on. The Majjhima Nikaya preserves a nice description of the daily life of the sangha:

> Lord, as to that, whichever of us returns first from the village with alms food gets the seats ready, sets out the water for drinking and for washing and puts the refuge bucket in its place. Whichever of us returns last eats any food left over if he wishes; otherwise he throws it away where there is no grass or drops it into water where there is no life. He puts away the seats and the water for drinking and for washing. He puts away the refuse bucket after washing it, and he sweeps out the refectory. Whoever notices that the pots of drinking water or washing water or water for the privy are low or empty sees to them. If any are too heavy for him, he beckons someone else by a sign of the hand and they move it by joining hands. We do not speak for that purpose. However, every five days we sit out the night together in talk on the Dhamma. It is in this way that we dwell diligent, ardent and self-controlled.[13]

In a society being wrecked by war, it is easy to understand how such simple austerity may have been attractive to many, not so dissimilar from our own time.

Nevertheless, the sangha was not popular everywhere or with everyone; many people accused the Buddha of being against the Vedic norms of procreation, marriage, and family. The rule of chastity was especially hard to bear for many, as witnessed by

---

13. MN 31.9.

numerous offences and subsequent rules for various sexual infrac-
tions recorded in the Vinaya.[14] The Buddha's popularity with the
political warlords of the time varied constantly, requiring the
Buddha to move from place to place. At least two schisms broke
out, the more serious one led by Devadatta, the brother of the
Buddha's wife, Yasodhara, and a cousin of the Buddha. The
"schisming" and scheming became so intolerable that the Buddha
withdrew into seclusion on more than one occasion, preferring to
live alone in the jungle with a tusker elephant.

Devadatta

Devadatta was a Buddhist monk and the cousin and brother-in-
law of the Buddha, and the brother of Ananda. Devadatta was
Koliyan. He split from the Buddha's community with five hundred
other monks to form their own sangha. Most of these are said to
have been Shakyan relatives of both Devadatta and Siddhattha.
Devadatta became self-righteous. He began to think that
he should lead the sangha, not the Buddha. Shortly afterward,
Devadatta asked the Buddha to retire and let him run the sangha.
The Buddha retorted that he would not even let his trusted disciples Sariputta or Moggallana run the sangha, much less one like
Devadatta, "who should be vomited like spittle."[15]

The Buddha warned the monks that Devadatta had changed for
the worse. Seeing the danger in this, Devadatta approached Prince
Ajatasattu and encouraged him to kill his father, the good King
Bimbisara; meanwhile, Devadatta would kill the Buddha. Devadatta then tried to kill the Buddha himself by pushing a rock down
on him while the Buddha was walking on the slopes of a mountain. When this failed, he got the elephant Nalagiri drunk and
sicked the enraged elephant on the Buddha while the Buddha was

---

14. See esp. I.B. Horner, trans., *The Book of the Discipline*, Vol. I, pp. 349–72.

15. Cullavagga VII:3 (V V). If the Buddha stated that he would not allow his
foremost disciples to lead the sangha, it seems unlikely that he would have allowed Mahakassapa, the third most trusted disciple, to do so either. This refutes
the claim that the Buddha implicitly appointed Mahakassapa to be the future
leader of the sangha by exchanging robes with him, especially since the Buddha
said the sangha should have no leader other than the dharma itself.

on alms round. However, the Buddha's loving-kindness (*metta*) was so great that it overcame the elephant's anger. Devadatta then tried to create a schism in the order.

He collected a few monastic friends and demanded that the Buddha accept the following rules for the monks: *that they should live all their lives in the forest, live entirely on alms obtained by begging, wear only robes made of discarded rags, dwell at the foot of trees, and abstain entirely from fish and flesh.* The Buddha allowed the monastics to follow all of these except the last if they wished. The Buddha refused to make any of these rules compulsory, however, and Devadatta went about saying that he was living in abundance and luxury – similar to the accusation made by the Group of Five before the Buddha's Enlightenment. Devadatta then created a schism and recited the training rules (*patimokkha*) apart from the Buddha and his followers, with five hundred newly ordained monks. The Buddha sent his two chief disciples, Sariputta and Moggallana, to bring back the erring young monks. Devadatta thought they had come to join his sangha. After asking Sariputta to give a dharma talk, he fell asleep. When he awoke, he discovered that the chief disciples had persuaded the young monks to return to the Buddha's group.

Last Years and Parinibbana

As the Buddha approached the age of eighty, his health began to decline. He describes his complexion as no more clear and bright, and his body as flaccid, wrinkled, and bent forward, with changed senses. He complains of backaches. The Buddha's former personal attendant, Sunakkhatta, was going about attacking the Buddha's dharma as mere rationalism and deriding his spiritual achievements. To make matters worse, his old friend, King Pasenadi of Kosala, had died after visiting the Buddha. Pasenadi's son, Vidudabha, used this visit as a pretext for staging a coup. In addition, his own people, the Shakyans, were slaughtered by King Vidudabha of Kosala after Vidudabha learned that his mother was a Shakyan slave. This wiped out most of the Buddha's own people.

In his eightieth year, the Buddha felt that his death was imminent. He set out the rules whereby the sangha should be governed following his death – to hold large and frequent meetings; to assemble and disperse in concord; to do their duty as members of the sangha in concord; to keep the rules of the sangha without adding or subtracting anything, subject to the proviso that the minor and lesser rules may be abolished; to honour seniority; to avoid craving; to live in the forest; and to maintain mindfulness, *each one for themselves.*

The Buddha proclaimed a sermon, entitled "The Mirror of the Dhamma,"[16] in which he declares that perfect confidence in the Buddha, the Dharma, and the Sangha, combined with perfect virtue, guarantees immortality.

It was during the rainy season at a place called Beluvagamaka that a severe sickness came upon the Buddha with violent and deadly pains. After recovering, he began to prepare Ananda for his inevitable death. During this time the Buddha's two foremost disciples, Sariputta and Moggallana, the arhants foremost in wisdom and spiritual powers respectively, also died. Finally, the Buddha came to the Capala Shrine in Vesali, where he told Ananda that he expected to die in three months. For the next three months, the Buddha continued to wander, visiting the sangha in various places and giving out final dharma teachings.

Finally, he came to Pava, to the park of Cunna the goldsmith's son, who invited him to the Buddha's infamous last meal. This was a meal of *sukara-maddava.* Some say that this was a dish of fatty pork, translated by such phrases as 'pig's delight' or 'hog's mincemeat' (literally, it may be translated as 'soft' or 'mild pig'). Others say it was a rice dish prepared with a special kind of mushroom, truffle, or bamboo shoots, relished by pigs. Others believe that it was a special medical preparation, designed to cure the Buddha of his illness. Still others suggest that it was poison, perhaps an assassination attempt or even suicide. Whatever it was, it disagreed violently with the Buddha, who directed that it be buried.

After the meal the Buddha collapsed and, overcome by thirst, drank polluted water from a stream nearby. Refreshed, the Bud-

---

16. DN 16:2.8f.

dha was able to make it to the River Kakuttha, in which he bathed and from which he drank, and went to a mango grove. Here he lay down on a robe spread on the ground, on his right side. After some time he got up and continued on to the Mallians' sal tree grove on the turn into Kusinara, on the further bank of the Hirannavati River. Here he lay down again on his right side between two *sal* trees. The Buddha gave Ananda advice about the disposition of his remains and places of pilgrimage. The texts portray the Buddha engaging in dharma talk right up to the end. Finally, he instructs the monastics to take the dharma and the discipline as their teacher in the Buddha's absence. The Buddha declared that after his death, the sangha should be based on seniority. He states that the sangha may abolish the lesser and minor rules of the *Patimokkha*. His last words were, "Indeed, bhikkhus, I declare this to you. It is in the nature of all formations to dissolve. Attain perfection through diligence."[17] Then the Buddha fell into a coma and died. The texts say that the *sal* tree flowered prematurely. This suggests late winter, i.e., late February, contrary to the unlikely tradition that puts the birth, Enlightenment, and *parinibbana* of the Buddha all on the same day in May.

Dr. Mettanando Bhikkhu, a medical doctor, has argued at some length in his article on the cause of the Buddha' death[18] that the account of the Pali texts is consistent with a diagnosis of mesenteric infarction, a common disease of the elderly in which blood supply to the bowel is constricted.

The First Council

Mahakassapa, who was regarded as foremost in asceticism, despite the fact that Buddha said that the sangha should have no leader other than the dharma, convened the First Buddhist Council shortly after the Buddha's death. Mahakassapa may have also brought an ascetic orientation to the council and, as with all organizations, had both supporters and detractors. Indeed, it is clear from the Cullavagga that Mahakassapa's group sponsored the

---

17. Ibid, 6.7.
18. "How the Buddha Died."

council, and that others were excluded.[19] The First Buddhist Council was held during the rainy season three months after the Buddha's death.

Since the rainy season retreat begins in June-July, it seems likely that the Buddha died in late February or March, which is consistent with the statement that the *sal* trees between which the Buddha died bloomed prematurely. I have already mentioned how the arhants at this council castigated Ananda for convincing the Buddha to ordain women and for failing to clarify which were the major and which were the minor rules of the Vinaya. Indeed, so deep was the misogyny of the arhants of this council that Ananda was castigated for allowing women to view the Buddha's body after his death, which (they claimed) was defiled by their tears.[20] Presumably, Ananda too had his supporters and detractors, so we see here how the politics of the First Buddhist Council may have played out. It is an open question whether all the monastics present at the First Council were men. Dr. Chatsumarn Kabilsingh, in her article, "The History of the Bhikkuni Sangha," argues that female monastics were also present.

---

19. See I.B. Horner, trans., *The Book of Discipline (Vinaya-Pitaka)*, Vol. V, p. 395, n.1.

20. Ibid, pp. 400f. If you are interested in learning more about the First Buddhist Council in the primary sources, you can read the 11th chapter of the Cullavagga in the Vinaya section of the Pali Canon at https://archive.org/stream/p3sacredbooksofb2olonduoft#page/392/mode/2up.

4
The Early Buddhist Schools

The Eighteen Schools

EVEN BEFORE HE died, the question of how best to preserve the dharma of the Buddha was already being debated. One group wanted to enshrine the Buddha's teachings in a kind of formalized textual transmission similar to the Vedas, but the Buddha declared that the teachings should be transmitted in the common language of the people.[21] The Pali Canon shows that Ananda was consciously memorizing the Buddha's talks, and there is even evidence of a power struggle that emerged in the wake of the death of the Buddha's two chief disciples, Sariputta, the disciple foremost in wisdom, and Moggallana, the disciple foremost in psychic powers, who was brutally murdered (it is not clear whether his killers were rival monastics or robbers). The Buddha himself had been the object of an abortive murder attempt by his cousin Devadatta, who thought that the rules of the sangha were too lax, an accusation that dogged the Buddha all through his life. Toward the end of his life the Buddha seems to be dissatisfied with the sangha, and when Ananda suggested that he appoint a successor, the Buddha refused to do so, stating that the dharma itself should be the leader and the teacher of the sangha after his death (*parinibbana*).

---

21. This is the prevailing modern interpretation. However, some scholars interpret the Pali in the opposite sense.

After the *parinibbana*, a faction arose within the Buddhist order (*sangha*) declaring that now that the Buddha was gone, the monastics could do whatever they pleased. At least this is the Theravadin interpretation. However, since the Buddha himself said that the minor rules of the Vinaya might be abolished after his death, it seems possible that this is also a politicized account by conservative monastics who were attached to the rules of the Vinaya and a more liberal group who wanted to institute a more liberal Vinaya based on the Buddha's statement. In any case, Mahakassapa, the disciple foremost in asceticism, convened a meeting of the sangha at which all of the rules of the Vinaya were upheld, including apparently intentionally discriminatory rules for female monastics.[22] Whether this was due to Mahakassapa himself is unclear, since Mahakassapa had declared that the number of monastic rules is inversely proportional to the spiritual development of the sangha, implying that the rules are in fact a symptom of degeneration and not the reverse (this is the opposite of the common view today that the Vinaya rules themselves are a sort of spiritual training).[23] This view also corresponds to the historical development of the sangha. Nonetheless, the First Buddhist Council instituted a rigorous Vinaya that was also explicitly misogynistic and which led ultimately to the disappearance of the female monastic order, the *bhikkhunisangha*.[24] All of this is documented in the Pali Canon.

---

22. Many modern scholars doubt the story that Ananda had to convince the Buddha to admit women to the sangha based on his reluctance to ordain his stepmother, Mahapajapati, based on contrary evidence in the canon that a nun's order (*bhikkhunisangha*) already existed when Mahapajapati presented herself to the Buddha. The account also makes no "theological" sense, since it implies that the Buddha was irresolute and did not know his own mind. The overall evidence of the canon is that the Buddha did not discriminate against women and ordained women on an equal basis with men. It is, however, possible that the Buddha delayed creating the *bhikkhunisangha* for a time due to social prejudice.

23. SN 16:13.

24. The eight "heavy rules" (*garudhammas*) for nuns include inconsistent textual references that indicate that it was not instituted by the Buddha, including references to a probationer ordination that did not exist at the time of Mahapajapati's purported ordination.

The Buddha emphasized the importance of the ideological unity of the Buddhist community and established rules by which future Buddhist teachings might be evaluated as well as a legal requirement of consensus or, failing that, majority rule in the context of respect for elders. This is set out in the Vinaya itself. Of course, sustaining such a democratic structure as the sangha expanded and diversified became increasingly difficult in a time when travel and communication were difficult to impossible. The sangha was actually unified for only about a century. During the Second Buddhist Council, a minority reformist group of elders advocated a new arrangement of the rules of the Vinaya, which included new rules – something that the Buddha himself expressly forbade – and when unsuccessful they broke away from the majority Mahasamghikas to found the Sthavira *nikaya*. Thus, the first schism was not a matter of doctrine but of monastic discipline and organization.

The next three hundred years saw the emergence of numerous schools and sects, many geographically based, splitting off from the original two, traditionally referred to as the Eighteen Schools. Different authorities present different lists of these schools, often referring to the same or similar schools by different names, including the Sri Lankan *Dipavamsa* (3rd–4th cent. CE); *Mahavamsa* (5th cent. CE); the *Samayobhedo Paracana Cakra*, a Sarvastavadin work attributed to Vasumitra; Vinitadeva, a Mulasarvastivadin monastic of the 7th–8th centuries CE; the *Sariputraparipriccha*, a Mahasamghikan history; and various Chinese Mahayana sutras. For my purpose here I have utilized a list based on noted University of Toronto Buddhologist A.K. Warder in chapters 8 and 9 in his *Indian Buddhism*, consisting of eighteen schools presented in approximate chronological order. Interestingly, he says that this list of eighteen schools corresponds to the status quo about 50 BCE, the approximate date when the texts of the Pali Canon were first committed to writing and the beginning of the emergence of the Mahayana literature as a distinct genre, beginning with the Prajnaparamita literature of the first century BCE. However, whereas Warder simply discusses these schools as they arise in his book, with numerous side references and repetitions, I have organized them into a chart to make the derivation of the schools clear, which Warder did not do. This diagram contextualizes the progressive development of the early schools of Buddhism for the 350-year period from c 400 BCE to c 50 BCE.

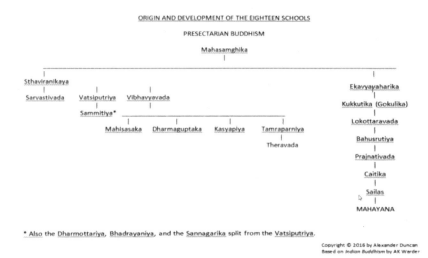

Keep in mind too that although I will allude to the Mahayana, *none of these schools is Mahayanist.* They are in fact all "Hinayana" schools, although of course that term is not appreciated by everyone, for which reason I refer collectively to the term "the Eighteen Schools" in my book, *Conversations with the Buddha,* instead of using the terms *hinayana* or *sravakayana.* After discussing the schools, I will conclude with some interesting implications and observations.

If you are keen, you might notice that the names of the schools on the chart, which follows Warder, differ slightly from the names of the schools in the corresponding sections. The reason for this is that I have used the equivalent Wikipedia headings where they differ from Warder in order make it easier for students to look them up. As with all Buddhist scholarship, opinions vary. In general, I have followed Warder and sought to effect a broad synthesis wherever possible.

1. *Sthavira nikaya*
(4th cent. BCE)

The Sthaviravada, literally, 'the sect of the elders,' precipitated the first Buddhist schism by splitting away from the Mahasamghikas during the Second Buddhist Council (about 334 BCE). Contrary to the last teachings of the Buddha according to the Pali Canon, the Sthaviravadins wanted to add new rules to the Vinaya, the Buddhist monastic code of discipline, against the will of the majority. Scholars now agree that the Mahasamghika Vinaya, which has fewer rules than the Sthavira Vinaya, is the oldest.

The Sthaviravadins split up into the Sarvastivada, Vatsiputriya, and Vinbhajyavada schools.

The Vatsiputriya split up into the Dharmottariya, Bhadrayaniya, Sammitiya, and the Sannagarika schools.

The Vibhajyavada split up into the Mahisasaka, Dharmaguptaka, Kasyapiya, and the Tamraparniya schools. The Tamraparniya school became known as the Theravada in the fourth century of the common era, and is the immediate precursor of the modern Theravadin school of Sri Lanka, Thailand, and elsewhere. As you can see, the Theravada is nine schools removed from the original pre-sectarian Buddhism, through the Sthavira which it claims as its own origin, and therefore cannot possibly be said to be identical with original Buddhism as claimed by its proponents, nor can the modern Theravada be accepted as a proxy for the Eighteen Schools of the Hinayana, which did not originate from the Theravada as we shall see.

2. *Mahasamghika*
(3rd cent. BCE)

Mahasamghika, 'the Great Sangha,' originated in Magadha, where the Buddha spent much of his time. It is regarded as the precursor of Mahayana Buddhism. The numerous *suttas* situated in Rajagaha (especially the Digha Nikaya) originated here. Several cave temples are associated with them. A Chinese account of the second century states that they wore yellow robes. A Tibetan source says that the robes bore the emblem of an endless knot or a conch. The doctrines of the Mahasamgha included:

- Ultimate and conventional truth;
- The trans-linguistic character of dharma;
- The conventional nature of language;
- Emptiness;
- The nature of bodhisattvas;
- The fallibility of arhants, making arhantship in effect an advanced stage of the path;
- The reification of Buddhahood;
- The infinity of the number of buddhas; and
- Intentional rebirth.

The Mahasamghikas regarded the Abhidhamma as non-canonical.

Since the Mahasamghikas were the majority and the Sthaviravada the breakaway minority, it is clear that the Mahasamghika must be regarded as the original post-sectarian Buddhist school with the Sthaviravadins as the schismatics. It is important to make this distinction from the perspective of Buddhist law, which seeks consensus, supports majorities, and shuns schismatics. In fact, to form a schism is a violation of the Vinaya, entailing initial and subsequent meetings of the community until the schism is resolved.

3. *Pudgalavada*
(3rd cent. BCE)

The Pudgalavada includes the Vatsiputriyas and the Sammitiyas. The Personalist school separated from the Sthavira about 280 BCE. The essential doctrine of this school was the reality of the person. The Theravada, Sarvastivada, and Madyamaka schools opposed this doctrine.

4. *Ekavyavaharika*
(3rd cent. BCE)

The 'single unified transcendent meaning school,' the Ekavyavaharika separated from the Mahamsamghika during the reign of Ashoka.

According to the *Samayabhedoparacanacakra* of Vasumitra, the Ekavyavaharikas, Kukkatikas, Lokottaravadins, and Mahasamghikas held forty-eight theses in common. The forty-eight views they held in common are connected with the nature of the Buddha, the bodhisattva, the arhants, and the stream entrants; mind and mental states; dormant passions and their outbursts; and the unconditioned. They also held that arhants are imperfect and fallible. They also held nine divergent views enumerated by Vasumitra concerning causation by self, others, and both and the coexistence of discrete thoughts.

5. *Kukkutika (Gokulika)*
(2nd–3rd cent. BCE)

The Kukkutika originated in the place-name of a major centre of the Mahasamghikas. The name means 'cinder,' and alludes to the universality of suffering. They held views similar to the Ekavyavaharika, Kukkutika, and Lokottaravada schools. Their centre was in Varanasi in eastern India. According to an Indian source, the Kukkutikans did not accept the Mahayana sutras as the 'word of the Buddha,' the *Buddhavacana.* They disappeared between the fourth and ninth centuries of the common era.

6. *Sarvastivada*
(3rd cent. BCE)

The Sarvastivadins – lit. 'the theory that all exists' – believed in the reality of the Three Times. They split from the Sthavira during the reign of Ashoka. The Sarvastivada influenced Buddhism for a thousand years, and were a major school. A Chinese source states that they wore dark red or black robes. They believed in three Buddhist vehicles – the way of the hearers, the way of the solitary buddhas, and the way of the bodhisattvas. They did not take refuge in the historical Buddha, but in the *dharmakaya,* the 'truth' or 'reality body.' Like the Mahasamghikas, they regarded arhants as fallible and imperfect. They also contested the view of the Mahisasakas that women are spiritually inferior. A nearly complete Sarvastivadin canon has recently been discovered in Afghanistan, the study of which should greatly add to our understanding of the early Buddhist canon.

7. Lokottaravada
(c 200 BCE)

Lit. 'those who follow the transcendent teachings,' the Lokottaravada emerged out of the Mahasamghika. They flourished in the northwest. The Lokottaravadins accepted the Mahayana sutras as *Buddhavacana*. Most of their canon has been lost, except for the Mahavastu, an early biography of the Buddha. The Infinite Life Sutra also owes much to their influence. The Ekavyavaharikas, Kukkutikas (a.k.a. Gokukkas), and the Lokottaravadins were doctrinally indistinguishable and were largely geographic rather than doctrinal in character. They distinguished two kinds of emptiness, emptiness of self and emptiness of phenomena. They upheld the Mahasamghika views concerning the transcendent nature of buddhas and bodhisattvas, the fallibility of arhants, and the Three Vehicles and provided special instructions for bodhisattvas, including the ten foundations (*bhumis*).[25] There are an infinite number of pure lands, buddhas, and tenth-stage bodhisattvas. All buddhas are equal in attainment. One thousand buddhas will follow the historical Buddha, including Maitreya, the Future Buddha of the Pali Canon.

8. Dharmottariya
(2nd cent. BCE)

Warder says that little is known of this school. It appears to have split from the Vatsiputriya along with the Bhadrayaniya, Sammitiya, and the Sannagarika during the second century BCE. He says that they were centred on the Aparanta region on the coast of Maharastra at the great port of Surparaka the capital. Their doctrines are similar to those of the Mahasamghikas from which they derived.

---

25. The ten *bhumis* describe the process by which ethics (1, 2), wisdom (3–6), and meditation (7–10) are perfected in the bodhisattva. The path of the bodhisattva includes that of the arhant (= eighth level bodhisattva).

9. *Bhadrayaniya*
(2nd cent. BCE)

The Bhadrayaniyas were located on the edge of the Maharastrian plateau behind the great port of Surparaka, called Nasika.

10. *Sammitiya*
(2nd cent. BCE)

The Sammitiya split from the Vatsiputriya school in the Sthavira tradition. According to Buddhologist Etienne Lamotte, the Sammitiya were the largest non-Mahayana sect in India. They affirmed the reality of the person. They were reputed to be extremely narrow-minded and intensely anti-Mahayana, destroying both texts and statues of the Mahayana and Vajrayana Buddhist schools.

11. *Sannagarika*
(2nd cent. BCE)

According to Titlin, this was the latest school of the Pudgalavada. He dates it to the third century CE.

12. *Bahusrutiya*
(3rd cent. BCE)

Lit. 'well learned,' the Bahusrutiya split off from the Mahasamghika school. It was founded by Yajnavalkya about 200 BCE. According to an Indian source, Yajnavalkya founded the Bahusrutiya school in order to promote a more profound discourse than that of the Mahasamghika, based on the idea of a superficial and profound meaning (conventional and ultimate truth). The Bahusrutiyas accepted both Hinayana and Mahayana teachings. Specifically, impermanence, suffering, emptiness, 'non-self-identity' (*anatta*), and 'emancipation' (*nibbana*) were considered to be ultimate truths, whereas the other teachings are mundane truths. They also believed that arhants are fallible. This school may have influenced the Tattvasiddhi Sastra.

13. *Prajnaptivada*
(3rd cent. BCE)

The Prajnaptivada school, reputedly founded by Mahakatyayana, seceded from the Bahusrutiya. They flourished in Magadha until the tenth century of the common era. Their main doctrine was that phenomena are the product of conceptualization. They distinguished between conventional and ultimate truth and between reality and mere concepts. Conditioned phenomena suffer because they are mere concepts or notions. They denied that suffering inheres in the *skandhas* or the five elements, contrary to the Sarvastivadins. The Noble Eightfold Path is eternal, immutable, and indestructible. The path cannot be cultivated through contemplation, but only through the cultivation of "all-knowledge" and the accumulation of merit. All attainments are the result of karma and merit. The Buddha's teachings are nominal, conventional, and causal. Therefore, they are only provisional. The Prajnaptivadins adhered to the two-truths doctrine, articulated the relationship between skillful means and wisdom, and may have influenced the great Buddhist philosopher Nagarjuna. The Bahusrutiyans and the Prajnaptivadins are particularly associated with the rise of the Mahayana.

14. *Mahisasaka*
(4th cent. BCE)

Founded by the monastic Purana, the Mahisasaka originated in the Vanti region of India during the Second Buddhist Council in the fourth century of the common era. They spread northwest and down to southern India including Sri Lanka, where they coexisted with the Theravada before they were absorbed by the latter. According to a Chinese source, the Mahisasakans were said to wear blue robes. They were said to be deeply involved in the practice of meditation, especially meditation on the Four Noble Truths. They held that everything exists in the present moment. A gift given to the sangha is more meritorious than a gift given to the Buddha. Early on, they rejected the doctrine of the intermediate state, but subsequently they came to accept it. The Infinite Life Sutra was composed by Mahisaskan monastics. The Mahisasakans were misogynists who believed that women could not become buddhas, a view that one also finds expressed in the Pali Canon. Because women cannot change the nature of their minds or bodies, they will cause Buddhism to decline.

15. Kasyapiya (Haimavata)
(c 190 BCE)

This school was named after Kasyapa, one of the missionaries of Ashoka sent to the Himalayan region. They split off from the Vibhajyavadin school in the second century BCE. They survived to the seventh century CE. According to a Chinese source they are described as wearing magnolia robes. They were an eclectic school and although nominally in the Sthavira tradition, they adopted doctrines from the Mahasamghikans. They believed that past events exist in the present in some form. They believed in the fallibility of arhants; because they have not completely eliminated desires, their perfection is incomplete and it is possible for them to relapse. The Gandhari Dhammapada may belong to this school. The Chinese canon also preserves an incomplete translation of the Samyutta Nikaya that may belong to this school.

16. Dharmaguptaka
(2nd cent. BCE)

The Dharmaguptakas split off from the Mahisasakas. Their Vinaya became the basis of Chinese, Vietnamese, Korean, and Japanese monasticism. Their name means 'preserver of the dharma.' They believed that the Buddha's teachings are superior to those of the arhants by virtue of his status as separate from the sangha. Therefore, venerating buddhas generates more merit than venerating the sangha (the opposite of the Mahisasaka view). They also advocated the merit of venerating stupas. They distinguished between the path of a hearer and the path of a bodhisattva. Thus, although formally in the Sthavira tradition, the views of the Dharmaguptaka are similar to those of the Mahasamghikas. They rejected the Sarvastivadin monastic rules on the grounds that the original teachings of the Buddha have been lost. According to a Chinese source, they wore black or deep red robes. Originating in

Aparanta, the Dharmaguptakas flourished in northwest India in the first century CE. Some scholars believe that they may have been founded by a Greek Buddhist monastic. They made major inroads in Iran, Central Asia, and China. Their Vinaya is still followed in China, Vietnam, and Korea. A Dharmaguptaka version of the Digha Nikaya is also extant in Chinese translation. It consists of four less *suttas* than the Theravadin version. A Dharmaguptaka Anguttara Nikaya is also extant, as well as a Dharmaguptaka Abhidharma. A sixth century CE Indian monastic named Paramartha identifies the Dharmaguptaka with the Mahayana.

17. Caitika
(1st cent. BCE)

The Caitika or Caityaka school flourished among the mountains of southern India, centred on Andhra, whence they derived their name. Led by Mahadeva, they emerged out of the Mahasamghika in the first or second century BCE. They are reputed to have owned the Great Stupa of Sanchi, commissioned by Ashoka in the third century BCE. They are also associated with the Ajanta Caves and the veneration of anthropomorphic Buddha images. They valued the path of the bodhisattva above that of the hearer, and they regarded arhants as fallible and subject to ignorance. They emphasized the transcendent character of the Buddha. A.K. Warder suggests that the Caitikas were the immediate precursor of the Mahayana. It has also been proposed that the great Prajnaparamita literature arose out of this school. They also elaborated the doctrine of the *Tathagatagarbha,* related to the Buddha-nature or Buddha-principle. They were also the reputed compilers of the ancient collection of Mahayana sutras entitled the Sutra of the Heap of Jewels (Maharatnakuta Sutra), consisting of forty-nine texts of varying lengths. The Caitika held that the Buddha's actions and speech were transcendent, but that some might only perceive the conventional or mundane interpretation.

18. Sailas
(1st cent. BCE)

The Apara Saila and Uttara (or Purva) Saila schools split from the Caitika around the Andhra city of Dhanyakataka, where the Caitikas also originated. The Madhyamaka Mahayana philosopher Candrakirti quotes the Purva Saila tradition in support of his doctrine that principles do not originate and cease in reality, so that the doctrine of interdependent origination (*paticcasamuppada*) is a conventional teaching only. The oldest parts of the Ratnakuta collection are also attributed to the Purva Saila school by various authorities.

The Five Points of Mahadeva

Mahadeva is a somewhat mysterious figure who, according to the Theravadin account, declared Five Points about thirty-five years after the Second Buddhist Council, about 300 BCE. However, some modern scholars have suggested that Mahadeva was actually the founder of the Caitaka school about two hundred years later, i.e., in the first century BCE. Although the historicity of this account is somewhat controversial, there is no doubt that the Five Points refer to an important controversy to do with the perfection of arhants on which the schools were thoroughly divided. These points or theses were:

1. Male arhants can have nocturnal emissions.
2. Arhants can be ignorant.
3. Arhants can doubt.
4. Arhants need guidance.
5. Arhants may attain the path by means of a verbal ejaculation [sic].

The gist of the first four of these points is that arhants are imperfect and fallible and therefore cannot represent the highest stage of the Buddhist path. As we have seen, the schools were divided on this question, including several Sthavira schools. The oldest Sthavira school to hold this view of the imperfection and fallibility of arhants was the Sarvastivada. The Sarvastivada also criticized the Mahisasaka view concerning the inferiority of women. In both of these respects, the Sarvastivada exhibits similarities to the Mahasamghika school, despite being a school in the Sthavira line. Warder dates the secession of the Sarvastivada from the Sthavira during the reign of Ashoka (third century BCE).

Views on Arhants

One of the interesting things that emerges out of the foregoing study is the position of the early schools on the status of arhants. We are accustomed to think of arhansthip as the ultimate goal of the Buddhist path, based on the Pali Canon, the only surviving complete early Buddhist canon, preserved by the Theravadins, yet the picture appears very differently when we catalog the positions of the early Buddhist schools on this question.

The Sarvastivada, Kasyapiya, Dharmaguptaka, Mahasamghika, Ekavyavaharika, Lokottaravada, Bahusrutiya, Pajnaptivada, and the Caitika schools all regarded arhants as imperfect in their attainment compared to buddhas and therefore fallible, despite being emancipated. I think that this ambiguity or paradox has to do with the doctrine of interdependent origination[26] as well as the historical fact of the primogeniture of the Buddha. Significantly, three of these schools fall under the conservative Sthavira, *the same school with which the Theravadins identify themselves.* Even the Mahisasakas – another Sthavira school – also appeared to believe that women could become arhants, but not buddhas, imply-

---

26. To recap, the chain of 'interdependent origination' (*paticca* + *sam* + *uppada*) includes two links (*nidanas*), craving (*tanha*) and ignorance (*avijja*), which are subject to intention, thus two points where the chain can be broken, resulting in liberation. Contact comes at the approximate midpoint of the chain, resulting from feeling and giving rise to clinging (desirous attachment), and is reversed through the practice of dispassion. Ignorance is the first link and therefore the root or "first cause" of the chain, resulting from birth, ageing, suffering, and death (interpreting the diagram as a cycle or "circle") and giving rise to 'constructive activities' (*sankharas*), and is reversed through the practice of wisdom, which is both the beginning and the goal of the path (Right View). Wisdom is the essential salvific principle, from which dispassion automatically follows. Interestingly, these two accomplishments, dispassion and wisdom, correspond exactly to the two stages of emancipation, the arhant and the Buddha respectively, with the Buddha pre-eminent due to the singular role of ignorance in the chain, which we see reflected in the primogeniture of the Buddha and the dependence of the arhants upon him.

ing that arhantship is inferior to buddhahood. Clearly, there was no consensus on this point. We are accustomed to thinking of the arhant as the ultimate goal of the Buddhist path, although the Pali Canon itself clearly considers Buddhahood to be beyond arhantship, because this is the view of the Theravadins, the only early Buddhist school to survive today.

The Buddha also prescribed different spiritual strategies for different people, based on their personal predilections and stages of development, including intentional rebirth, deva rebirth, and rebirth in the Brahma worlds, which are clearly not the highest goal according to the Buddha. There is even an arhant rebirth (in the Pure Abodes). The *metta* or loving kindness meditation, which is often mentioned all through the Pali Canon, by itself does not lead to arhantship.[27] As we have shown, the Theravadin claim to be identical with pre-sectarian or original Buddhism is historically false. On the other hand, the doctrine, associated with Mahadeva, that arhants are imperfect and fallible explains certain difficulties with the arhant concept in the Pali Canon, including the fact that it is a non-Buddhist concept generally (but not universally) associated with an intermediate *samana* stage (e.g., by the Jains) and the Buddha's statement and the evidence of the Pali Canon that it could be achieved relatively easily, in as short a time as one to seven days depending on the text, which seems an awfully short time to achieve the complete transcendent self-perfection that the Buddha took eons to develop, even with the aid of the *Buddhavacana*!

The Forty-Eight Doctrines of the Mahasamghikas

When Martin Luther decided to challenge the dogmas of the Roman Catholic Church in November 1517 he summarized his "disputation" in ninety-five theses, which he nailed to the front door of the All Saints Church in Wittenberg. Similarly, the Doctrines of the Different Schools (*Samayabhedoparacanacakra*) of Vasumitra records forty-eight special theses attributed to the Mahasamghika, Ekavyavaharika, Lokottaravada,   and   the Gokulika

---

27. Richard Gombrich holds a contrary view, but it is not widely accepted.

schools. Vasumitra was a monastic who led the Fourth Buddhist Council in Kashmir about the second century and helped to compile the Great Commentary of the Abhidhamma. Whether this is the same Vasumitra who wrote the Doctrines of the Different Schools is unclear. The book exists in English translation under the title *Origins and Doctrines of the Early Indian Buddhist Schools*. These are summarized on pages 18 to 32. Many of these propositions correspond to insights that I have had because of my study of the *suttas* of the Pali Canon. I have only just begun to study these, but in simplified summary form, they are as follows:

The Forty-Eight Theses of the Mahasamghika
1. *Buddhas are transcendent.*
2. *The Tathagata is undefiled.*
3. *Tathagatas preach the righteous law.*
4. *The Buddha can expound all of the doctrines in a single utterance.*
5. *The speech of the Buddha is always true.*
6. *The* sambhogakaya *or 'energy body' of the Buddha is infinite.*
7. *The divine power of the Tathagata is infinite.*
8. *The Buddha is immortal.*
9. *The Buddha never tires of enlightening beings.*
10. *The Buddha neither sleeps nor dreams.*
11. *There is no hesitation when the Buddha answers a question.*
12. *The realization of the Buddha is trans-linguistic.*
13. *The Buddha understands everything at once.*
14. *The wisdom of the Buddha is infinite.*
15. *Buddhas know that they have extinguished all defilements and will not be reborn.*
16. *Bodhisattvas are not gestated in the normal way.*
17. *The bodhisattva's final birth is indicated by the appearance of a white elephant.*
18. *Bodhisattvas are born by Caesarian section. Caesarian section was known in India as early as 1500 BCE, which also might explain the reason for Maya's reputed death seven days after the Buddha's birth.*

19. *Bodhisattvas do not harbour thoughts of greed, anger, or harming others.*
20. *Bodhisattvas may be reborn in good or bad states to help others.*
21. *One who has realized truth can meditate on all of the aspects of the Four Noble Truths simultaneously.*
22. *The five sense consciousnesses conduce to both passion and dispassion.*
23. *Beings in the form and formless worlds all possess all six sense consciousnesses.*
24. *The five sense organs in themselves are impercipient.*
25. *One can speak even in a meditative state.*
26. *Perfected beings are unattached.*
27. *Stream entrants know their own state.*
28. *Arhants are subject to temptation, ignorance, and doubt, are dependent on others, and the path is realized by utterances.*
29. *Suffering leads one to the path.*
30. *The words of suffering can help one to realize the path.*
31. *By wisdom, one annihilates suffering and experiences bliss.*
32. *Suffering is a kind of food.*
33. *One can remain in a meditative state indefinitely.*
34. *A Buddhist in an advanced state of realization can still retrogress.*
35. *A stream entrant can retrogress but an arhant cannot (because they have no passions).*
36. *There is no worldly right view or right faith.*
37. *Everything is good or bad. Nothing is morally neutral.*
38. *A stream entrant has destroyed all of the bonds.*
39. *Stream entrants cannot commit matricide, patricide, murdering an arhant, causing a schism, or cutting a Tathagata.*
40. *All Buddha* suttas *are inherently perfect.*
41. *There are nine ultimate or absolute things: extinction realized by wisdom, extinction not realized by wisdom, ordinary space, infinite space, infinite consciousness, nothingness, neither perception nor non-perception, karma, and dharma.*
42. *Mind is inherently pure.*

43. *Subconscious passions are neither mental nor do they become conscious.*
44. *Conscious and unconscious passions differ.*
45. *Past and future are not real.*
46. *Mental objects can be known or understood.*
47. *There is no intermediate state of existence between death
and rebirth.*
48. *Stream entrants are capable of meditation.*

Theravadin Claim to Historical Primacy

The earliest reliable historical accounts situate the origin of the
Theravada – the 'doctrine of the elders' – in Sri Lanka about 200
BCE, two hundred years after the *parinibbana.*[28] According to tradition they were founded by Mahinda, the son (or brother) of
Ashoka, who became a Buddhist monastic. Originally, they were
called the Tamraparniya, 'the Sri Lankan lineage.' Warder does
not include either the Tamraparniya or the Theravada in his list of
the eighteen original schools. Warder does not refer to either of
these schools in his book, *Indian Buddhism.* Disputes concerning
doctrine and practice caused the school to divide into three sub-
schools, the Mahavihara, Abhayagirivihara, and the Jatavanaviha-
ra, each of which was named after its associated monastery. These
schools were reunited in the 12th century by the Sri Lankan king,
under the guidance of two forest monastics of the Mahavihara
school. Thus, Theravada Buddhism became associated with na-
tionalism and even fascism.

The Tamraparniya/Theravada is an offshoot of the Vibhavyava-
da school, which derived from the Sthavira minority that split off
from the Mahasamghikas, through six intermediate schools (see
chart). As I have already explained, this schism was illegal under
Buddhist ecclesiastical law and thus all subsequent developments
were also illegal. The Theravadins clearly have no direct succession from original or pre-sectarian Buddhism, contrary to their
dogmatic claim to represent the original teachings of the Buddha.

---

28. 344 years if one accepts the traditional Theravadin date of the *parinibbana*
of 544 BCE.

Moreover, the term 'Theravada' did not come into use before the fourth century of the common era, when it was used in the *Dipavamsa* to designate the national spiritual heritage of Sri Lanka. According to a Chinese source, Mahayana Buddhism was also practised in Sri Lanka in the seventh century. The Mahayanists were associated with the Abhayagiri monastery, whereas the "Hinayana" Buddhists were centred on the Mahavihara monastery. As I have mentioned, Sri Lankan Buddhism itself was not unified until the twelfth century. Buddhaghosa codified Theravada doctrine in the fifth century of the common era. Thus, the Theravada is one of the latest of the so-called "early" schools.

Theravadins consider buddhas and arhants to have reached the same level of spiritual development; thus, arhants must be perfect and infallible. As I have shown, this view was by no means universally accepted by the early schools. Since the arhants of the First Buddhist Council and the Pali Canon itself are clearly misogynistic, this commits modern Theravadins to the view that women are spiritually inferior to men, a position still held in Thailand. The *bhikkhunisangha* died out in Sri Lanka during the thirteenth century. Some scholars (e.g., Melford Spiro, *Buddhism and Society*) consider Theravada Buddhism to be a composite of many separate traditions, overlapping but still distinct. The Theravadin Vinaya, with 227 rules for monks and 311 for nuns, both enshrines the misogyny of the First Buddhist Council and preserves a larger number of rules than the Mahasamghika, for which reason the Mahasamghika Vinaya is considered the oldest Vinaya extant. According to Mahakassapa, a larger number of rules indicates degeneracy, not spiritual superiority, which also corresponds to the historical account of the Pali Canon.[29]

According to Ajahn Sucitto ("What Is Theravada?"), a British-born Theravada Buddhist monastic,

> It was not originally a counterpoise to Mahayana, although it became subsequently defined, and has defined itself, as such. In fact, the term 'Mahayana' came into being around the first century, long before the term 'Theravada' was applied to a 'school' of Buddhism. The German

---

29. See n. 23.

scholar, Hermann Oldenberg referred to 'Theravada' to describe the Pali Vinaya texts he was translating – and published in 1879, but it wasn't until the early years of the twentieth-century that the term 'Theravada' was employed (by the English bhikku, Ven Ananda Metteyya) to describe the Buddhists of Sri Lanka, Burma and S.E. Asia. Even then, the term was not officially used in the Asian homelands until the gathering of the World Fellowship of Buddhists in Colombo in 1950.

Theravada Buddhism has been characterized by a series of collapses and revivals. Each time, the tradition became more consolidated, which of course also implies a loss of diversity. This phenomenon of simplification over time is well known to students of hermeneutics. According to Ajahn Sucitto, the Sri Lankan sangha disappeared during the eighteenth century and had to be revived from Thailand. This is the oldest lineage in Sri Lanka today – a mere three hundred years old.

David Chapman, in his essay, "Theravada Reinvents Meditation," notes that

in the early 1800s, vipassana had been completely, or almost completely, lost in the Theravada world. Either no one, or perhaps only a handful of people, knew how to do it. Vipassana was reinvented by four people in the late 1800s and early 1900s. They started with descriptions of meditation in scripture. Those were vague and contradictory, so the inventors tried out different things that seemed like they might be what the texts were talking about, to see if they worked. They each came up with different methods. Since then, extensive innovation in Theravada meditation has continued. Advocates of different methods disagree, often harshly, about which is correct. ...

In the mid-1800s, these texts were revered because supposedly they showed the way to nirvana. However, the way they were practiced was for groups of monks to ritually chant the text in unison. This is like a bunch of people who don't know what a computer is reading the manual out loud, hoping the machine will spring to life, without realizing you need to plug it in. ...

In the 1880s, there is no evidence that anyone in Sri Lanka knew how to meditate. One biography of [Anagarika] Dharmapala [a Sri Lankan Buddhist revivalist and writer] says flatly that 'the practice had been neglected and then forgotten.' It's possible that there were a few monks somewhere who still practiced vipassana, but there is no evidence for that. We do know that he travelled extensively in Sri Lanka, and 'in spite of all his enquiries he never succeeded in finding even a single person, whether monk or layman, who could instruct him in... meditation practices.'

Chapman makes two further points that are of interest here:

•   Asian Theravada repeatedly reinvented meditation under the influence of Western ideas. Chapman might be thinking of Theosophy or modernism here.

•   "Guys" [males] who were "into" extreme asceticism, which the Buddha expressly forbade, reinvented Theravada meditation. This fascination with asceticism continues in Theravada today, but is it Buddhist?

5
The Oldest Buddhist Scripture

Introduction

ANY TRADITION THAT attributes a special authority to one or more founders faces the same problem of documentation: how do we know what the original teachings were and, once we identify them, how are we to understand their meaning? The latter ranges from the problem of translation to the problem of understanding the meaning of meaning itself, while the former also relates to the problem of preservation. This aspect of Buddhism is like any other religion. Islam has the Quran, Christianity the Gospel, the Jews the Torah; Hindus have the Vedas, the Taoists have the Tao Te Ching. The historicity of some of these texts is ambiguous; in the case of traditions that emphasize an historical teacher more than the teaching, the hermeneutical problem is intensified. In the case of Buddhism, the primary historical source represents a developmental period of 375 to 387 years (404 BCE–29 or 17 BCE, following Wynne).[30] Even if we reject the naïve hermeneutic that a later text is automatically invalid, identifying the historical core of the original teaching is interesting, subject to the proviso that we cannot conflate "earliest" with "literally identical to the words of the Buddha."

Even more vexed is the question whether originality even matters? Are the literal words of the Buddha necessarily definitive? The Buddha, like all historical phenomena, existed in a

---

30. Wynne, "How Old Is the Sutta Pitaka?"

relative and contingent samsaric context, and therefore all of his manifestations and appearances are karmically conditioned, including whatever insights concerning dharma that the Buddha bestowed directly upon his contemporaries and upon those of us who hear them indirectly. Even if we accept the archaic claim that the Buddha was omniscient in some sense, we may question the omniscience of his disciples. Theravadins, anticipating this problem, insist that the arhants were infallible, but even this leaves open the questions of unknown teachings, lost texts, and subsequent misinterpretations by non-arhants. The evidence of the texts themselves is that the Buddha tailored his teachings to his audience. The true object of study in Buddhism is not the person or circumstances of the historical Buddha, it is what the Buddha himself indicated in his thoughts, words, and actions, i.e., the dharma, at which he pointed like the famous finger pointing at the moon. The Pali Canon says that the Buddha de-emphasized leadership and directed his followers to understand the dharma directly for themselves. Thus, Buddhology is based on a false premise. Any study of the oldest Buddhist scripture must have for its objective the revelation of the one true object of study, the dharma itself. This is a significantly larger study than historicism or linguistics can comprehend. The Pali Canon says that the Buddha hesitated to teach, and finally only agreed to teach after being petitioned by God himself; he said that he knew much, much more than he taught; he taught differently to different people, based on their circumstances and needs, including religion to the householders, meditation to the monastics, and wisdom to the arhants. Dharma is protean and adjusts itself continuously to the circumstances of the time. For this reason alone, fundamentalism is fatuous.

Stratification in the Pali Canon has been a special subject of study for a century now, largely based on the linguistic studies of Pali specialists, but most of the progress in the field was made by the time that Pande published the first edition of his *Studies in the Origin of Buddhism* (1957), which he updated till his recent death in 2011. In that book, he cites a theory of stratification proposed by the great early 20th century Buddhist translator T.W. Rhys Davids. Law's elaborate critique[31] only reinforces Rhys Davids's conclusion, with a few changes that do not affect our argument here. According to both Rhys Davids and Law, the first (i.e., oldest) four items in the list are:

1. The simple statements of Buddhist doctrine now found, in identical words, in paragraphs or verses recurring in all the books.
2. Episodes found, in identical words, in two or more of the existing books.
3. The Silas, the Parayana, the Octades, the Patimokkha.
4. The Digha, Majjhima, Anguttara, and Samyutta Nikayas.

Despite being written in elegant verse, its location in the Khuddaka Nikaya (generally considered to consist of more recent texts), and having none of the ordinary signs of oral transmission (e.g., turgid repetitiousness, stock phrases and lists, etc.), according to no less authorities than Rhys Davids and Law, the oldest extant doctrinal parts of the Pali Canon, setting aside the non-doctrinal ethical precepts and the rules of training, are the Parayanavagga ('chapter of the final goal') and the Octades (Atthakavagga, 'groups of eight'). This is confirmed by H. Saddhatissa,[32] whose translation of the Sutta Nipata is used by Bhikku Bodhi in his talks on the Sutta Nipata (Saddhatissa adds I:3 as contemporary with the Atthaka and Parayana *vaggas*),[33] and by K.R. Norman,[34] among others. Paradoxically, these are now found in the Sutta Nipata in the Khuddaka Nikaya, which is demoted to number five in Rhys Davids's list. Although a few more potentially archaic texts have been suggested, e.g., the Udanas, Itivuttaka, etc.,[35]

---

31. Law, "Chronology of the Pali Canon."
32. Saddhatissa, *The Sutta-Nipata.*
33. This is the Khaggavisanasutta, the famed Rhinoceros Sutta, which advocates the life of a homeless wanderer, "as a beast unbound in the forest goes feeding at pleasure," free of emotional entanglements.
34. Norman, *The Group of Discourses (Sutta-Nipata).*
35. Not accepted as early by Rhys Davids or Law. Law put these works at #7 out of 10, more recent than the *nikayas* and even the Jatakas. Gombrich seems to place the composition of most of the *nikayas* in the mid-fourth century CE, about fifty-five years after the *parinibbana*. Rupert Gethin thinks that they are somewhat more recent. However, Gethin's own statement that they are the product of the "first few generations" after the Buddha' death places them no

the consensus view seems to be that the fourth and fifth chapters (*vaggas*) of the Sutta Nipata, denominated the Parayanavagga and the Atthakavagga,[36] are among the oldest if not the oldest canonical texts to survive today. It is therefore interesting to examine the teachings of these texts, considering the possibility that they are close to, if not identical with, the original teachings of the historical Buddha. According to Lebkowicz, Ditrich, and Pecenko,[37] they are pre-monastic. Fausböll says that "we see here a picture not of life in monasteries, but of the life of hermits in its first stage. We have before us not the systematizing of the later Buddhist church, but the first germs of a system, the fundamental ideas of which come out with sufficient clearness."[38] Since Buddhist monasticism was founded by Gotama Buddha himself, and the lands and buildings had already begun to be donated and built during his lifetime, this must have been very early indeed, when many monastics still lived or wandered solitary or in small groups. Alexander Wynne, citing the Atthakavagga, suggests that "much of what is found in the Suttapitaka is earlier than c. 250 B.C., perhaps even more than 100 years older than this,"[39] i.e., about 350 BCE at least. This is fifty-four years after the *parinibbana,* for which Wynne accepts Gombrich's date of 404 BCE. If we allow a margin for error of about twenty years, this is 30 to 80 AB approximately. In the Christian tradition, this would correspond to the late canonical period (approx. 60–110 CE).[40]

The Atthaka and the Parayana *vaggas* constitute the fourth and fifth chapters of the Sutta Nipata in the Minor Tradition (Khuddaka Nikaya). The Sutta Nipata (lit. 'falling down *suttas*') consists of mixed verse and prose in five sections. The Atthakas and Paraya-

---

later than about 300 BCE. See Rupert Gethin, "Gethin on Gombrich: 'What the Buddha Thought.'"

36. The Atthakavagga also survives in Chinese translation as an independent work.

37. Lebkowicz et al., *The Way Things Really Are.*

38. Fausböll, *The Sutta-Nipata,* p. xii.

39. Wynne, "How Old Is the Suttapitaka?"

40. For comparison, the Christian canonical period extends from 30 to 160 CE. This period includes many non-canonical texts as well, especially after 95 CE. Q, the original Christian scripture (reconstructed), is dated to 40–80 CE.

nas consist of sixteen and seventeen short *suttas* or *sutta*-like texts, thirty-three in all. In English translation, it consists of sixty-eight pages, approximately thirteen thousand words, somewhat longer than the Tao Te Ching (10,000 words) or Q (6,000 words). They do not appear to have been nearly as edited as the *nikayas,* probably because they are written in verse (Pande notes that verse form is more conservative in the Pali Canon though he rejects the assumption that verse must be automatically older than prose in the same text). The terminology and conceptual structures seem to be pre-*nikaya* and still in a process of formation (e.g., an interdependent origination (*paticcasamuppada*) consisting of seven *nidanas* instead of ten or twelve, with similar but more protean terminology, while ignorance is referred to but in a somewhat different way). The syntax is fresh and lively, full of vitality and enthusiasm. The tone is positive, even heroic. It is exciting to think that this may be the oldest surviving *sutta* collection, a literal remnant of the Buddha himself and one of the original seeds of the *suttas* of the Pali Canon.

I have used the English translation of V. Fausböll, published in 1881 in Max Muller's Sacred Books of the East series. Although there are more modern and literary translations of the Sutta Nipata, Fausböll's literal translation has the virtue of adhering closely to the Pali as far as I can see so that there is less danger of misconstruing an interpretation of a modern translator for an original view of the Buddha. I have also compared several other translations, especially that of K.R. Norman.

The Atthakavagga addresses such basic concerns as desire, attachment, philosophy, mindfulness, detachment, the nature of Buddhahood (referred to as the *Muni,* or 'Sage,' similar to the Tao Te Ching, and *Bhagavat,* 'Lord'), and the path. The *suttas* emphasize the importance of independence and disdain philosophizing and seeking salvation through others. We must save ourselves. The Buddha opposes the doctrine of self-purification through the cultivation of inward peace to the doctrine that one is purified by the practice of philosophizing based on speculation and argument. Even at this early date, we see the Buddha celebrated and even worshipped as a descendent of the Sun, a *Muni,* an *Isi,* and a

Sambuddha ('perfectly or self-enlightened'). The Buddha is said to
have been reborn from the Tushita ('satisified') heaven, associated
with the bodhisattva doctrine. The Buddha is described as having
the thirty-two marks of a great man and as having the psychic
power of telepathy. The realm of the deities (devas), including
earthbound devas and Mara, are also referred to. The path is described as both gradual and instantaneous. The Buddha prohibits
some of the same superstitious practices, especially prognostica-
tion, that he criticizes in the first *sutta* of the Digha Nikaya, the
Net of Confusion (Brahmajala Sutta). As observed by Mrs. C.A.F.
Rhys Davids, asceticism is deemphasized.[41] Pain is observed, but
not cultivated. The liberated person is free from attachment *and
revulsion* and sees happiness everywhere. They are friendly and
tolerant to all, much like the sage of Laozi. These texts, especially
the Parayanavagga, introduce the same question and answer format that structures almost all of the *suttas,* suggesting that this
may have been the major teaching method used by the historical
Buddha.

The study of the Atthaka and Parayana *vaggas* provides a win-
dow into the archaic dharma of the Buddha. It gives us an opportunity among other things to test the rationalist assumptions of
the so-called modern or secular Buddhist movement. [42] In
these *vaggas* one recognizes a broad range of doctrinal topics, including a system of epistemological, soteriological, ontological,
cosmological, Buddhological, and ethical world-views that antici-
pate similar doctrines that we find more thoughtfully worked out
in the *nikayas.*

---

41. See the Introduction to her translation of the Dhammapada in Rhys Davids, *The Minor Anthologies of the Pali Canon,* Part I, pp. vii–xxxix, esp. pp. xi,
xxviii f., and xxxxi.

42. Some other cognate terms are secular Buddhism, agnostic Buddhism, "ig-
nostic" Buddhism, atheistic Buddhism, pragmatic Buddhism, modern Theravada,
progressive Theravada, original Buddhism, core Buddhism, mainstream Buddhism, Protestant Buddhism, British Buddhism, and academic Buddhism. See
Buddhist Modernism (https://en.wikipedia.org/wiki/Buddhist_modernism) and
Secular Buddhism (https://en.wikipedia.org/wiki/Secular_Buddhism).

In the following sections, I will summarize the world-views implicit in these texts in broad outline.

1. Epistemology

The Buddha affirms that the only eternal or ultimate truth is consciousness, and that truth is unitary. Thus, it is trans-dual. For this reason, the Buddha rejects sectarianism, scholasticism, asceticism, rationalism, dogmatism, and debate, and proposes a philosophy of no philosophy, which is identified with wisdom.

2. Soteriology

For there to be salvation there must be a fall. Thus, the Buddha identifies ignorance and desire as the primary binary that binds us to "reiterated existence" (rebirth) in time. He repudiates desire, grasping, and the body and stresses the inferiority of the body, existence, and the householder life of possessiveness, territoriality, and war. The Buddha rejects self-purification by knowledge, actions (i.e., karma, as in Jainism), tradition (Brahmanism), sacrifice, or by following others. He proposes that one must purify oneself through the progressive practice of detached indifference, the cultivation of inner peace (tranquility) and mindfulness or "thoughtfulness," sitting in secluded meditation in the wilderness, at the foot of a tree, in a cemetery, or in a cave on a mountain. The Buddha posits a mode of knowledge by which one is purified, which is unitary and trans-dual and can be realized by the practice of mental concentration. By these means, a transcendent state of realization is progressively induced that leads to the perfect, immortal, and timeless security of nirvana, in which desire itself is extinguished. Elsewhere meditation is described as the realization of emptiness, nothingness, or the void, which corresponds to the fundamental ontological state. Nirvana is a state beyond consciousness itself. Those who attain this state are described as "men who have crossed the stream." The realization of nirvana itself is instantaneous, immediate, and uncharacterizable.

3. Ontology

Existence is described as suffering and impermanent. Beings are trapped in an endless cycle of rebirth, but the very impermanent and temporary nature of existence implies that it is possible to escape into non-rebirth by transcending the whole sevenfold system of interdependent origination by which name and form (individuality) lead to "touch" (contact), decay and origin, pleasure and pain (feeling), will (intention), grasping, and finally suffering (ignorance is mentioned elsewhere as "the head"). We recognize here a primitive form of the familiar doctrine of *paticcasamuppada* (lit. 'following from anything as a necessary result with coming into existence'). The law of cause and effect (*kamma*) driven by mental activity (*sankhara*) is the essential kinetic principle. At the same time, the world is described as essentially illusory, empty, and void.

4. Cosmology

The Atthaka and Parayana *vaggas* allude to the familiar elements of Buddhist cosmology, including other worlds, deities or devas, Mara, and the Tushita heaven (IV:16. 1), the latter the heaven from which the Buddha-to-be was reputedly reborn. This corresponds to the bodhisattva idea, whereas the rhinoceros (of the Rhinoceros Sutta) is a symbol associated with the *pratyekabuddha.* The rhinoceros is as unlike the contemporary image of the monastic as one can imagine.

5. Buddhology

The Buddha is referred to by his family or clan name of Gotama and described as a man, as well as by the mysterious term *tathagata*, 'he who having come this way has thus gone that way to suchness.' He is described as wise and great, a World Teacher, as well as being omniscient, that is, he has perfect understanding. He is distinguished by the thirty-two marks of a great man, and is identified as a descendant of the Sun and symbolically with both the sun and the moon.

6. Ethics

The Buddha advocates an ordinary ethical life of moderation and self-restraint.

Although it would be a logical error to infer that because this is the oldest surviving text, it necessarily is complete and therefore exclusive of all other texts – many other similar texts were presumably lost or subsumed into later texts – what the text does say is of more than passing interest since this is the closest we can get to what the Buddha actually taught, composed perhaps no later than twenty years after his death. The text has a fresh and lively voice and originality of diction that radiate the vigour and vitality of beginnings, even in translation. In particular, it appears as a virtual hologram of the doctrines found in the *nikayas,* including such advanced concepts as trans-duality, the unity of truth, the philosophy of no philosophy, gradual and instantaneous realization, rebirth, karma, Mara, devas, other worlds, the Tushita "heaven," and the transcendent nature of Buddhahood itself. Far from being late ideas, these doctrines are clearly inherent in the fundamental substrate of the Buddhist oeuvre. This contrasts sharply with the modern secularist view that the historical development of Buddhist doctrine represents a degeneration from an original ideal devoid of "superstitious" elements. The Atthaka and Parayana *vaggas* are extremely sophisticated philosophical documents, comparable to or surpassing even the Tao Te Ching.

A close evaluation of the Atthaka and Parayana *vaggas* discovers allusions to trans-dualism; trans-rationalism; rebirth (which some modern or secular-minded modern Buddhists would like to abandon); ethical indifference (very like Yeshua's injunction not to judge); individualism; the nirvana element or "realm"; emptiness; instantaneous enlightenment; the planes of existence; and the omniscience and perfection of the Buddha, including the thirty-two "supernatural" marks of a great man. The Atthaka and Parayana *vaggas* do not support the view that these doctrines are later accretions. Rather, the whole oeuvre appears to inhere in its historical ground. To say that they do not originate with the Buddha is therefore a dogmatic and unprovable assumption.

Prologue of the Parayanavagga

The Atthaka and Parayana *vaggas* consist mostly of direct teachings of the Buddha or short question and answer sessions with individuals with little or no additional historical or biographical details. The single exception is the Prologue to the Parayanavagga, called the Vatthugatha (lit. 'story in verse'). Because of its singular nature in the context of these texts, I am going to summarize it here. Both Rhys Davids and Law place the Parayanavagga before the Atthakavagga, but Law specifically excepts the Prologue, suggesting that it is later, though he does not mention it elsewhere in his scheme. It may, therefore, be the oldest Buddhist historical account.

The story is situated south of Savatthi, the capital of Kosala, where many of the later *suttas* are also located. Bavari, a *brahmana*, whose name means 'enemy of worldly existence,' dwelled near Alaka, on the banks of the Godhavari, a river in the territory of Assaka, "wishing for nothingness." Assaka was the most southern *mahajanapada*. The Godavari river is the second longest river in India, after the Ganges, and runs from west to east across central India. Like many ascetics of the time, including the Buddha, Bavari lived outside a village where he could obtain the requisites, including enough money, apparently, to hold a great sacrifice in the Brahman tradition. After this, another *brahmana* arrived, "with swollen feet, trembling, covered with mud, with dust on his head,"[43] who immediately demanded five hundred pieces of money! Bavari treated the other *brahmana* with the utmost courtesy and respect, but apologetically explained that, having spent all of his money on a great sacrifice, he had no money left to give to the *brahmana*. Offended, perhaps even enraged, the *brahmana* proceeded to curse Bavari, declaring that after seven days his head would cleave into seven pieces. This was a common curse repeated elsewhere in the Pali Canon.

Bavari became sorrowful and began to waste away, taking no food, but at the same time he continued to delight in meditation. After some time the benevolent deity of the place, presumably a

---

43. Sutta Nipata., V:1.5(980).

benign earthbound deva, appeared to Bavari and explained to him that the other *brahmana,* now departed presumably, is a hypocrite and an impostor, knowing nothing about heads or head splitting, thus rather strangely segueing into the topic of the story and indeed of the *vagga.* Thus, the Parayanavagga is in fact a precis of the salvific wisdom of the dharma itself.

Bavari asks the deva to explain to him about heads and head splitting, but the deva does not know anything about it, saying that this knowledge is limited to buddhas. Bavari asks the deva who he can approach for an explanation, and the deva tells Bavari that a World Ruler, a descendent of King Ikshvaku (Skt. *Okkaka*), the first king of the Ikshvaku or solar dynasty, has gone out of Kapilavatthu, the capital of the Shakyans. This identification of the Buddha as a descendent of the righteous and glorious king Ikshvaku suggests the descent of Yeshua from King David. The solar dynasty is also important in Jainism, since twenty-two out of twenty-four of the Jain *tirthankaras* belonged to this dynasty, and to Hindus, whose culture hero, Rama, of the Ramayana, also belonged to the solar dynasty. According to the Buddhist texts the founder of the solar dynasty was Mahasammata, the first king of the current age, who was democratically elected (approximately ten trillion years ago according to the Sinhalese and Burmese chronicles). The deva describes the Buddha as "light-giving": "He is, O Brahmana, the perfectly enlightened (Sambuddha); perfect in all things, he has attained the power of all knowledge, sees clearly in everything; he has arrived at the destruction of all things, and is liberated in the destruction of the upadhis," referring to the "fuel of life" that precipitates rebirth. "He is Buddha, he is Bhagavat in the world; he, the clearly-seeing, teaches the Dhamma" (V:1.17). *Bhagavat* means 'the Adorable One,' and in Hinduism is a term for Krishna or God. This passage again alludes to the salvific knowledge or "power of truth."

Bavari, his spirits revived, asks the deva where he might find this chief of the world, the first of men, so that he might go there and worship him. Referring to the Buddha by the Jain term *Jina,* 'Victorious One,' and as a "bull of men," the deva tells Bavari that the Buddha is staying in Savatthi. Bavari then goes to his sixteen *brahmana* disciples, including the great *isi* (rishi) Pingiya, to go to Savatthi to see the Buddha for themselves. His disciples ask Bavari how they will recognize him. Bavari tells them that the hymns, referring presumably to the Vedas, refer to thirty-two marks of a great man, and that they can recognize him by these signs. Interestingly, no such hymn has ever been identified. Bhikku Sujato has suggested that they might be Babylonian in origin.[44] Whatever their origin, their presence in the Prologue of the Parayanavagga clearly indicates their archaic origin. Bavari tells his disciples that such a one will either become a peaceful and just World Ruler or a saintly Sambuddha who will remove the veil from the world. Bavari also tells them that they will also know the Buddha because he will answer the questions that are in their minds without asking.

Bavari's disciples travel north to Savatthi to find the Buddha, along with a large number of their own students. Bavari's disciples are described as advanced philosophers and meditators, with matted hair or dreadlocks and wearing animal hides. They travel through a succession of cities, including Savatthi, but finally they find the Buddha at the top of a mountain near Vesali, Magadha, in the Barabar Hills north of Gaya, called the Rock Temple (*pasanaka cetiya*, lit. 'stone tope'), southeast of Savatthi.[45] Here the Buddha was teaching dharma to the monastics, "like a lion roaring in the forest."[46] Ajita, apparently the leader, beholds the Buddha as a sun or a moon, and perceives all of the thirty-two marks of a great man on his body. Asking the questions concerning Bavari in his mind, the Buddha tells him that Bavari is 120 years old; his name; that he has three of the marks of a great man (long tongue, tuft of hair between the eyebrows, and a sheathed penis), and that he is perfect in the three Vedas. Satisfied, Ajita gets to the point, and asks the Buddha about the head and head splitting. The Buddha tells Ajita that the head refers to ignorance, and that knowledge

---

44. Sujato, "On the 32 Marks." Coincidentally, there are thirty-two base pairs that define the sixty-four codons of the human genetic code.

45. Dhammika. "Footprints in the Dust."

46. Sutta Nipata, V:1.40(1015).

cleaves the head, along with belief, thoughtfulness, meditation, determination, and strength.

This metaphorical identification of ignorance with the head and head splitting – the destruction of ignorance – with knowledge is exceptionally interesting, and proves among other things that the Buddha's criticism of "philosophizing" clearly does not extend to a rejection of knowledge or wisdom as such. The implication rather is that knowledge or wisdom is the salvific principle, as we have discussed elsewhere. Thus, two kinds of knowledge are distinguished. Ignorance of course becomes the root or "head" of the doctrine of interdependent origination.[47] Ajita puts his animal hide on one shoulder, "falls down" before the Buddha, and "salutes him with his head,"[48] perhaps kneeling before the Buddha and touching his forehead to the ground in an act of prostration. Ajita apparently has Bavari's warrant to act on his behalf, for he tells the Buddha on behalf of Bavari and his disciples that they all pay homage to the Buddha's feet (perhaps Bavari was too old to make this long journey himself, despite his former expression of his wish to do so). The Buddha wishes Bavari and Ajita, described as a young man, well. Wishing them happiness and long life, the Buddha invites Ajita and the disciples to ask him whatever questions they wish. Ajita and the other disciples ask the Buddha a series of philosophical and soteriological questions in the next sixteen *suttas*, which make up the Parayanavagga.

Now I will take a closer look at nine specific topics of the Atthaka and Parayana *vaggas* in greater detail. These explanations represent a collation of the relevant references in these texts and follow the texts closely, with a minimum of interpretation, which I will leave for the Conclusion.

The Philosophy of No Philosophy

I am going to start with epistemology, the study of knowing, first, because of the weight that these two *vaggas* put on what I

---

47. Ignorance is also described as a shroud that covers the world in the Parayanavagga (2.2.).
48. Sutta Nipata, V:1.52(1027).

have chosen to call "the philosophy of no philosophy." Philosophy, philosophizing, and/or philosophers are discussed in no less than eight *suttas* of the Atthaka *vagga* (IV:3, 4, 5, 8, 9, 11, 12, 13). The Buddha says that "the dogmas .of philosophy are not easy to overcome."[49] On the other hand, the independent one, i.e., the follower of the Buddha, "has shaken off every (philosophical) view."[50] One is reminded of the first *sutta* of the Digha Nikaya, the Brahmajala Sutta, where the Buddha disdains philosophizing as a "base art." Ironically, this discussion of conflict avoidance breaks out into an open argument between Magandiya and the Buddha (9.6, 7). The Buddha makes it quite clear that "if a man's purification takes place by (his philosophical views), or he by knowledge leaves pain behind, then he is purified by another way than the *ariyamagga*, i.e., the noble way" (4). The Buddha considers that philosophizing creates division and discord (5.1), Therefore a bhikku "does not depend even on knowledge. He does not associate with those that are taken up by different things, he does not return to any (philosophical) view" (5.5). The Pasurasutta (IV:8) includes an extensive description of philosophical debates that we find elsewhere described in the Pali Canon. "Seeing this," says the Buddha, "let no one dispute, for the expert do not say that purification (takes place) by that" (8.7). Nevertheless, the Buddha acknowledges that philosophy can take one part of the way (IV: 8.11, V:14.3), and appears to distinguish between understanding and "philosophical views" (IV:9.13). In antithesis to the view that philosophical knowledge is salvific the Buddha declares that the truly salvific thing is a state of inward peace and outward indifference. Only this state confers true wisdom and happiness, yet wisdom is also praised (16.15; V:12.1; 17. 13, 15, 17); "inward peace" itself is referred to as "truth" (dharma) and trans-rationalism or the trans-linguistic (V:7.6–8). He also asserts that the sage does not reject anything (IV:9.5) and is liberated by knowledge (V:1.51). Clearly, the relationship between knowledge and wisdom is subtle and complex. This notion of the true sage being indifferent to

---

49. Ibid, IV:3.6.
50. Ibid, 3.8.

formal learning or academic knowledge reminds one of the Tao Te Ching.

Meditation

Buddhism is not merely or even primarily a theory. The Buddha says that he understood the theory of emancipation prior to his Enlightenment, but it was not until he understood the praxis of emancipation that he became enlightened and began to teach others. Therefore, it is of special interest to know what the Buddha said about meditation in the Atthaka and Parayana *vaggas*.

The Buddha advises his followers to "cultivate the mind of a recluse" (IV:6.7). Instead of seeking salvation through philosophical argument, knowledge, virtue (ethics), or "holy works" (merit), the Buddhist should seek salvation through the cultivation of "inward peace" and tranquility, and the cultivation of an attitude of perfect tolerance, neither accepting *nor rejecting* anything. The Buddha identifies three types of consciousness that are not conducive to liberation, including "natural consciousness," insanity, and unconsciousness, the latter being an error that is identified in later *suttas* as leading to rebirth in the *Asanna satta,* the realm of unconscious beings, just below the Five Pure Abodes, the place where non-returners and arhants with residue are reborn interestingly. Thus, the Buddha makes it clear that a type of superconsciousness, for lack of a better term, characterizes the attainment of nirvana, also referred to as the "cessation of consciousness," but it is clear from the text that cessation of consciousness does not imply unconsciousness. Rather, it seems to refer to the absence of sensation (V:14.7) of a "dispossessed mind" (V:16.26). Once again, we see the importance of collating all relevant texts to avoid misunderstandings. The Buddha advises his followers to be still, without desire; to be meditative; watching; and to sit down quietly. One is to "drive off the agitations of the mind" with an equanimous, calm, composed mind; thoughtful, with mind liberated; intent on a single object (concentrated).

The Buddha appears to equate meditation with "wishing for nothingness" or "having in view nothingness," neither grasping *nor rejecting* anything. Interestingly, the Parayanavagga says that

85

the knowledge of "heads and head-splitting" is only found in bud-dhas, the head being equated with ignorance and head splitting with the abolition of ignorance. Ignorance of course became the root of the interdependent origination in later texts: "Ignorance is the head, know this; knowledge cleaves the head, together with belief [faith], thoughtfulness [mindfulness], meditation [concen-tration], determination [resolution], and strength [energy]" (V:1. 51). Clearly, therefore, the Buddha is making a distinction between philosophical argument and another sort of knowledge ("having been delivered in the highest deliverance by knowledge" [V:7.3f]), characterized as wisdom, and referred to as the Divine Eye (*dibba-cakkhu*, the *ajna* chakra). A passage in V:10.4 seems to allude to the yogic doctrine that one stops breathing in advanced stages of meditation (jhana), which one also finds in Patanjali. The culmin-ation of meditation is *nibbana*, the 'extinction' of desire. Yet even the Buddha meditates, the text tells us, a fact reiterated in the lat-er *suttas*.

Arhant and Bodhisattva

The Atthaka and Parayana *vaggas* make a clear distinction be-tween those who live in the cave, rather strikingly anticipating Plato's parable of the cave (Fausböll equates the cave with the body)[51] and those who have crossed the stream (gone to the other shore). This then is the fundamental soteriological project of Bud-dhism.

Those who have liberated themselves from "reiterated existenc-es" (*samsara*, 'rebirth' but also time) are called *muni* ('sage'), *brahmana* ('knower of the Absolute or Ultimate Reali-ty'), *isi* ('seer,' a Vedic rishi), and "men who have crossed to the other shore."[52]

The Buddha too is referred to as *Muni, Brahmana*, and *Isi*, but is also associated with a separate set of specialized terms, includ-ing *Bhagavat* ('holy,' 'fortunate one'), Gotama (the reputed family name of the Buddha, meaning 'one whose brilliance dispels dark-

---

51. Ibid, IV:2.1(772).
52. Dhammapada, 6:6(85).

ness'), "kinsman of the *Adiccas*" ('solar dynasty'), Buddha ('awakened'), *Sakka* ('able,' the name of the Buddha's clan), "the light-
giving," *Sambuddha* ('omniscient' or 'self-enlightened'), "clearly-
seeing" ("all-seeing one"), "chief (*naga*) of the world," "perfectly
enlightened," "first of men," *Jina* ('conqueror,' 'victor,' a Jain
term), "bull of men," *Tathagata* ('he who has thus come and gone
to that'), noble ('*naga*'), "thou with the born eye (of wisdom)," as
well as hero, divine, exemplary, supreme, and lord.

Brahmanas are reputed to be perfect buddhas (V:15.4) (alternatively, the Buddha declares himself a perfect *brahmana*; unlike the
brahman caste of the later *suttas* that are criticized for their
worldliness, these *brahmanas* are holy men). [53] The *brahmana* Bavari defers to the Buddha and refers his students (described
as youthful) to the Buddha and recommends that they go to visit
him (V:1.23). Posala and Pingiya both become followers of the
Buddha, despite being described as a *brahmana* and
an *isi* respectively themselves. The venerable Pingiya says, "There
is only one abiding dispelling darkness, that is the high-born, the
luminous, Gotama of great understanding, Gotama of great wisdom" (V:17.13), thus affirming the primogeniture and singularity of
the Buddha, who is self-enlightened, and credits the Buddha for
teaching him, a rishi, the dharma (V:17.14; cf. 17).

The superiority of the Buddha is, therefore, implicit in these
texts. Moreover, the texts also imply that the Buddha is referring
back to an ancient tradition that underlies Brahmanism itself as a
sort of "spiritual Brahmanism." While the bhikku who succeeds in
the Buddhist project is clearly emancipated from samsara, his attainment is distinguished from that of the Buddha, who is omniscient, all-seeing, chief of the world, perfectly enlightened, first of
men, and supreme. Moreover, the texts refer to the Buddha's having been reborn from the Tushita heaven, which is later identified
in the Pali *suttas* with the place from which bodhisattvas are reborn. Thus, *the same distinction between the concepts of "arhant"
and "bodhisattva" is clearly implied.* There is therefore no eviden-

---

53. Presumably these were orthodox Brahman recluses contemporary with the
Buddha. Norman simply refers to them as "brahmans."

tiary or necessary logical basis for the dogma that the distinction between the arhant and the bodhisattva is not original.

The Deathless

The Buddha talks about crossing the stream and going to the other shore, but what does this mean? Is salvation only psychological, or is it also ontological? The Buddha raises this issue when he asks the question, putting it in the mouths of the greedy, "What will become of us, when we die away from here?" The Buddha's answer is clear insofar as the wicked are concerned: desire for re-iterated existence leads to rebirth in unfortunate states. But what of those who liberate themselves from sensual desire? What sort of future state do they experience? The Buddha makes it clear that salvation does not imply rebirth in any other world, because all worlds are subject to the same suffering. Therefore, the liberated *muni* ('sage') neither longs for rebirth nor is reborn in any state. Does this mean that they, not being reborn, cease to exist in any sense? Is the Buddha here teaching some sort of mystical nihilism? The *muni* is beyond designation, because they do not cling to any philosophical view. They are uncharacterizable, because they do not cling, neither accepting *nor rejecting* anything. "Having gone to the other shore, such a one does not return" (IV:5.8).

The Buddha says that "only the name (*nama*) remains undecayed of the person who has passed away" (IV:6.5). According to the PED,[54] this *nama* is the immaterial aspect of *namarupa*, 'name and form,' which constitutes the individual. *Nama* itself consists of four mental factors; *vedana* ('feeling'), *sanna* ('sensation'), *sankhara* ('mental activity' or thinking), and *vinnana* ('consciousnness' or intuition), corresponding neatly to the four Jungian functions of the psyche. Therefore, *nama* = psyche. The implication of this passage for the *muni* is obscure, however, because the *muni* is said to be nameless. The Buddha may simply be referring to the continuity of rebirth, in the context of the post-mortem survival of the human personality (cf. IV:6.4), or even

---

54. Rhys Davids and Stede, *Pali English Dictionary*.

ironically to the memory of one's heirs and descendants, so this passage is ambiguous.

However, the Buddha also says that the *muni* "does not enter time, being delivered from time" (IV:10.13; cf. 13. 17). He neither belongs to time, nor is he dead (IV:13.20). The Buddha also says that consciousness is an eternal truth (IV:12.9). This implies that consciousness itself persists in an eternal "now-state." For the *muni* there is no death and no rebirth (IV:13.8). He goes to the immortal [deathless] region (IV:16.6).[55] The 'deathless' is one of the main themes of the Pali Canon, referred to by the Buddha frequently.

The Way of the Trans-dual

Whether the Buddha taught the doctrine of the trans-dual is one of the most hotly debated questions in Buddhist studies. Bhikku Bodhi commits Theravada to a dualistic view in his essay, "Dharma and Non-duality."[56] Therefore my defence of trans-dualism (not, note, non-dualism; trans-dualism includes both non-dualism and dualism, including the dualism of non-dualism and dualism itself, with trans-dualism as the fourth point of the quaternary or "tetralemma") in this context is bound to be controversial. However, I see no other context in which to interpret the transcendence of good and evil (IV:4.3), the non-existence of "notions" or concepts such as equality, lowness, and distinction or equality and inequality (IV:5.4, 9.9, 10.8, 13), "no desire for both ends" (i.e., extremes) (IV:6), "single truths" (the context makes it clear that the Buddha is referring to mutually exclusive or contradictory statements, i.e., to the law of non-contradiction) (IV:8.1), the binary character of dharma (11.7), 'name and form' (*namarupa*) (11.11, V:2.6, 12.5), "the truth is one, there is not a second" (IV:12.7),

---

55. *Gaccato amatam disam*, lit. 'goes to the ambrosial quarter.' Pali *amatam* refers to amrita, a.k.a. soma, the mind-altering drink of the gods that confers deathlessness or immortality in Indian tradition, the recipe for which has been lost.

56. "The teaching of the Buddha as found in the Pali Canon does not endorse a philosophy of non-dualism of any variety, nor, I would add, can a non-dualistic perspective be found lying implicit within the Buddha's discourses."

the "double *dhamma*, truth and falsehood" (the implication being that the true *dhamma* is transcendent) (12.9), and ultimate (eternal) and relative truth (relative truth is dualistic, and eternal truth is trans-dual) (12.9), as well as numerous additional references in the later *suttas*. There is in fact only one eternal or absolute truth, mind or consciousness itself, which is trans-dual and inherently empty yet infinitely differentiating itself in samsara by means of the illusion of difference (= *atta*, self-identity or ego), driven by the ultimate kinetic principle (will or intention) expressed in the principle of proliferation and the law of cause and effect (karma).

This is moreover the synthetic positon, reconciling all other views. It comes as no surprise to discover the theme of the transdual in the Atthaka and Parayana *vaggas*. The identification of realization with the trans-dual and the essential nothingness, emptiness, or voidness of all extremes is a universal feature of all wisdom traditions everywhere and therefore a part of the perennial philosophy (= the ancient tradition). If the lock is complex and the key fits, then the key is the truth. The doctrine of voidness (see below) also implies the trans-dual because it is empty yet all-inclusive ($0 = 1$, the primary binary in unity or the *yabyum* of existence, the cosmic egg).

Any paradox essentially indicates the trans-dual.

The World Is Void

The Buddha says that "the world is completely unsubstantial" (IV:15.3); "look upon the world as void" (V:16.4). The realization of the impermanent, insubstantial, illusory, ephemeral, and mirage-like nature of the world corresponds to the experience of the void, nothing, nowhere. Thus, the void, nothing, nowhere become designations of the ultimate nature of the world of samsara, the ground of which is reality itself.

The Planes of Existence

An equilateral cross with a central point (V:5.7, 6.8, 13.3) represents samsara. This symbol is a universal archetype, similar to the swastika, the Tibetan vajra, the Ethiopian cross, and the central symbol of the Rosicrucian order, among others. The horizontal

plane represents the ordinary world of three-dimensional extension,[57] which Buddhists and Taoists describe as the ten thousand
worlds – the infinitely differentiated and differentiating order of
stars, galaxies, and universes. The vertical vector or ray represents
the extraordinary world of vertical extension, ranging from lowest
frequency or vibration (the material or sensual polarity referred to
as the *kamaloka*) to the highest (the spiritual polarity referred to
as the *arupaloka*). The central point is the individual point of
view, the mind stream, which is not a "self" but rather a trans-
temporal sentient continuity that has no extension and therefore
no self-identity yet is the root of differentiation itself, without
which samsara itself is inexplicable.

The complete Buddhist cosmology of thirty-one planes of existence divided into various worlds and groups of worlds is not
found in the Atthaka and Parayana *vaggas*. However, there are
tantalizing references to other worlds, devas, Mara, and especially
the Tushita heaven, the only world to be specifically named in
these texts. The Tushita or 'satisfied' world is four realms above
the human world, third of the sensual realm and twenty-third in
the realm of samsara. The Tushita devas include the bodhisattvas,
who according to tradition are born here prior to their final birth
as a human being. It is intriguing that this specific world is the
only one named in these texts and that the Buddha is specifically
mentioned to have been reborn in the human world after having
resided in the Tushita realm.

The Cosmic Buddha

The Buddha is referred to by a number of honorifics, including
Muni ('sage'), *Bhagavat* ('holy,' a follower of Vishnu; the Hindus
regard the Buddha as an avatar or emanation of Vishnu), *Jina*
('Victorious,' also a Jain term), supreme Buddha ('awakened'), *Gotama* ('the one who dispels darkness by brilliance,' the reputed
family name or clan name of the Buddha), *samana* ('recluse'),

---

57. The possibility that the universe that we experience is a three-dimensional
projection of a two-dimensional diffraction pattern or hologram at the event
horizon of a black hole is a serious theory of modern science.

kinsman of the Adiccas ('sun'), "the Isi ('seer' or rishi, a direct allusion to the Vedic tradition) of exemplary conduct," *Sambuddha* ('one of clear or perfect knowledge'), Shakyan ('able', referring to the Buddha's people), *Tathagata* ('one who having come thus has gone to suchness'), master, teacher, bull of men, the man of excellent understanding, the all-seeing one, "hero free from lust," "thou with the born eye (of wisdom)," "he who shows the past," "a perfect, accomplished *Brahmana*," and "this man who sees what is good."

The Buddha himself is characterized as venerable, light-giving (luminous), perfectly enlightened, clear-sighted (clearly seeing), first of men, best of men, chief of the world, of great understanding (of excellent wise knowledge or great wisdom), "unyoked," free from passion, "skilled in head-splitting" (i.e., dispelling ignorance, located in the head), accomplished, cultivated, houseless (homeless), free from commotion, "liberated, who leaves time behind," doubtless, accomplished in all things, aware of past shapes, leaderless, "knowing all the faces of consciousness," divine, famous, "darkness dispelling," high-born, and free from harshness.

Thus, the Buddha is described as extremely wise or even omniscient; ecstatic; transcendent or god-like; virtuous or self-controlled; noble; and enlightened or luminous. The Buddha is clearly distinguished from the "men who have crossed the stream" by a significant number of superlative qualities.

Beyond Good and Evil

The monastic should not desire extremes. The one who clings not abides in a state of "inward peace"; they do not grasp *or reject* anything. The *brahmana* does not cling to virtue or holy works, either to their presence *or to their absence*. Holy works do not lead them. The dharma sage does not prefer anything. They are indifferent and tolerant. The "philosophizers" call what they devote themselves to "good" (the irony is palpable). Fools make their own views the truth, therefore they hold others be fools (IV. 12.5). Therefore, the *brahmana* does not cling to virtue, holy works, merit, good, *or evil* (IV:4.3). He lets it all go.

Conclusion

Barring a major new discovery, the Atthaka and Parayana *vaggas* are as close as we can get to the actual utterance of the historical Buddha – the Buddhist Q. At the same time, they are interpretations developed over the course of the first few decades after the Buddha's death, presumably in all sincerity based on an oral transmission that there is no reason not to believe began soon after the *parinibbana*. Once we recognize that the true object of Buddhist studies is not the Buddha but the dharma, the historical problem becomes less significant since the person of the Buddha, himself merely one of a series if we believe the Pali Canon, becomes less significant. Contrast this with Christianity, for which the central fact of the resurrection assumes preëminent importance since without this magical or supernatural act humanity is doomed to damnation.

According to the *vaggas*, the Buddha encouraged independent inquiry, denied that anyone could save another, and referred all spiritual seekers to their own judgments. He rejects salvation by philosophical argument, ordinary knowledge, good works, merit, or others. The Buddha encouraged his followers to be tolerant and appreciate different points of view, for the dharma is transrational, trans-linquistic (see Norman, *Group of Discourses*, V:7.1076), and experientially and ultimately individual, though it can also be understood (being trans-dual) as a collective phenomenon too. Nonsectarianism and the rejection of fundamentalism both follow logically from these premises, and the Buddha strongly emphasizes the futility of philosophical debate and argument. In later texts, the Buddha is portrayed as one who seeks out common ground, is compassionate and concerned, and addresses the individuality of those who come to him for guidance.

The dharma is not reducible to a formula. It is an active search for the meaning of the transcendental object translated into the four dimensions of human experience, which are always changing. The dharma is a wheel that turns forever and cannot be stopped. Thus, today we might understand the omniscience of the Buddha as perfect metaphysical understanding through the actual experience of the clarity of enlightenment, whereas those of earlier ages had another understanding such as that of the Jains. The universe overall may be ultimately entropic, but the introduction of the transcendental object creates negentropic patterns and equations that also have the capacity to disseminate themselves across space and time. This is the definition of a "dharma age."

The concurrence between the Atthaka and Parayana *vaggas* and the *nikayas,* which constitute the next stratum of development in the Rhys Davids/Law chronology, is remarkable, showing the care with which the originators of these texts assimilated earlier material. The development of the Pali Canon is not haphazard, accidental, or arbitrary, and we see many of the same tropes that we have identified repeated and expanded in subsequent *suttas.* From this perspective, we may regard the whole Pali Canon itself as a continuous meditation on the original teachings of the Buddha. There also appear to be many similarities between these ideas and those of the legendary Laozi in the Tao Te Ching, a book that must be earlier than the earliest known text, which has been dated to the late fourth century BCE. According to tradition, these teachings go back to the sixth century BCE. Thus, even though the Buddha may or may not have been influenced by this text specifically, it is possible that the same pan-Himalayan wisdom centre that the compilers of the Tao Te Ching drew on as well influenced him. In this context the speculation that the Buddha was of mixed Aryan-Mongol race, suggesting the possibility of a Mongol or even Chinese influence on Buddhism, is fascinating. Taoist tradition makes Laozi and the Buddha contemporaries, which need not be historically factual to allude to a symbolic or even initiatic truth.

The Atthaka and Parayana *vaggas* present a comprehensive world-view, including theories of knowledge, salvation, the nature of being, the universe, the Buddha, and ethics, remarkably similar to recent developments in modern philosophy and quantum physics, including the centrality of the act of observation (reality of consciousness), wave-particle duality (the trans-dual), and quantum entanglement (interdependent origination). The Buddha rejected sectarianism, dogmatism, and intolerance, affirmed the primacy of consciousness and the value of the human individual, saw the central problem of human beings as their ignorance of the nature of reality, and called upon us as individuals to wake up and to take personal responsibility for the implications of our thoughts, words, and actions; we must each save ourselves through radical *real*ization. In particular, the Buddha articulated the mechanics of ethics - the Law of Karma - whereas Western philosophy has fallen into ethical nihilism in the wake of the "death of God." The Buddha saw that religion, with its exoteric reliance on dogmas, rites, and rituals, completely fails to solve the human problem.

Unlike the poetic mysticism of the Tao Te Ching, with which the Atthaka and Parayana *vaggas* exhibit many other affinities, the Buddha expounds a rational spirituality that is articulate, profound, clear, and explicit yet leads beyond rationality and mysticism alike to the direct experiential realization of the Absolute. Against those who would like to eliminate rational inquiry altogether, the Buddha spent the last forty-five years of his life engaging in question and answer sessions with all those who came to him seeking answers. Not merely a mystic, he was also a philosopher and a political and ethical activist, though he disdained argument and debate and realized that reason leads beyond itself to something greater. Thus, he criticized, realized, and transcended religion, both in his person and in his teachings.

6

Final Teachings of the Buddha

THE MAHAPARINIBBANA SUTTA is interesting because it is the oldest and longest biographical account of the Buddha, located in the Digha Nikaya, including his final and most mature teachings.

Almost forty fundamental spiritual principles are embedded in the narrative but are easily overlooked if one focuses on the biography.

Thus, the Mahaparinibbana Sutta constitutes one of the most important foundational documents of historical Buddhism.

First Recitation Section

Principle #1: Tathagatas Never Lie (1.2). King Ajatasattu of Magadha uses the Buddha as an oracle because tathagatas, having achieved self-perfection, are in perfect synchrony with themselves and with reality itself, as they must be if they have reached identity with their ground. This passage highlights the paradox of the coexistence of the corrupt and violent nature of northeast India in the fifth century BCE and the deep spiritual faith of the people, including many of their rulers.

Principle #2: The Political Philosophy of the Buddha: Social Democracy/Anarcho-Syndicalism (1.4). The Buddha sets out a comprehensive political philosophy, thus showing that even a transcendent being continues to care for the inhabitants of the world of samsara. Indeed, the political organization of society is a recurring theme in the Pali Canon. These principles include government by assembly, peacefulness, traditionalism, respect for elders, women's rights, public religion, and a national spiritual organization. These precepts follow the organizational principles of the quasi-democratic Vajjian republic, which were also similar to the principles of the Shakyan republic of the Buddha's clan.

Principle #3: Precepts for the Sangha: Communitarianism (1.6). The precepts for the monastics also parallel those of the Vajjians, and include government by assembly, peacefulness, self-control (replacing traditionalism), respect for elders, dispassion (replacing women's rights), forest dwelling (replacing public religion), and mindfulness (replacing a national spiritual organization).

Principle #4: Communism (1.11). The sangha is to be organized based on commonality of property, but does not supersede civil society, which supports the sangha so that the sangha is a function of civil acceptance, and not the reverse (thus, the concept of a Buddhist religious government is a contradiction in terms, despite the references to a national spiritual commonality). Interestingly, the northern continent of Sumeru, Uttarakuru, which is the home of the longest-lived and most advanced race of the four races of human beings, with longevity of a thousand years, is communistic. Presumably this will be the social system of Shambhala when, according to the Kalachakra, it appears in the twenty-fifth century of the common era.

Principle #5: Wisdom Is the Salvific Principle (1.12). A recurring theme that runs all through the Mahaparinibbana Sutta, almost like a refrain, is the mutual relationship between morality, ethics, virtue (self-control); one-pointedness, concentration, or meditation; and wisdom or gnosis. This is called the threefold training or the threefold partition, and is not attributed to the Buddha, but to the nun Dhammadinna (in the Culavedalla Sutta, MN 44), who the Buddha declared to be the nun foremost in wisdom. In some sects of religious Buddhism today this threefold division has virtually replaced the Noble Eightfold Path. The path is presented as beginning with the cultivation of virtue, followed by meditation. Because of these two things, wisdom, identified with enlightenment, arises spontaneously.

The Buddha states that meditation, imbued with morality, brings great fruit and profit, and that wisdom, imbued with meditation, brings great fruit and profit, but that it is the mind imbued with wisdom that brings about emancipation. Thus, the sequence is morality (since meditation cannot be imbued with something that it does not have), meditation, and wisdom. Note, however, the subtle distinction made here between morality and meditation on the one hand and wisdom on the other. Morality and meditation are skilled means (*upaya*), but wisdom is the essential salvific principle, which brings the threefold partition into alignment with the Noble Eightfold Path, the first "limb" of which is Right View (or Wisdom) that leads the aspirant to the attainment of the first crucial stage of the stream entrant. It seems, then, that the proper sequence of the path is wisdom, morality, and meditation. Wisdom is not merely something that is attained. It is also something that is cultivated. This view is confirmed in the doctrine of interdependent origination (*paticcasamuppada*), the radical or first principle of which, ignorance (*avijja*), is resolved by wisdom. Wisdom is also the essential attainment of a buddha, whereas ethics and meditation, leading to the state of dispassion, are the essential attainments of an arhant. If one reads the Pali Canon in its entirely, it is clear that it is the realization of wisdom that brings about emancipation. There are many stories of aspirants attaining emancipation simply by listening to a dharma talk of the Buddha or another follower of the Buddha, followed by a period of meditation as short as five days. Similarly, the Buddha himself says that emancipation is available after a period of meditation as short as seven days. Meditation, though essential, is not primary.

Principle #6: Sariputta and the Buddha Debate on the Greatness of the Buddha (1.16). Sariputta, renowned for his wisdom, affirms to the Buddha that the Buddha is the best and most enlightened ascetic or brahman, past, present, or future. Rather than accept this praise, the Buddha turns it against Sariputta, first chidingly affirming him – "You have spoken with a bull's voice, Sariputta, you have roared the lion's roar of certainty" – and then questioning him – "Have all the Arahant Buddhas of the past appeared to you, and were the minds of all those Lords open to you?

Have you perceived all the Arahant Buddhas who will appear in the future? Do you even know me as the Arhant Buddha?" To all of these questions Sariputta is forced to acknowledge that he does not know. Thus, the Buddha ironically concludes, "You have spoken with a bull's voice, Sariputta; you have roared the lion's roar of certainty."

Such is my reading of this text, which might be read by a religious as an affirmation of Sariputta's faith, were it not for the emphasis the Buddha placed on questioning and Sariputta's defensive reply. Rather, the Buddha challenges Sariputta to justify his claim. Sariputta's reputation for wisdom was not misplaced, for he turns the tables on the Buddha, and proves to the Buddha that his respect for the Buddha is not based on faith or clairvoyance, but on his knowledge of the 'drift of the dharma' (*dhammavaya*). This recurs to the Buddha's statement that, though we may not know the dharma, we can judge the dharma by its effect – true dharma always yields good karma; something that has bad karma cannot be true dharma, reminiscent of the statement by Yeshua that one can judge a tree by its fruits.

However, one must be careful not to conflate real and apparent goodness. Goodness does not necessarily "feel good," or even "look good," whereas something that does not "feel good" is not automatically bad. The Buddha has no response, thus acceding (by silence) to the wisdom of Sariputta's reply.

Principle #7: Comprehensive Dharma Versus Dharma in Brief (1.18). Comprehensive dharma is often contrasted with dharma in brief or 'in short' (*samkhittena*). As Peter Masefield points out in *Divine Revelation in the Pali Canon*, the distinction is obscure, since the content of comprehensive dharma and dharma in brief often seems to be similar.[58] Dharma in brief is frequently requested before an aspirant goes into the forest for a period of intensive solitary meditation, often culminating in arhantship. It seems that it might be similar to an oral transmission or empowerment, as in the tantric traditions.

Principle #8: The Motif of the Axis Mundi (1.22). The Pali Canon frequently presents the Buddha as sitting with his back

---

58. Masefield, *Divine Revelation*, pp. 101f.

against a pole or pillar. The monastics sit behind the Buddha, facing the lay followers, who sit in the east facing the Buddha. Thus, to the sangha the Buddha appears in the place of the rising sun, and to the lay followers in the place of the setting sun, foremost of the sangha, with the sangha as "support."

The motif of the pole or pillar alludes to the tree of awakening (the Bodhi tree, ficus religiosa), sitting under which the Buddha attained Enlightenment. The Buddha also experienced his first meditative state as a child while sitting under a rose apple tree, and died between two sal trees, while lying on the ground in accordance with Indian custom. He was also born under a sal tree. Similarly, the Buddha enjoins his followers to live in the forest as a place of refuge. India has a long history of sacred trees and forests, as well as many other societies. When the Buddha broke his vow of abstinence when he was on the verge of dying, he was seated under a tree, and Sujata, who offered him a bowl of rice cooked in milk, believed that he was the spirit of the tree to which she had come to make a food offering. The sacred tree is representative of the polar or vertical axis, like Mount Sumeru, through which communication with the higher worlds becomes possible. The pillars of Ashoka also recur to this symbolism, all of which represent the axis mundi – the cosmic axis, world axis, world pillar, *columna cerului,* center of the world, or world tree, the omphalos (navel) of the world, and is a universal motif of the *philosophia perennis* with its origin in prehistoric shamanism.

Principle #9: The Path of the Householder: The Way of Karma (1.24). Buddhism is not merely a spirituality of monastics, ascetics, and recluses. In fact, originally the Buddha emphasized the teaching of lay people.[59] The Buddha had many followers who were householders, and some of these attained arhantship. Thus, the Buddhist science of spirituality also includes the path of the householder, which is sometimes called the lunar path or the way of the valley. The path of the householder is based primarily, but not exclusively, on the path of karma, i.e., removing bad karma through self-purification and acquiring merit through the cultivation of good karma. Thus, Buddhism is not divorced from practi-

---

59. See Hajime Nakamura, *Gotama Buddha,* Vol. 2, p. 57.

cal life, and reveals itself to be a pragmatic spiritual philosophy. This is shown by the Buddha's summary of the perils and advantages of good and bad morality, which he designates as failure and success in morality. The advantages of success in good morality, i.e., good karma, include wealth, reputation, confidence and assurance, dying unconfused, and rebirth in a higher world.[60] It is clear from this and other passages that though the sangha was organized in a communitarian and, indeed, communistic way, the Buddha realized that the extension of that system of social order to civil society as a whole was not practical. It does not seem that the Buddha opposed property and wealth in civil society, for example, though it is clear from other passages that he saw wealth as imposing special social obligations on the wealthy, and that he advocated social redistribution of property and wealth for the general good. However, it is clear that the Buddha sees the development of money and property as socially pernicious factors that lead to criminality, violence, and war.

Principle #10: The Cohabitation of Devas and People (1.26, 3.50). *Deva* is usually translated as 'god,' but this is a very unsatisfactory translation. The English word means 'that which is called or invoked,' whereas the Sanskrit/Pali word means 'shining,' referring to a celestial being of light, rather like Plato's bisexual flying spheres. According to the PED, devas are splendid, mobile, beautiful, good, and luminous, as well as continuous with the life of humanity and all beings. They are beings who occupy higher worlds in the system of vertical extension that, along with the horizontal dimension, defines samsara as a quaternary, but it is clear from this passage that some devas also coexist with humanity. These earthbound devas are described as minor devas. These include ugly dwarfs (*kumbhandas*), aerial spirits connected with trees and flowers that live in the fragrance of nature (*gandharvas*), great snakes that can take human form and live in streams, oceans, and caves (nagas), nature fairies associated with woods and moun-

---

60. Curiously, the Pali Canon emphasizes rebirth in a higher world as a valid goal, especially for householders, though emancipation from a deva state is considered to be more difficult than from the human state, if not impossible, and devas are always reborn in a lower state, not necessarily human.

tains, which also appear as ghosts that inhabit wilderness areas and threaten travellers (*yakshas*), and finally large humanoid birds (*garudas*).[61] Interestingly, Patna or Pataligama is one of the oldest continuously inhabited places on earth and the largest city in the world between 300 and 195 BCE. About 300 BCE, a hundred years after the death of the Buddha, its population was 400,000. As one can see from the text, thousands of devas invisibly inhabited this city, influencing the minds of the inhabitants telepathically.

This passage is interesting because it implies that the Buddha's dharma is not directed to humans only, but that it is also directed at devas.

Principle #11: The Divine Eye: *Ajna* Chakra (1.27). The Divine Eye is referred to frequently all through the Pali Canon. In the Pali Canon, this is one of the six gnoses (*chalabhinna*). In this context, it refers to knowing the karmic destinations of others. However, it has a larger meaning as well. It is enumerated as one of the three wisdoms (*tevijja* or *tivijja*), along with the memory of past lives and the extinction of the mental intoxicants. In the Mahasaccaka Sutta (MN 36), the Buddha says that he obtained the Divine Eye during the second watch of the night (10 pm–2 am) of his Enlightenment. In the Mahaparinibbana Sutta, it is by means of the Divine Eye that the Buddha sees devas. The Divine Eye is also a universal symbolic motif or archetype. In Egyptian and Indian mythology, one finds the eye of Horus and the eye of Shiva respectively. It also appears in Freemasonry, where a semi-circular glory appears below the eye, which is enclosed in a triangle. In Christianity, it represents the Eye of Providence, where clouds or sunbursts surround it. The Eye of Providence also appears on the Declaration of the Rights of Man and of the Citizen of the French Revolution, as well as the American dollar bill.

In the Indian chakra system, the eye appears as the *ajna* chakra, the eye of intuition and intellect, located in the centre of the forehead. In Tibetan Buddhism, the "third eye" is the upper end of the central energy channel that runs up the spine to the top of the

---

61. These are not merely myths. No less celebrated a bhikku than Ajahn Brahm has declared that he has seen both nagas and *garudas*. See his "Buddhism and Alien Abductions" and Jacques Vallee, *Passport to Magonia*, etc.

head. This centre is also important in Qigong, Sufism, and Cabala. In human beings, the Divine Eye corresponds to the pineal gland, in the centre of the brain, a vestigial third eye that actually appears in lizards, amphibians, and fish. Descartes calls this organ "the seat of the soul." Modern research has discovered that the pineal gland is the source of naturally occurring dimethyltryptamine (DMT), the most powerful psychedelic known, which is also widely found all through nature. Interestingly, DMT facilitates vivid otherworldly visions including encounters with non-human entities of exactly the sort that we have been describing.

Principle #12: The Buddha Was Not an Extreme Ascetic (1.30). Although it is well-known that the Buddha rejected the extreme asceticism of the proto-Shaivite *samanas* with whom he associated prior to his Enlightenment, the Buddha is still regarded as moderately ascetic, illustrated for example by the quite rigid rules of the Vinaya. Nevertheless, it is clear from the Pali Canon that the Buddha's life, while simple, also had its pleasures. There are numerous examples in the Pali Canon in which the Buddha and his entourage are invited to the home of a wealthy local person, usually either political figures or celebrities, to be entertained with a fine meal of choice food, which they invariably ate to their satisfaction. Since the Buddha travelled extensively, this must have occurred fairly frequently. The Buddha and his entourage also often occupied comfortable parks and other places of great natural beauty. These facts stand as useful correctives to the extreme view that the Buddha was exclusively ascetic.

Principle #13: A Meaningful Miracle: More Evidence of Proto-tantra (1.33). Although the Pali Canon is largely naturalistic in its descriptions of people and events, it does attest to the reality of psychic powers, and sometimes these appear as full-blown miracles, as in the story of the Buddha and his entourage transporting themselves from one side of the Ganges to the other. This is especially ironic in view of the disparagement of miracles by the Buddha in the Patika Sutta (DN 24:1.4). Similarly, Yeshua disparages those who seek for a sign, declaring that no sign will be given to them, yet the Gospels and the Church continue to ascribe miracles to him as the proof of his divinity.

The Buddha correctly saw that the belief in miracles leads to a superstitious reverence for the person or the power rather than the one true miracle, the miracle of the dharma itself, which leads to emancipation. *Nevertheless,* the presence of miracles of this type in the Pali Canon is another indication of the early development of proto-tantric literary motifs even in the first period of pre-sectarian Buddhism, much as Gnosticism appeared early in the development of Christianity. One can derive valid messages from such stories even if they are not literally or historically true.

Second Recitation Section

Principle #14: The Mirror of Dharma (2.8). The Mirror of Dharma presents a method whereby the aspirants can realize for themselves the state of stream entry, whereby they realize the fact that they will achieve emancipation within no more than seven rebirths. The method is to cultivate *absolute confidence* in the Buddha, the Dharma, and the Sangha. This method must be differentiated form Christian faith, however, which is virtually defined as "belief for belief's sake," whereas the Buddha states that the "unwavering confidence" to which he refers is based on "inspection, leading onward, to be comprehended by the wise *each one for himself*" (italics added). Moreover, the *morality* of such an aspirant must be perfect. By this method, one can know for oneself as a matter of certainty that one has achieved stream-entry.

Principle #15: Mindfulness (2.12, 2.13). The Pali word translated as 'mindfulness' is *sati*. According to the PED, the etymological meaning of this word is 'memory,' 'to remember'; also, 'recognition,' 'consciousness,' 'intentness of mind,' 'wakefulness of mind,' 'mindfulness,' 'alertness,' 'lucidity of mind,' 'self-possession,' 'conscience,' 'self-consciousness.' The Sanskrit word is *smrti,* which also refers to the oral recitation tradition of the Vedas. The reference to self-consciousness is somewhat disconcerting, given the Buddha's apparent rejection of the *atta* (Skt. *atman*) theory, commonly identified with the self. Mindfulness is probably also connected with the recollection of past lives, which is emphasized all through the Pali Canon. Mindfulness begins with mindfulness of the body, and is then extended to feelings, mind, and mind-objects.

Principle #16: A Courtesan Entertains the Buddha (2.14). As we have seen, though the Buddha clearly lived a very modest and simple life, it was not without its pleasures, in the form of the choicest food when prominent people in various communities entertained him and his entourage. It is also clear that the Buddha interacted with and taught women without distinction. A striking confirmation of both of these observations is the Buddha's interaction with Ambapali, a wealthy *ganika* who lived in the Licchavi city of Vesali, part of the Vajjian confederacy. Although Walshe politely renders the Pali word *ganika* by 'courtesan,' comparing her to the Japanese tradition of the geisha, the PED simply renders the word as 'harlot,' 'one who belongs to the crowd,' i.e., a common woman or, perhaps, a promiscuous woman, though Ambapali was a royal harlot. Nonetheless, Ambapali was a wealthy and beautiful woman who was a *nagavradu*, a 'royal courtesan' who was also a prominent citizen of the town.

The Buddha stayed in her mango grove, taught her the dharma, and went to her home for his morning meal, accompanied by his monastic entourage. Clearly, the Buddha did not see this as a violation of the Vinaya rule against consorting with women, and a prostitute at that. Clearly, the Buddha was neither a fundamentalist nor a judgmental prude. He consorted with women, taught them the dharma on an equal basis with men, and was not above enjoying a fine meal or the company of a beautiful, but high class, prostitute. In this and in many other ways, the Buddha seems to be similar to Yeshua. Ambapali made a gift of her mango grove to the sangha and later became an arhant.

Principle #17: Energy, the Force of Life, Health, and Longevity (2.23, 3.40). Here we encounter the first major sign of the Buddha's impending illness, characterized by diarrhea and sharp pains so severe as to suggest dying. The monastics remained at Ambapali's park in Vesali, whereas the Buddha spent his last rainy season in Beluva, a small town outside the southern gate of Vesali. What is most interesting about this passage, however, is the reference to energy and a "force of life" by which the Buddha was able to overcome his illness and postpone its effects so that he could take his leave of the order of monastics. The Buddha recommends the cultivation of energy all through the Pali Canon, but only in a few places is it clear that this energy is an *iddhi*, a psychic power that has intrinsically healing and vitalistic effects, comparable in fact to kundalini, which the Buddha seems to have experienced during his ascetic period. This brings the Buddha's teachings into relation with kundalini yoga, the Tibetan concept of *tummo*, the Chinese concept of *qi*, and other cognate concepts that we find worldwide.

Principle #18: Inner and Outer Dharma (2.25). Here and elsewhere the Buddha indicates that his teaching has no "inner" and "outer," that he has no "teacher's fist" in respect of doctrines. This is widely interpreted to mean that Buddhism is exoteric, and that there is no esoteric dharma, no "secret wisdom," such as Vajrayana, Tantra, Theosophy, etc. imply. However, this is not, strictly speaking, what the Buddha says. The Buddha says that he makes no distinction between inner and outer, teaching everything to everyone openly and without secrecy. Walshe himself recognizes this when he states that there is no contradiction here between this passage and the Simsapa Sutta (SN 56:4.31). In the latter, the Buddha distinguishes between knowledge that leads to liberation and other forms of knowledge, "vast as the leaves in the *simsapa* forest." The latter is of the same order as the former, and is known because of realization: "Even so, bhikshus, much more is the direct knowledge that I have known, but that has not been taught. Few is that which has been taught." The distinction that the Buddha is making seems to be between praxis and gnosis, the latter the goal of the former. Thus, the latter does in effect constitute a secret wisdom, an untaught knowledge that is nonetheless the object of realization. What the Buddha is actually saying here is that he openly teaches the entirety of wisdom, but that he emphasizes the praxis first, because it is through the latter that one realizes the former. In the Simsapa Sutta, the practice referred to is the Four Noble Truths. Clearly, however, the Buddha taught a great deal more than the Four Noble Truths. This is the only interpretation that reconciles and harmonizes all relevant passages, and shows the importance of not selecting the passages that one likes, but rather referring to and collating all relevant passages in order to arrive at a synthetic understanding.

Principle #19: The Sangha Has No Leader (2.25). In this very significant passage, the Buddha makes it clear that he does not want to be succeeded as head of the sangha. In other passages the Buddha disdains being thought of as a "leader," referring to himself rather as a friend among friends. Later in the Mahaparinibbana Sutta, the Buddha states that the monastics should take the dharma as their leader. Nevertheless, after the Buddha's death, and backed by King Ajatasattu, the sangha appointed Mahakassapa, at his own instigation, as its leader at the First Buddhist Council, followed by Ananda. Since the appointment of a leader violates the Buddha's dictum with respect to the organization of the sangha, one may question the legitimacy of the early Buddhist councils; the legitimacy of the arhants did become an issue when the Sthaviras (lit. 'elders' or 'arhants') – precursors of the Theravada – split from the Mahasamghikas – the majority – after the Second Buddhist Council over questions re the rules of the Vinaya and the infallibility of the arhants. This split became the basis of the division between the Eighteen Schools and the Mahayana and the Mahayana's adoption of the path of the bodhisattva as its goal.

Principle #20: The Dharma Is the Only Refuge (2.26). The monastics are to live freely as individuals, within a cooperative sangha, with themselves and the dharma as their only refuge (sometimes translated as 'retreat'). Again, the reliance on the self is paradoxical in light of the *anatta* doctrine. Some scholars believe that the formula of the Three Jewels, i.e., taking refuge in the Buddha, the Dharma, and the Sangha, is a later innovation that arose about the time of Ashoka (third century BCE), and that the original refuge formula referred to the Dharma only.[62] Clearly, the kind of sangha described by the Buddha is very different from the hierarchical, authoritarian sangha that we often see today. Although the Buddha did respect seniority, the sangha is supposed to emphasize independent self-inquiry and free thought and consensus (failing which, majority rule), without excessive attachment to

---

62. Rhys Davids, *The Minor Anthologies of the Pali Canon,* Part I, p. xliv.

rules, rituals, or beliefs and without a singular leader. Recently, the Dalai Lama, to his credit, has honoured the Buddha's dictum by stepping down as the political leader of the Central Tibetan Administration and fostering a democratic constitution. In this regard, as in many others, the Buddha seems to be exceptionally modern.

Third Recitation Section

Principle #21: The Four Roads to Power (3.3). The Four Roads to Power are another example of magical or proto-tantric thinking in the Pali Canon. This practice is not aimed only at awakening or enlightenment but also at the development of psychic powers – in this context, longevity. In Walshe's translation, success in this practice would enable the practitioner to live for a hundred years, close to the maximum longevity of a human being. Specifically, had Ananda taken the hint, he might have asked the Buddha to extend his life by this means and live another twenty years.[63] However, Ananda – who is represented in the *sutta*s as a bit dull – did not take the hint.

The four roads to power (*iddhipada*) are not explained further in the Mahaparinibbana Sutta, but we know what was involved from the Viraddha Sutta (SN 51:2). In this *sutta*, the Buddha states that the practice consists of the development of four qualities: will (*chanda*), energy (*viriya*), intention (*citta*), and investigation (*vimamsa*), which are in turn based on the cultivation of concentration (*samadhi*) and concentrated mental aspiration (*padhana-sankhara*).

Principle #22: The Dharma, the Power of Truth, and Merit (3.7). We see again a reference in the "dhamma of wondrous effect" to the universal ideas that pervade the Pali Canon, especially the Jatakas, of the Power of Truth and the Act of Truth. This is a pan-Indian idea, in which the ultimate truth of things itself exercises an influence that is beneficial and powerful. Mahatma Gandhi utilized this as a political principle, which he called *satyagraha*. This is also the principle of merit. Like mantra, the study,

---

63. This is the prevailing modern interpretation.

teaching, or recitation of dharma is held to be intrinsically efficacious and beneficial.

Principle #23: Conscious Dying (3.10). According to this passage, the Buddha did not die as a matter of accident or involuntar-
ily; he deliberately renounced the life principle, mindfully and
with clear awareness. One might be inclined to regard this as my-
thologization, but one would be mistaken. This principle of conscious dying is also found among the Tibetan lamas, some of
whom are reputedly able to will themselves to die at will. This skill
is widely attested. This practice is portrayed in the movie, *Little
Buddha*. In Tibetan Buddhism, this practice is called *phowa*. It is
the highest of the Six Yogas of Naropa. Dzogchen meditation is
considered the highest, greatest, and most essential *phowa* practice.

Principle #24: Two Nirvanas: With and Without Remainder
(3.20). There are two types of nirvana, the final 'going out' or extinction of desirous attachment: one with and one without "remainder." The arhant who attains nirvana ceases to make new
karma due to the absence of desirous attachment, but existing
karma still needs to work itself out. This suggests that karma is
not entirely destroyed by nirvana. If all karma were destroyed by
nirvana, then one would die immediately. If the destruction of
karma were the precondition of attaining nirvana, then the attainment of nirvana would be impossible. The Buddha appears to
teach that the attainment of nirvana destroys *much* karma, *but not
all*. This view of nirvana also corresponds to the Buddha's life. After he attained Enlightenment, the Buddha remained in an altered
state of consciousness for a whole week, after which he returned
to ordinary consciousness. He continued to live, and the evidence
of the Pali Canon is that he continued to engage in spiritual retreats, practising mindfulness of the breath – this behaviour
makes no sense if the Buddha were already a perfected being. Rather, it implies a being who still needs and benefits from spiritual
practice. Finally, the Buddha exhausted his remaining karma and
renounced the last vestige of attachment to life. He died, attaining
the state of perfection called *parinibbana*, 'final emancipation,'
characterized by absolute transcendence.

Principle #25: Eight Liberations: The Eight Ecstasies (3.33)

1. Rapture and happiness born of seclusion;
2. Delight and happiness born of concentration without applied or sustained thought;
3. Quiet, subtle, and pervasive happiness, subtle enjoyment of mindful and equanimous mind, without rapture;
4. Stability, stillness, and equanimity, without happiness;
5. Infinite space;
6. Infinite consciousness;
7. Nothing;
8. Neither perception nor non-perception – opening to the transdual;
9. Cessation of feeling and perception.

Principle #26: The Buddha's Enlightenment Experience (3.34). The Buddha describes his monumental Enlightenment experience, referring to having just attained supreme Enlightenment. This seems to be an early statement, there being no reference to the three watches of the night, consisting of recalling past lives, karma, and interdependent origination, respectively. At sunrise, he attains full Enlightenment, characterized by the encounter with Mara and the absolute cessation of desirous attachment. Here, however, the Buddha simply attains supreme Enlightenment in a moment, suggesting the instantaneous theory of liberation. The name of the place is Uruvela, located in the state of Bihar; the river is Neranjara; and the tree is the Goatherd's Banyan tree. Goat herders, having gone to the shade of the Banyan tree, would gather there, hence the name. Interestingly, the commentaries claim that this tree was located to the east of the "awakening tree," whereas the *sutta* seems to suggest that this was the "awakening tree."

Fourth Recitation Section

Principle #27: The Four Criteria of Authentic Dharma (4.8). After the death of the Buddha, the Buddha's sermons were remembered and recited by the sangha, especially by Ananda, who had been the Buddha's personal attendant for the last twenty-five years of his life. Since only Buddhist arhants were permitted to participate in the First Buddhist Council, we are fortunate that Ananda, rather conveniently it seems, attained arhantship on the night before the council met, since without his participation many of the Buddha's teachings would have been lost. Thenceforth, the sangha would come together to rehearse the teachings of the Buddha based on the memories of the participants. As the participants died off, the nature of this transmission changed. From being memories of the actual hearers, the recollections increasingly focused on questions of preservation, clarification, and codification of doctrine. These traditions were handed down in this way for almost three hundred years. With the passage of time, it became increasingly important to verify the validity of these teachings.

Therefore, it is of interest to read in the Mahaparinibbana Sutta the criteria that were applied to verify the validity of the teachings that were passed down. The *sutta* identifies four primary sources of such teachings that may be considered: the Buddha himself, but also the community of elders and teachers; a meeting of the elders; and a single elder. The sources of authority are clearly the Buddha himself and the senior bhikkus or *theras,* both as individuals and together with others. According to the PED, any monastic of any seniority may be called *thera* because of their wisdom; the Mahaparinibbana Sutta says that any monastic may claim to have heard a teaching from "the Lord's own lips."

So much for the admissible sources of teachings. The Buddha then cautions that any such claim is neither to be approved nor not approved. Rather, "his words and expressions should be carefully noted and compared with the Suttas and reviewed in the light of the discipline [Vinaya]." *If the teaching conforms to the* suttas *or the discipline, it is to be accepted. If it does not conform, it is to be rejected.* Thus, a continuous preservation of tradition is guaranteed. The Buddha does not say who is sanctioned to verify the teachings. However, elsewhere he says that decisions are to be made by consensus of the sangha, or, failing consensus, by majority rule.

An important point to note in this validation procedure is that *it is ideological, not historical.* The primary criterion is not whether the words and circumstances of the teaching are historically accurate or not, but whether they conform to the established truth of the dharma based on previously accepted teachings. In other words, is there a reasonable continuity of teaching? Receiving a teaching from the Lord's own lips is the first criterion, *but not the only one.* Thus, the accusation that is frequently made against the Mahayana sutras that they are false because they are non-historical is irrelevant. The truth or falsity of the Mahayana sutras is to be validated based on the same criteria as the Pali *suttas* themselves, i.e., do they conform with the established teachings of the Buddha as handed down by tradition? In this context, therefore, do they conform with the Pali *suttas*, which are doubtless older than all but the oldest Mahayana sutras (about first century BCE). In the same way, the conformity of the Pali texts with each other must also be subject to the same scrutiny. The method of logical syncretism or synthesis follows logically from such considerations.

Principle #28: The Buddha's Last Meal: Not Food Poisoning (4.18). The Buddha's final meal is translated by Maurice Walshe as 'pig's delight,' thus glossing over the obscurity of the Pali phrase, *sukara-maddava,* which may refer to pork or to a kind of truffle. This story has led to the speculation that the Buddha died of food poisoning. However, Dr. Mettanando Bhikkhu, in his article, "How the Buddha Died," suggests that food poisoning is an unlikely explanation of the Buddha's sickness, first, because the Buddha felt the onset of the sickness very quickly, whereas food poisoning takes several hours to incubate and, second, because food poisoning does not cause the bloody diarrhea mentioned in the *sutta.* He also rejects chemical poisoning, peptic ulcer, and hemorrhoids. Dr. Mettanando's conclusion, based on the symptoms described in the *sutta,* is that the Buddha died of mesenteric infarction, a medical condition in which inflammation and injury of the small intestine result from inadequate blood supply – a common disease of the elderly that is lethal after ten to twenty hours. Thus, it was not his final meal that killed the Buddha, but old age, though the size of the meal that the Buddha consumed may have been the trigger that brought about the second and final episode of the disease that we know from previous passages had begun to afflict the Buddha some eight or nine months before. The cogency of Dr. Mettanando's analysis also gives us confidence in the historical accuracy of the Mahaparinibbana Sutta.

Fifth Recitation Section

Principle #29: Women (5.9). As I discussed in "The Status of Women in Ancient India and the Pali Tradition," there are two distinct attitudes toward women expressed in the Pali Canon. One attitude disparages women, grudgingly admits that women are capable of enlightenment, and admits women to the sangha as "second-class citizens," whereas the other makes no distinction between men and women, and admits women to the sangha, apparently on an equal basis with men. As we have seen in our discussion of the Mahaparinibbana Sutta, the Buddha was not above enjoying a fine meal with a courtesan. Here, however, we see another, quite incompatible attitude toward women: we should not look at them, we should not speak to them, and if they speak to us, we should be very careful. This is mild compared with other passages in the Pali Canon, which we will not discuss here. The Buddha spoke to Ambapali. He delivered a talk on the dharma to her, which (the text states) instructed, inspired, fired, and delighted her. It is possible that the rest of his entourage remained discreetly silent all through the meal. Perhaps. On the other hand, perhaps what we are seeing here is two opposed views of women that are mutually incompatible, as Bhikku Bodhi has suggested in his introduction to the Anguttara Nikaya. If we accept Bodhi's view, then we must believe that the Buddha held two incompatible views simultaneously; that he abandoned one view in favour of the other at some point in his career – perhaps when Ananda "convinced" him to allow women to be admitted to the sangha; or that one of these views is an imposition by anonymous misogynistic monastic redactors of the Pali Canon. My view, which I consider the common sense one, is the last one, since the first two views imply that the Buddha was unenlightened and are, frankly, absurd.[64]

Principle #30: Ananda (5.13). It is ironic that Ananda, who was called the Guardian of the Dharma due to his photographic memory, was both the Buddha's closest disciple and the least accomplished. In many ways, he is portrayed in the *suttas* as being a bit thick. Nevertheless, he served the Buddha faithfully as his personal attendant during the final twenty-five years of the Buddha's career, when the Buddha was 55 to 80 years old, and was the source of much of the *sutta* tradition collected together in the Pali Canon. Ananda and the Buddha were first cousins through their father, Suddhodhana. The Buddha described him as kind, unselfish, popular, and thoughtful, as well as chief in conduct, service, and memory. Nevertheless, Ananda's participation in the First Buddhist Council, convened by Mahakassapa, the Buddha's disciple who was foremost in asceticism, was contested because he was only a stream entrant. The Pali Canon portrays Ananda as an imperfect, but sympathetic, figure, lonely and desolated after the death of the Buddha. Nevertheless, he rather conveniently attains nirvana on the eve prior to the convention of the First Buddhist Council, where he was severely criticized by the arhants for persuading the Buddha to ordain women, as well as his failure to ascertain from the Buddha which were the major and which were the minor rules of the Vinaya. As a result, the rules of the Vinaya remain unchanged to this day!

Principle #31: The Gradual Versus the Instantaneous Path (5.27). The reference to four grades of attainment recalls the discussion that one finds in various places between advocates of the gradual path and advocates of the non-gradual path. That is, is enlightenment a process of gradual development or is enlightenment attained instantaneously?[65] The four grades are the attainments of stream entrant, once-returner, non-returner, and arhant.

---

64. This does not stop the Thai sangha from declaring that an ordained nun is guilty of the "crime" of impersonating a monastic, or for expelling Ajahn Brahm for his importunate defence of women's rights.

65. Gradualism is the Indian view, subitism the Chinese view. Both views are referred to in the Pali Canon. From the trans-dual perspective, they are equivalent.

However, this path, the path of the arhant, which the Buddha doubtless taught, is not the path of the bodhisattva (lit. 'wisdom-being'), which the Buddha himself followed, and the Pali Canon makes it clear that the ten powers of an arhant are not the same as and apparently inferior to the ten powers of a Tathagata Buddha.[66] An essential difference, moreover, is that a bodhisattva/buddha is self-ordained by definition, as in the original *samana* tradition, which reappears later in the Brahma Net and Srimala sutras, whereas an arhant always receives the dharma from a Buddha; thus, an arhant always follows and is, thus, inferior to a buddha. The Buddha himself is also referred to as an arhant. The distinction between an arhant and a buddha became a point of contention after the Second Buddhist Council, which resulted in the great schism between the Mahasamghika majority, which subsequently developed into the Mahayana, and the Sthaviravada minority, which subsequently developed into the Eighteen Schools, and the Theravada.

Sixth Recitation Section

Principle #32: The Dharma Retreat (6.1). The imminent death of the Buddha obviously raised the problem of how the sangha should be organized after the Buddha's death. In these passages, the Buddha addresses this issue. First and foremost, the Buddha states that the dharma and the discipline – the Dharma-Vinaya, which is the name that the Buddha always gave to his teaching – is to be the teacher after his death. In addition, whereas during the Buddha's lifetime the sangha was egalitarian, in which all members of the community addressed each other – even the Buddha – as 'friend' (*avuso*), rather like the Quakers, the Buddha declared that after his death the sangha should be organized as a decentralized hierarchy based on seniority, in which the junior monastics would address the senior monastics as 'Lord' (*bhante*) or 'Venerable Sir' (*ayasma*). Some scholars also hold that the formula of the Three Jewels, i.e., the Buddha, the Dharma, and the Sangha, originated during the time of Ashoka (third century BCE), whereas the

---

66. AN 10:90; MN 12:9–21.

original formula was singular. That is to say, the original Buddhists only took their refuge (more properly, "retreat") in the Dharma alone.[67]

Principle #33: The Minor Rules of the Vinaya (6.3). Contrary to the fundamentalism that seems to affect many followers of the Vinaya today, the Buddha further declared that the "lesser and minor" rules of the Vinaya might be abolished. Unfortunately, when the Buddha said this, Ananda did not ask the Buddha which of the rules were major and which were minor, so the First Buddhist Council, led by Mahakassapa, the so-called Father of the Sangha, took the conservative approach of abolishing none of them. There are six Vinayas known today – that of the Theravada, Mahasamghika, Mahisasaka, Dharmaguptaka, Sarvastivada, and Mulasarvastivada, three of which are still followed by the Theravada, East Asian Buddhists, and Tibetan Buddhists respectively, but the scholarly consensus is that the Mahasamghika Vinaya is the oldest.[68] The Mahasamghika subsequently developed into the Mahayana.

Although many religious Buddhists strongly emphasize the rules of the Vinaya, the original Buddhist sangha did not follow any fixed set of rules for six years. These developed gradually over the course of the Buddha's life in response to specific situations, therefore reflecting the social conventions of the time. Apparently, the Buddha was quite flexible about the observance of these rules. For example, according to the Vinaya itself the rules may be abrogated if required to do so for reasons of health or to prevent a crime. Alcohol and drugs were permitted for the purpose of healing.[69] The Buddha frequently warns the monastics against attachment to rules, rituals, and dogmas. A Vajjian monastic complained to the Buddha that he could not stand such training with so many rules and regulations. Far from reprimanding him, the Buddha asked him whether he could stand the threefold training in higher morality, higher thought, and higher insight. In Mahayana, these became the three higher trainings (AN 3:84). Once

---

67. Rhys Davids, *The Minor Anthologies of the Pali Canon,* Part I, p. xliv.
68. Andrew Skilton, *A Concise History of Buddhism,* p. 48.
69. Ariyesako, *The Bhikkus' Rules.*

proficient in this, lust, malice, and delusion would be abandoned and no wrong deed would be performed without needing to follow the rules as such. The implication, then, is that slavish adherence to the letter of the rules is not required to attain emancipation. Interestingly, the Vajjians also brought about the great schism in the Buddhist order during the Second Buddhist Council on this very question of rules.

The core of the Vinaya is given in the *patimokkha*. When one analyzes these rules, one finds just about ten essential rules, very similar in fact to the Bodhisattva Precepts. These are grouped into rules that entail automatic expulsion from the sangha for life (*parajika*), rules requiring an initial and subsequent meeting of the sangha (*sanghadisesa*) that result in a period of probation, indefinite rules (*aniyata*) based on acknowledgment of the offence, rules entailing confession with forfeiture (*nissagiyya*), rules entailing confession (*paccitiyya*), violations that must be verbally acknowledged (*patidesaniya*), and training rules (*sekhiyavatta*).

The Brahma Net Sutra (mid-fifth century) is one of the oldest summaries of the Bodhisattva Precepts, which exist in many variations. The ten major Bodhisattva Precepts are:

1. Not to kill;
2. Not to steal;
3. Not to engage in licentious acts;
4. Not to use false words and speech;
5. Not to trade or sell alcoholic beverages;
6. Not to defame the sangha;
7. Not to praise oneself and speak ill of others;
8. Not to be stingy;
9. Not to harbour anger;
10. Not to speak ill of the Buddha, the Dharma, or the Sangha (lit. 'the Three Jewels').

These precepts also prohibit encouraging others do so. In addition, there are forty-eight minor rules, which are not always regarded as mandatory. Note that the consumption of alcohol is not expressly forbidden, only trade. Mrs. Rhys Davids argues in the introduction to her translation of the Khuddaka-Patha that it is not the "sensible use" of liquors, but rather the habit, frequency, and occasions for indulging in them, which was originally prohibited.[70] In any case, it is clear that the Vinaya regards it as a relatively minor offence, being the fifty-first of ninety-two *pacittiyas*, requiring confession only, preceded by "not to witness military activities" and followed by "not to tickle." We know from the first *sutta* of the Digha Nikaya, the Supreme Net (Brahmajala Sutta), that the Buddha regarded ethical and moral rules to be *oramattakam silamattakam* – 'merely profane (mundane), merely ethical (practices).'

Principle #34: Earthbound Devas (6.11). In a previous section of the Mahaparinibbana Sutta, we learned that at least some lower devas, the spiritual or celestial beings of light who occupy the higher planes or dimensions of the thirty-one planes of existence, also co-exist with human beings and influence them telepathically. The Buddha himself claimed to be aware of such devas and to have received teachings (*dhamma*) from them. We know that at least three deva realms have intercourse with human beings, including the Four Great Kings, the Thirty-Three Gods, and the Brahma realms, and that the anti-gods seem to occupy nearly the same plane as humans, viz., the one world ocean.

Here we encounter another interesting bit of lore about the devas, for Ananda asks Anuruddha, a cousin of the Buddha and one of his five principal followers, which devas he is aware of. Anuruddha was ranked as one of the foremost in the attainment of the Divine Eye. Anuruddha refers to sky devas and earth devas whose minds are earthbound in contrast to devas who are free from craving. The last category implies that devas are capable of practising dharma and of attainment, something that is implied all through the Pali Canon, despite the dogma that only human beings are capable of emancipation. The *anti-gods* are another example of earthbound devas, having been cast down from the realm of the Thirty-Three Gods, perhaps due to their association with samsara and the powers of nature. The earth devas refer to the Four Great Kings, the realm of what we describe as the sprites, tree spirits, elves, fairies, pixies, gnomes, Japanese *yokai*, the Span-

---

70. Rhys Davids, *The Minor Anthologies of the Pali Canon*, Part I, p. xlvii.

ish and Latin-American *duende,* various Slavic fairies, and other similar beings of all times and climes.

Principle #35: Subhadda and the First Buddhist Council (6.20). Subhadda was the last monastic to be ordained by the Buddha. Maurice Walshe states in a note that this Subhadda is not the same as that one, perhaps because this Subhadda, a barber, ordained late in life, whereas the other Subhadda was a *samana* ('wandering ascetic') of another sect. It is certainly a coincidence that two monastics with the same name were associated with the Buddha's death and the period immediately afterward, but not impossible. On the other hand, some translations of the Mahaparinibbana Sutta refer to Subhadda the barber as "the late-received one," referring perhaps to his being the last follower to be personally ordained by the Buddha rather than to his age. The Pali Canon denigrates him, and this may be the reason why he is distinguished from the *samana* Subhadda, but this may also reflect a sectarian prejudice. We know that the First Buddhist Council was contentious, and that this contentiousness persisted in later councils too. In any case, Subhadda the barber suggested that the rules might be relaxed (something that the Buddha himself advocated), precipitating the First Buddhist Council.

The First Buddhist Council was called together shortly after the Buddha's death by Mahakassapa, who was regarded as foremost in asceticism, despite the fact that the Buddha said that the sangha should have no leader other than the dharma. Presumably, Mahakassapa also brought an ascetic orientation to the council and, as with all organizations, had both supporters and detractors. Indeed, it is clear from the Cullavagga that Mahakassapa's group sponsored the council, and that others were excluded.[71] The First Buddhist Council was held during the rainy season about three months after the Buddha's death. Since the rainy season retreat begins in late June or July, it seems likely that the Buddha died in March, which is consistent with the statement that the sal trees between which the Buddha died bloomed prematurely. I have already talked about how the arhants [sic] at this council castigated Ananda for convincing the Buddha to ordain women and for

---

71. See I.B. Horner, *The Book of Discipline,* Vol. V, p. 395, n.1.

failing to clarify which were the major and which were the minor rules of the Vinaya. Indeed, so deep was the misogyny of the ar-hants of this council that Ananda was castigated for allowing women to view the Buddha's body after his death, which (they claimed) did their tears defile.[72] Presumably, Ananda too had his supporters and detractors, so we see here how the politics of the First Buddhist Council may have played out. It is an open question whether all of the monastics present at the First Council were men. Dr. Chatsumarn Kabilsingh, in her article, "The History of the Bhikkuni Sangha," argues that female monastics were also present.

---

72. Ibid, pp. 400f.

7

Beyond Good and Evil: The Story of Angulimala

CERTAINLY THE MOST notorious and interesting arhant in the Pali Canon is Angulimala, whose monastic name literally means 'finger garland,' alluding to his reputed habit of killing passersby in the Jalini forest near Sravasti and wearing a garland or necklace of their finger bones before entering the Buddhist sangha and attaining nirvana. This story, startling and even macabre, is highly paradoxical and serves as an invaluable indication of original Buddhist beliefs concerning the nature of enlightenment, karma, and the Act of Truth and the bizarre forms in which they may manifest. The story is so distasteful and unconventional that its historicity seems certain; the confusion that resists any conventional explanation suggests a deeper meaning, as has been proposed by Buddhist scholar Richard Gombrich in his book, *How Buddhism Began*.

First, let us summarize the conventional story as it appears in the Pali Canon and its commentaries. Angulimala, whose birth name was changed from Himsaka ('harmful') to Ahimsaka ('harmless'), was the son of the brahman Bhaggava Gagga and his wife Mantani. Bhaggava was a spiritual advisor (sometimes rendered 'chaplain') to King Pasenadi of Kosala, one of the sixteen great regions of ancient India from which the Buddha himself came. Pasenadi himself was a disciple of the Buddha who was subsequently dethroned by another of his advisers and died of exposure while trying to regain his throne. The Magadha kingdom later annexed Kosala after a series of wars.

In accordance with the custom of the time, Ahimsaka's horoscope was cast when he was born and it was discovered that he was born under the *nakshatra* ('lunar mansion') Aslesha, the so-called "robber constellation," corresponding to the second and third decanates of Leo in Western astrology, which predestined him (according to the *sutta*) to a life of violence and criminality. However, Aslesha is not only associated with robbery. It is also associated with sorcery, a fact the significance of which will become clear. The name Ahimsaka was chosen by his parents in order to attempt to circumvent this. He was sent to the great university of Taksasila (present-day Taxila), where he became the best student of his teacher. Generally, a student entered Taksasila at the age of sixteen. The Vedas and the Eighteen *Silpas* or Arts, which included skills such as archery, hunting, and elephant lore, were taught, in addition to law, medicine, and military science. The institution is very significant in Buddhist tradition since it is believed that Mahayana Buddhism developed there.

So far, the story is quite unexceptional and believable. However, according to the commentaries Ahimsaka became embroiled in a scandal in which he was accused of having an affair with his teacher's wife. Whether this was true or not, his teacher, who is presented improbably in the *sutta* as a fool, believed it and demanded that Ahimsaka complete his instruction by giving him the bizarre gift of one thousand human fingers. Bound by the ancient rule of fealty to the guru, Ahimsaka was obliged to comply with his teacher's maliciously motivated demand, which in turn activated Ahimsaka's innate predisposition to violence. Ahimsaka then went to the Jalini forest, where he became a serial killer, described as a bandit in the Angulimala Sutta (MN 86). He was one finger short of fulfilling this project by murdering his mother when he met the Buddha.

The absurdity of the foregoing story is palpable, and Richard Gombrich has suggested as an alternative that in fact Ahimsaka was a proto-tantric practitioner, the left-hand form of which included sexual yoga and even murder in an attempt to free oneself from all human limitations and to awaken the innate divine Shakti. In this context, the fact that Taksasila subsequently became the original source of the Mahayana teachings, considered heretical by the reactionary redactors of the Pali Canon, is suggestive. The earliest evidence for human sacrifice in the Indian subcontinent dates back to the Bronze Age Indus Valley civilization. If this interpretation is correct, it puts the significance of the Buddha's encounter with Angulimala and the Buddha's subsequent acceptance of him in a completely different light.

The Angulimala Sutta tells the story of how the Buddha, in the twentieth year of his ministry, i.e., about 375 BCE, after alms round, left Sravasti on the road that led directly to Ahimsaka, now called Angulimala, described as a bloody-handed, violent, merciless mass murderer, despite warnings from the local people not to go. This was not a casual outing, but a journey of some distance.

It seems clear the Buddha's intention was to confront Angulimala directly. However, the Buddha's interaction with Angulimala is extremely peculiar. Angulimala comes running up behind the Buddha, calling on him to stop – a rather odd thing for a bandit to do. The Buddha is said to have replied to Angulimala, and said, "I have stopped, Angulimala. You too stop!"[73] Startled and intrigued by the Buddha's reply, and perhaps recognizing the Buddha as a holy man, instead of killing him Angulimala asks the Buddha what he is talking about, whereupon the Buddha delivers a sermon to Angulimala on the nature and significance of "stopping," i.e., the transcendence of karma and samsara and the attainment of nirvana, whereupon Angulimala declares, "at long last this recluse, a venerated sage, has come to this great forest for my sake."[74] Angulimala then converts to the dharma and becomes the Buddha's personal attendant, taking Angulimala as his ordination name. According to the Vinaya, the Buddha himself would have given this name to Angulimala, which is in itself astonishing insofar as it is a direct allusion to his purported criminality.

If Angulimala were an ordinary murderer, the foregoing story makes no sense at all. To all appearances, the Buddha is rewarding

73. MN 86:5.
74. Ibid, 6.

a psychopathic serial killer with the gift of ordination in the sangha and allowing him to become his personal attendant, even giving him the name Angulimala as his monastic name! In fact, this is how the Buddha's actions were perceived by the local people, at whose insistence the Buddha agreed to amend the Vinaya to prohibit criminals from being allowed to be ordained in the Buddhist sangha henceforth, which begs the question even more forcefully of why the Buddha did it in the first place. However, the Buddha did not stop there. After returning to Jetavana Monastery near Sravasti with Angulimala as his personal attendant, the Buddha defended Angulimala to King Pasenadi, followed by another bizarre story that also seems to have a deeper implication.

While begging for alms in Sravasti, Angulimala sees a woman giving birth to a deformed child (some translators interpret this as referring to a painful or difficult labour). Once again, the macabre seems to follow Angulimala wherever he goes. After telling the Buddha about this, the Buddha tells Angulimala to effect an Act of Truth. The Act of Truth, also described in the Jatakas, is a pan-Indian practice based on the idea that truth (dharma) has an intrinsic power that can be called on to produce apparently miraculous effects based ultimately on the law of karma. It may also be described as the law of righteousness and was the basis of Mahatma Gandhi's political strategy that he called "satyagraha" (Pali *saccagaha*). The Buddha instructed Angulimala to return to the woman, and utter these words with the intention of healing the child: "Sister, since I was born I do not recall that I have ever intentionally deprived a living being of life. By this truth, may you be well and may your infant be well!"[75]

What is most bizarre about this is that, based on the story, the Buddha was instructing Angulimala to lie, something that a Buddha is supposed to be incapable of doing. The obvious contradiction is immediately resolved in the *sutta* by having Angulimala point out to the Buddha [sic] that this was a lie, whereupon the Buddha amended the words to "since I was born with the noble birth," thus turning the Act of Truth into a pun based on the sig-

---

75. Ibid, 15.

nificance of Angulimala's dramatic transformation. However, a more plausible explanation is that Angulimala was in fact not a mass murderer at all, and that the whole *sutta* is an elaborate confabulation based on an original story that was so unacceptable to the Sri Lankan redactors of the Pali Canon that it had to be disguised or distorted. Subsequently, Angulimala is represented as attaining nirvana after a relatively short time, thus completing the transformation from a notorious bandit to an arhant. According to the Dhammapadatthakatha, Angulimala died soon after.

The Angulimala Sutta also provides a fascinating insight into the inner workings of karma for, even after achieving nirvana, no one, not even an arhant or a Buddha, is exempt from the inexorable operation of the law of karma. Thus, one morning during the alms round a crowd gathered around Angulimala and started throwing objects at him, including a clod of earth, a stone or a stick, and a potsherd, cutting his head, breaking his bowl, and tearing his outer robe. Returning to the Buddha in this state, the Buddha told him, "Bear it, brahmin! Bear it, Brahmin! You are experiencing here and now the result of deeds because of which you might have been tortured in hell for many years, for many hundreds of years, for many thousands of years."[76] The commentaries explain that not even an arhant or a Buddha is exempt from karma, even the Buddha himself having been injured after an attack by his cousin Devadatta, who blamed the Buddha for not enforcing a more rigorous Vinaya on the sangha, including strict vegetarianism, which the Buddha rejected. However, a deeper implication appears as well, for, if past karmas must work themselves out even in the case of an arhant, and arhantship represents the final rebirth of an emancipated being, and if even a murderer can become an arhant, all of which follow logically from the story, then it also follows that it may be that an arhant may be severely afflicted by all of the unresolved karmas of their past births, thus having the appearance of being the very opposite of an arhant, an anti-arhant in fact! It appears that Angulimala may have been an arhant of just this type!

---

76. Ibid, 17.

Such considerations lead us directly to considerations of Tantra, which would subsequently develop into the Vajrayana tradition and, in Tibet, the *mahasiddhas*, including adept practitioners of the type represented by Padmasambhava and others, whose appearance and behaviour were directly contradictory to conventional ideas of enlightenment. Was this the underlying motivation for the redactors of the Pali Canon to conceal the person of Angulimala beneath the absurd self-contradictions and bizarre self-justifications of the *sutta* commentaries? They could not deny the historicity of Angulimala. The Vinaya itself attests to his existence, but they desperately tried to whitewash the real story with the story of a murderer whose evil life was transformed by the miraculous charisma of the Buddha, which bizarrely has become one of the most popular children's stories of Theravada Buddhism!

So what are we to make of the story of Angulimala in the light of the foregoing? I suggest that Angulimala was in fact born under the *naksatra* of Aslesha, and subsequently studied some sort of proto-tantric spirituality under a guru at Taksasila, where he was initiated into sexual tantra and acquired a reputation as a brilliant student and a highly realized practitioner. This is more than hinted at when his guru instructs him to make a necklace of human fingers in order to make the science that he has learned efficacious. Tantrics, including Padmasambhava, typically spent years meditating in charnel grounds where the construction of such a necklace would have been easy. Perhaps this was the token by which his final meditations were completed. Interestingly, one of the austere practices (*dhutanga*) to which Angulimala was committed after becoming a Buddhist monk included meditating in cemeteries!

After the completion of his studies, he became a solitary forest dweller in Jalini, inspiring the veneration and fear of the local people. So great was his reputation that he came to the attention of the Buddha in Sravasti, who made a significant trek to visit him. This is in itself extremely unusual, the Pali Canon usually representing officials and people as visiting the Buddha, not the reverse. When the Buddha met Angulimala, he recognized him as an advanced spiritual practitioner and instructed him in the *Bud-*

dhadharma, and Angulimala was so impressed that he became a Buddhist monk and the personal attendant of the Buddha, and they returned to Sravasti together. Subsequently Angulimala attained nirvana and became an arhant, but also incited the violent enmity of the crowd due to his reputation as a tantric sorcerer. The Buddha, however, recognized him as a powerful tantric healer and explicitly declared by means of the Act of Truth that Angulimala was innocent of any crimes. To placate the crowd the Buddha also agreed to prohibit criminals from entering the sangha. The redactors of the Pali Canon, who could not accept that the Buddha would thus honour a tantric practitioner, even if he did convert to the *Buddhadharma*, subsequently covered all of this up. This is not the only place in the Pali Canon where the Buddha speaks positively about Tantra. In the Ambattha Sutta (DN 3), for example, he refers positively to Kanha, a negro and the son of a slave girl who became a powerful shaman.

8

Near-Earth Realms, Fallen Angels and Human Beings in Buddhist Cosmology

BUDDHIST COSMOLOGY IS *nowhere explained in the Buddhist sut-*
tas in its totality as a system. Yet its essential architecture appears
in all schools, both Hinayana and Mahayana, with only minor dif-
ferences, based on a systematic analysis and synthesis of scattered
references found all though the Pali Canon. Thus, it must have been
a topic of intense scrutiny, having arisen during the pre-sectarian
period that is closest to the original teachings of Shakyamuni Bud-
dha. Consequently, this discussion cannot be assigned to any par-
ticular sect. It underlies and unifies the whole Buddhist world-view,
even the Theravada, some of whose followers commonly claim that
the Buddha did not present an ontology. I will present a synthetic
overview of Buddhist cosmology and ontology in the context of con-
temporary post-Newtonian science and explore its implications for
the spiritual path. One is struck by the degree to which the Buddhist
world-view broadly anticipates contemporary scientific discoveries,
once one overcomes the twin misosophies of "scientism" and "philo-
sophical materialism," which true science transcended long ago.
That this is not generally recognized or accepted testifies to the ig-
norance that masquerades as enlightenment today. Nor is ontology
irrelevant to the topic of spiritual development, as some might as-
sert, based on a selective reading of the texts. Rather, in the light of

the Buddhist revelations concerning the fundamental and ultimate nature of reality, Buddhist beliefs concerning spiritual practice acquire a clarity that only enhances the prevalent psychological interpretation, which also suffers from the accusation of subjectivity. As with ethics, any spiritual praxis implies a corresponding ontology.

Unfortunately, what Evans-Wentz referred to as the "long dark age of the West" still blinds us to the insights that might be derived from realizing that scientism, as distinct from science, does not only not present a comprehensive picture of reality – it actually blinds us to it, in the service of a contemporary ethos that increasingly threatens to destroy the world of nature and humanity in its relentless pursuit of competition, property, and mindless consumption that stands opposed to the three primary facts of existence: non-self-identity, impermanence, and suffering as taught by the Buddha.

Buddhist cosmology divides experience both vertically and horizontally. Horizontally, the Buddhist *suttas* describe worlds or world systems separated by vast regions of empty space. These worlds appeared in great spheres that emerged out of a state of potentiality, expanded, contracted, and disappeared over long periods ranging from millions to trillions of years. In the largest sense, this fourfold process of origination, evolution, devolution, and potentiality has no beginning and no end – it is infinite and eternal in extent and duration. The spherical universe is itself organized into (more or less) spherical stars and galaxies that themselves move in (more or less) spherical orbits, and even larger collections of galaxies. The latter fact that has only been recently substantiated by science. The Buddha also describes the destruction of solar systems by supernovas, which proceed in seven stages or phases (the so-called "seven suns"), characterized by the cessation of rain and the consequent disappearance of vegetation over a period of hundreds of thousands of years, followed by the drying up of the rivers and oceans and finally the incineration of the earth itself. Some string theorists also posit that universes themselves coexist as holographic diffraction patterns in two-dimensional planes that appear in our universe as black holes.

While not specifically indicated by Buddhist cosmology, such a view is certainly consistent with it.

This quaternary dynamic structure of states of origination, evolution, devolution, and potentiality also describes the very small. In fact, it is the fundamental process structure of becoming itself (samsara). Phenomenal reality is nothing other than process, cycles within cycles within cycles, driven by the law of karma (causality). What we call "matter" is not a "stuff," but rather a particular kind of process or system of processes. This description largely accords with the modern scientific conception of the physical nature of reality since the downfall of philosophical materialism. The mathematician Alfred North Whitehead in his book, *Process and Reality,* describes it, for example.

The Buddha also describes a vertical dimension, ranging from a high-energy, abstract polarity to a low-energy, "material" polarity that also accords very well with the world-view of modern physics. Buddhist cosmology divides this vertical continuum in various ways, starting with a twofold division into material and immaterial "realms" (*lokas* or *dhatus*) and ending with a division into thirty-one fundamental planes of "vibration" or existence. According to this world-view, matter or form is only one aspect of reality.

According to Buddhist cosmology, human beings inhabit the fifth realm, counting from the bottom, or the twenty-seventh realm, counting form the top, of these thirty-one planes of existence. The human realm is also the lowest (seventh) realm of the so-called "happy destinations," represented as a flattened inverted triangular island-continent that floats in the world ocean to the south of Mount Sumeru (the North Pole), the shape of which suggests the Indian subcontinent. This represents the earthly realm (*manusyaloka*) consisting of four continents.[77] Sumeru (lit. 'excellent' or 'wondrous mountain') is the Buddhist rep-

---

77. These are Jambudvipa ('land of the Indian blackberry tree'), Purvavideha ('land of the thorn tree'), Aparagodiyana ('land of the *kadam* tree'), and Uttarakuru ('land of the kalpa tree'), located in the south, east, west, and north respectively. Uttarakuru is the abode of the most advanced humans, who live for a thousand years and are, interestingly, free-loving communists. Our own species of human lives on Jambudvipa, characterized by the shortest lifespan of the four types.

resentation of the universal archetype of a central world axis, usually represented as a mountain, tree, or pole. Commonly identified with Mount Kailash or Kangrinpoque in the Tibetan Himalayas, this identification is clearly symbolic. In fact, geographically, and here I am primarily interested in physical facts, Sumeru clearly represents the rotational and magnetic axes of the earth. The four continents represent the continents of the earth. The shape of the southern continent, where human beings live, clearly corresponds to the Indian subcontinent. Thus, the western continent would correspond to the African-South American landmass, which we now know was originally joined; the northern continent to North America and Greenland; and the eastern continent to Eurasia. It is now known that several supercontinents have formed and separated all through the earth's history. The Buddhist description appears to allude to a specific moment in the earth's geologic history when the continents had just this formation. According to at least one animation I have seen, this was the situation about 120 million years ago. In this interpretation, then, the "peak" of Mount Sumeru would correspond to the North Polar Axis of the earth, the magnetic pole of which, like Shambhala, "wanders." The ocean around its base corresponds to the "one world ocean" in which the continents drift. The "one world ocean" is clearly shown in the Dymaxion map invented by R. Buckminster Fuller.

Mount Sumeru includes the realm of the asuras, who inhabit its base; the realm of the Four Great Kings, who occupy its four slopes;[78] and the realm of the Thirty-Three gods, Vedic and post-Vedic demigods who occupy its truncated apex. Thus, Mount Sumeru is represented as a truncated four-sided pyramid. This architecture resembles that of Mount Kailash as well as the ziggurats, built in the ancient Mesopotamian valley and western Iranian

---

78. These are Vaisravana, 'he who hears everything'; Virudhaka, 'he who causes to grow'; Dhrtarastra, 'he who upholds the realm'; Virupaksa, 'he who sees all,' associated with the colours yellow, blue, white, and red; the north, south, east, west; and various symbols, including the umbrella, mongoose, stupa, sword. *pipa* ('lute'), serpent, stupa, and pearl. The function of the Four Great Kings is to report to Sakra, the chief of the realm of the Thirty-Three Gods, on the state of humanity.

plateau, and similar structures, called step pyramids, also found in Egypt, Europe, Mesoamerica, South America, North America, and Indonesia. Floating in the air above Mount Sumeru are the realms of the *yama* devas, joy or contentment (the *tusita* devas), two realms associated with creativity, and three God-realms (the Brahma devas). Below the realm of the humans and the asuras are the realms of ghosts, animals, and hell-beings, the latter divided into eight hot and eight cold hells.

It is fashionable to interpret the realms of Buddhist cosmology psychologically, as representative of various types, stages, or degrees of consciousness or conscious realization. This point of view is certainly valid, but this does not mean that the thirty-one planes of existence are *merely* psychological symbols in the modern sense. According to the *Buddhist* world-view, psychological and ontological states are opposite sides of the same coin. Reality itself is ultimately resolvable into mental states, matter itself being merely a delusion of consciousness. In this discussion, I intend to focus on the neglected ontological aspect of the Buddhist cosmic conception. In particular, I will focus on the realms that we perceive and/or that interact or communicate with our own, "earthly" realm. I am well aware that this description corresponds to some aspects of certain modern speculative theories associated with various Theosophical, National Socialist, UFO, and conspiracy theories. Jacques Vallee is one of the more reasonable individuals currently exploring this area. However, while these correspondences may be interesting, it is not my intention here to argue for or against these theories or to endorse any particular point of view, but simply to present the anterior Buddhist cosmology from an historical and scientific perspective.

According to the *suttas,* all of the thirty-one planes of existence, corresponding as they do to "levels" of conscious realization, are inhabited by sentient beings. This must be true because, as in quantum physics, it is the act of observation that gives rise to phenomenal reality. A world devoid of sentient beings is a world in a state of potentiality. This is also true of the horizontal dimension of samsara. The difference is that the sentient beings that inhabit the realms above the human realm are far more intelligent, knowledgeable, beautiful, powerful, faster, and long-lived than we are, by many orders of magnitude. *They are not, however, necessarily more spiritual than humans. Many are decisively less spiritual.* Because of their great gifts, inherited from past karma, many of these beings are relatively complacent, and simply enjoy their lives, which can last millions, billions, or even trillions of human years (to them, however, such vast durations need not appear as they do to us, any more than a dog or a cat feels itself to be short-lived). However, at the lower end of the scale, the inhabitants of the Brahma worlds (*mahabrahmas*) may and do take an interest in human affairs. These beings occupy the highest realm that actually interacts with humans. The Brahma world is the lowest world in the system of thirty-one planes that is not subject to periodic destruction, whereas all of the planes below the Brahma realm are subject to the fourfold process of origination, evolution, devolution, and potentiality already discussed.[79] Beings within these realms are, however, still subject to this process. Otherwise, their merit would not be exhausted and they would not be reborn. Thus, the Brahma world is the highest and subtlest plane of phenomenal existence. They live approximately one trillion years. The best-known inhabitant of this world is Mahabrahma Himself, a.k.a. "God," who erroneously believes Himself to be the Creator of the Universe, because He is the first being to be reborn after the destruction and reappearance of the universe in a lower world due to loss of merit. In Gnosticism, He is called the Demiurge (*demiourgos,* 'creator'). The Mahabrahma Sahampati convinced the Buddha to preach following his Enlightenment for the sake of all sentient beings. Thus, although ignorant and deluded in some ways, *mahabrahmas* are not actually malicious. The Buddha encouraged his disciples to be reborn there, as an intermediate step towards enlightenment, and provided the well-known *maitri* meditation to achieve this goal.

The so-called 'divine race' (*devaputra*) inhabits the next lower world associated with creativity (*parnimirmita-masavartin*). These are the original capitalists, divine beings (devas) who delight in desire and enjoy the offerings given by others. These correspond

---

79. Not all of the sources are consistent in this regard, however.

to the anthropomorphic gods of the pagan polytheistic pantheons, which in many traditions (e.g., Vodun) are literally nourished and sustained by the offerings they receive. These beings live for about nine billion human years. Mara, the tempter of the Buddha, is often said to reside in this realm, although he is also associated with the demonic asuras.

Next are the bodhisattvas, who are reborn in the human world as buddhas. Each Buddha initiates an eon, era, epoch, or dispensation of dharma, which does not end until his dharma is forgotten. Thus, we are now in the Buddha dispensation of Shakyamuni Gautama, which will last for only about five thousand years. We are now at the *midpoint* of the Shakyamuni dispensation. The bodhisattvas inhabit the Tusita ('joyful') realm, the second realm above the human. These beings live for 576 million years.

The realm of the Four Great Kings is the closest realm next above our own. The nature spirits, dwarfs, fairies, dragons, goblins, trolls, and similar beings of all traditions, of varying degrees of ethical purity, inhabit it. These beings live for nine million years (other sources say ninety thousand years).

Finally, we find the asuras and four human types. The latter range in longevity from ten to a thousand years or more. Our own human species, which is merely one of many, lives to the south of the base of Mount Sumeru. Currently we live about 120 years, although originally we were much longer-lived than this. During the age of the *chakravartins* (lit. 'rulers of the universe') human beings of the different continents were able to travel between the continents, using a flying machine called a *cakraratna*.

Whereas human beings inhabit four great continents in the one world ocean that surrounds the base of Mount Sumeru, the asuras inhabit the ocean itself immediately surrounding the base. "A-sura" was interpreted to mean "non-sura," i.e., not a *sura*, a synonym for deva (literally, a 'shining being' or energy being of light). Deva can also be translated 'celestial dweller' or 'star.'

Asura is often translated 'Titan, demigod, anti-god, or demon.' The asuras are described as addicted to the passions of wrath, pride, envy, insincerity, falseness, boasting, and bellicosity. They are dominated by ego, force, and violence. At least some asuras are actually malevolent. As with all of the six classes of sentient beings, asuras may be reborn as human beings, and human beings may be reborn as asuras. Because humans and asuras occupy essentially the same plane, i.e., the one world ocean surrounding the base of Mount Sumeru, there is considerable interaction between them. Asuras enjoy a much more pleasurable life than humans do, but they are plagued by envy for the devas.

Asuras and human beings are alike in that we both have shared a similar fate. Both human beings and the asuras originally occupied a much higher realm in the Buddhist hierarchy. Asuras originally lived in the realm of the Thirty-Three Gods on the peak of Mount Sumeru, but they were cast down to the foot of the mountain due to their drunkenness. Thus the asuras and the devas of the Thirty-Three Gods engage in constant conflict, in which human beings also become embroiled.

The asuras were not always regarded as evil beings. In the Rigveda (c 1500–1000 BCE) asuras were a type of deva, such as Asura Varuna, the god of the celestial ocean, the underwater world, and law and order, moral and societal affairs, and nature. *Asuras* (lit. 'lord') were originally a term associated with individual devas, not a class of beings in their own right. Asuras become a distinct class of being during the late Vedic period (c 1000 BCE–500 BCE). Originally the asuras were the older and stronger siblings of the devas, powerful and beneficent. The later Vedic texts begin to document a conflict between the asuras and the devas, in which the asuras were invariably victorious. According to the Bhagavad Gita, the asuras are described as vicious, proud, arrogant, conceited, angry, harsh, and ignorant. This reflects a growing conflict between the older, dominant cult of asura worship and a newer but rising cult of deva worship. Originally, the asuras were non-anthropomorphic and formless gods, in contradistinction to the more anthropomorphic devas. The asuras were the guardians of the natural and moral laws of rita, the great principle of cosmic order that regulates and coordinates the operation of the universe, comparable to dharma and karma. The deva worshippers, on the other hand, were concerned with power, might, fear, submission, and the status quo.

Interestingly, it was also during the late Vedic period that women were stripped of their traditional rights and privileges and demoted to the status of property, something that the Buddha opposed but which was reinstated immediately after his death (*parinirvana*) about 400 BCE by the "arhants" of the First Buddhist Council. Thus, the division between the asura and deva worshippers appears to correspond to a social schism that occurred during the late Vedic period and culminated in the *sramana* counterculture of the fifth and sixth centuries BCE. In Buddhism, the asuras are seen as inferior deities who are never satisfied and who always strive to improve themselves. This is paradoxical because the Buddha opposed the brahmanic establishment based on caste, supported by the deva worshippers, as a degenerate remnant of the primordial tradition that the Buddha sought to restore. This schism reflects a conflict between the adherents of the old gods that continues today, in which the worshippers of the old gods seek to restore their worship to a position of primacy, against the more recent gods of oppression. One finds a similar conflict in Egyptian mythology, in which the old gods, like Set, now associated with evil, were originally not regarded as evil at all. This principle of cosmic conflict became entrenched in later religions, such as Zoroastrianism and Christianity, as well. In the Iranian tradition, the asuras, especially Asura (*Ahura*) Mazda, the personification of Wisdom, retained their privileged status and it was the devas who were demonized and cast down.

Similarly, human beings originally occupied the radiant or splendid realm (*abhasvara*), next above the Brahma world. Here we dwelled as beings of light or pure energy, characterized by delight and joy, with lifespans of approximately ten trillion years. The original trans-humans or deva-humans were psychologically individual but physically alike. Plato describes them as celestial bisexual spheres of pure energy. When a universe re-emerges from a state of potentiality (the so-called *vivartakalpa*), it is immediately populated by humans from the Abhasvara realm. According to modern scientific reckoning, this occurred about fourteen billion years ago. The first humans were not like modern humans. They shone in their own light, moved through the air without mechanical aid, lived for a very long time, and did not require physical nourishment. They were more like a type of inferior deity than contemporary human beings. This was the age of the *chakravartins* (lit. 'universal rulers'). However, gradually we developed a taste for physical food and sensation. Our bodies became heavier and more material. We lost our intrinsic luminosity. Our bodies became more differentiated. Our lifespan decreased. We divided into two genders and began to reproduce sexually. We began to hunt and eat the flesh of animals. Territoriality, property, greed, theft, violence, and criminality gradually overtook us. Social distinctions and government arose. The critical transition to humanity appears to have begun during the hunter-gatherer stage of human civilization. This arose about two million years ago according to the archaeological record, corresponding to Homo erectus, who is also credited with the discovery of fire. It culminates in the Neolithic Revolution, which occurred about ten thousand years ago. This appears to be the period when the deva-humans began to enter into the physical primate evolution through the process of rebirth or transmigration. This was perhaps facilitated by the ingestion of psychedelic plants by early primates, as suggested by Aldous Huxley, Terrence McKenna, Graham Hancock, and others, thus opening a "door" to the higher realms (the so-called "stoned ape" hypothesis).

Asuras perceive devas in the same way that animals perceive humans. Humans perceive animals consistently, unless they are tiny, but devas and asuras only rarely. Asuras are often confused with hell beings. The objection to devas that we do not see them disappears entirely when one realizes that one is comparing orders of sentient beings potentially comparable to the difference between an ant and a man.[80] A deva is no more visible to a man than a man is to an ant, even though the latter may be crawling

---

80. Ants appeared in the evolutionary record about one hundred million years ago. *Homo* appeared about 2.5 million years ago. Consequently, the difference between ants and men is only about 97.5 million years, far less than the trillion year life span of devas, so it is clear that the difference between devas and men is of an order of magnitude of at least ten thousand times greater than that between ants and men.

across his hand. The argument works the other way too. When was the last time you chatted with an ant? Yet ants and human beings inhabit the same terrestrial space. It is not necessarily true that the planes of samsara are ontologically separate, any more than the higher dimensions of strings are separated from space and time in string theory. All of the dimensions may co-exist and yet be invisible to each other. Similarly, we have millions of radio and television programs and cell phone conversations passing through our bodies right now, but we do not perceive them. We literally live within an invisible 4D electromagnetic space. Perhaps this is the reason why we have yet to "discover" extraterrestrial civilizations, some of which must be millions or even billions of years older than Homo sapiens. Perhaps they are right here, right now, but we simply cannot see them, or see them only rarely.

In order to appreciate a higher-energy being, one must adjust one's own energy vibration to their frequency. This is possible in theory by concentrating consciousness, increasing or decreasing its "vibration." Mind itself is the universal substrate of reality. Thus, all of reality is, in principle, accessible to it. This can be achieved through meditation or a variety of mind-altering techniques, both physical and psychological, including the ingestion of psychedelic substances, but one's perceptions will be limited by one's cognitive capacity, which is largely a matter of karma, since all human beings are capable of enlightenment in principle. This capability is the *tathagatagarbha,* the Buddha-potentiality. On the other hand, a Buddha has transcended samsara completely. Therefore, he is able to travel in a "mental body" to any part of samsara and communicate with the beings that inhabit other realms without limitation or distortion. Thus, he has a perfect comprehension of reality.

Vertical Phenomenology of Samsara

Realm	Sub-realm	Sanskrit	Location	Inhabitants	Lifespan	Meditative State
NORTHERN POLARITY: A HIGH-ENERGY, IMMATERIAL STATE CHARACTERIZED BY BEING-CONSCIOUSNESS-BLISS (NIRVANA)						
(14 additional planes do not interact with the earth-plane)						
FORM WORLD (RUPA LOKA)						
Radiant devas				Human beings (before they fell)		2nd jhana
	Streaming radiance	Abhasvara	409,600 miles above the earth[81]		8 e.[82]	
	Unbounded radiance	Apramanabha	204,800 miles above the earth		4 e.	
	Limited radiance	Parittabha	102,400 miles above the earth		2 e.	
Brahma devas				Brahma gods		1st jhana
	Great Brahmas	Maha-brahma	51,200 miles above the earth		1.5 e.	
	Ministers of	Brahma-purohita	25,600 miles		1 e.	

81. The original sources of course do not indicate miles. To arrive at miles I have used an equivalence of 1 *yojana* = 5 miles (8.0467 km). The distance from the Radiant Devas to Mt. Sumeru is comparable to the distance between the earth and the moon.

82. According to one interpretation, an eon (*mahakalpa*) equals 1.28 trillion years, so the Abhasvara devas live about ten trillion years. ("Trillion" here is defined as one thousand billion, or ten followed by eleven zeroes.) In another interpretation it is 10 to the power of 140 (i.e., ten followed by 140 zeroes) – a much larger number.

Brahma		above the earth		
Retinue of Brahma	Brahma-parisadya	12,800 miles above the earth		0.5 e.[83]
DESIRE WORLD (KAMA LOKA)				
Happy Destinations (apaya)				
Creative devas				
Devas wielding power over others' creations	Parinirmitavasavartin	6,400 miles above the earth		9.2 b.y.
Devas de-lighting in creation	Nirmanarati	3,200 miles above the earth		2.3 b.y.
Contented devas	Tusita	1,600 miles above the earth	Bodhisattvas	576 m.y.
Temporal devas	Yama	800 miles above the earth		44 m.y.
33 devas	Trayastrimsa	Peak of Mount Sumeru, elevation 400 miles[84]	Asuras (be-fore they fell)	36 m.y.
Four Great Kings	Caturmaharajikakayika	Slopes of Mount Sumeru, max. eleva-	Nature spir-its, trolls, goblins, fairies, etc.	9 m.y.

83. The previous three figures are as given in the Sarvastivada tradition. The Vibhajyavada tradition has 1, 0.5, and 0.3 eons respectively.

84. This figure corresponds very closely to the outer limit of the earth's atmosphere, the exobase (approx. 434 miles).

		tion 200 miles			
Humans	Manusyaloka	Islands in the ocean surrounding Mount Sumeru			
	Jambudvipa	Southern continent	10–120 y.		
	Purvavideha	Eastern continent	250 y.		
	Aparagodaniya	Western continent	500 y.		
	Uttara-kuru	Northern continent	1,000 y.		
Unhappy Destinations (sugati)					
Asuras	Asura	Base of Mount Sumeru			
Animals	Tiryayoniloka				
Ghosts	Pretaloka				
Hell beings (divided into eight hot and eight cold hells)	Naraka				
SOUTHERN POLARITY: A LOW-ENERGY, MATERIAL STATE CHARACTERIZED BY ILLUSION-IGNORANCE-SUFFERING (SAMSARA)					

When we consider spiritual development in this way, from the perspective of Buddhist cosmology, we see that we must "ascend" the "great chain of being" from the realm that we inhabit, the so-called earth realm, level by level. The life of the Bodhisattva Gautama is the paradigm of this process in the current eon. Even Gautama experienced two false starts before attaining Enlightenment, after renouncing the world at the age of 29. First, he endeavoured to achieve transcendence by refining his consciousness to the ultimate degree. Although he experienced the highest possible meditative state, the fourth formless meditation, in which he realized the highest plane of samsara, the sphere of neither perception nor non-perception, he rejected it as unsatisfactory. Subsequently he plunged into a six-year experiment in extreme asceticism (*tapas*), including self-mortification, living and sleeping in charnel grounds, mind control, breath control, and extreme fasting. Despite all this effort, all he achieved was bringing himself to the verge of dying. It was only after rejecting all of these practices as intrinsically worthless that he approached the periphery of Enlightenment. He simply sat beneath a tree, and practised mindfulness of the breath and the body with intense mental concentration, insight, and detachment. Then he experienced his final challenge – his famous encounter with Asura Mara.

The character of Mara appears to have two different aspects which may be related to the conflict between the asuras and the devas. In one aspect he is a deva, a resident of the plane of the devas that wield power over the creations of others, the highest realm of the *kama loka*. Mara is commonly understood to be the chief of this realm; in another aspect, he is a demon or asura. It appears to be in the latter aspect that the Buddha encountered him on the cusp of his Enlightenment. This story is well known and need not be repeated here. My main point is that Mara was intensely opposed to the Buddha's Enlightenment, for by becoming enlightened Gautama would not only escape Mara's dominion; Mara knew that he would lead countless others to do so too. Here we see the envy and hatred of the devas for which the asuras are famous. Yet in order to become enlightened Gautama also had to conquer Mara, as the chief of the asuras who block the way to the higher planes. From this we may infer that the asuras, in their war against the devas, are also opposed to human spiritual progress. Psychologically, we would say that the asuras are the personification of the blind forces of desirous attachment, the instinctual complexes that bind humanity to samsara and the animal state, *which must be encountered and overcome* in order for the spiritual quest to be successful. *This is, of course, the central axiom of Tantra.* All of the spiritual traditions of humanity attest to this "dark night of the soul," the experience of agitation, confusion, and suffering without which the spiritual quest is fruitless. Nevertheless, as I have already mentioned, this Western psychological interpretation is only one side of the coin; the other side is the objective ontological existence of the asuras themselves. Thus, contemporary humanity is situated at a great crux. On the one hand, we can remain in the state of samsaric attachment, which is where the asuras want us to be, in the same state as the asuras themselves – ignorant, lustful, violent, and self-destructive. On the other hand, we can dare to encounter, challenge, and overcome the asuras themselves, and through an act of will, master them. This cannot be achieved by repression, however, or by reliance upon some fatuous vicarious atonement, for the asuras stand guard as sentinels at the base of Mount Sumeru, challenging and obstructing all those who endeavour to ascend. They cannot be avoided or evaded. They arise out of the watery depths of the collective unconscious, and strive with all their power and might to possess and overwhelm all those who dare challenge them, dragging us down into the very chaos in which they exist themselves. This is the lesson par excellence of the Enlightenment of the Buddha.

One is struck by the profound correspondence between Buddhist cosmology and the post-Newtonian scientific understanding of the nature of reality. This is all the more remarkable when one compares the Aryan cosmic conception with the Semitic world-view, with its limited notions of a six-thousand-year-old universe, creation biology, flood geology, the unique spiritual status of the human species, racialism ("the chosen race"), geocentricity, vicarious atonement, etc., which led to the conflict between the new science and the Church that in turn has led to the virtual abandonment of any semblance of a vertical (spiritual) axis of existence in the West. This has led to the disasters of scientism, philosophical materialism, "scientific" socialism, social Darwinism, capitalism, and fascism, the results of which not only threaten human civilization, but now the very survival of the planet itself. I have documented some of these remarkable correspondences, including:

- That reality has no origin and no creator;
- The primacy of the mind (the quantum act of observation);
- The non-uniqueness of human sentience;
- The universality of sentience and thus the complete interconnectedness of all living beings, with no essential difference between them;
- The reality of higher dimensions, characterized by different frequencies or vibrations of energy, all real but many of which are invisible and intangible to each other;
- The non-reality of matter;
- Process philosophy;
- The big bang and the expansion, contraction, and ultimate destruction of, not just this universe, but many universes besides our own;
- Interstellar space;
- The reality of astronomical distances and vast cycles of time, including other stars, worlds, and sentient beings all through the universe and beyond;
- The complete interdependence of phenomena, which was only proved in the 1960s by Bell's Theorem;
- The ubiquity of the law of causality;
- Periodic destruction of planets by supernovas;
- Continental drift;
- One world ocean;
- Vast cycles of terrestrial, historical time, characterized by periodic world cataclysms;
- The depth of the earth's atmosphere;
- The distance from the earth to the moon;
- Multiple human species;
- The precise genetically programmed longevity of Homo sapiens of 120 years;
- The reality of air and space travel;
- And, finally, the reality of psychic abilities, which are just beginning to be classified and studied by science.

I hope the foregoing will convince even the most skeptical that the belief, prevalent in some schools of religious Buddhism, and based on an over-reliance on a few texts, that the Buddha did not teach a theory of the nature of reality, is factually false. Thus, we may open our minds up to the realization that we do not pursue meditation in a vacuum. Spiritual development is not a purely mental or subjective activity. Spirituality is not onanism! Rather, it expresses a profoundly real universal teleology through which one may discover, not merely abstract metaphysical or psychological insights, but profound realizations concerning the fundamental nature of what we choose to call "physical" reality.

Appendix

At the request of a student I have added the following account of the preta world, i.e., the world of the spirits of the dead, commonly but mistakenly referred to as 'hungry ghosts,' from the Chinese *èguǐ* (餓鬼). The pretas inhabit the *paraloka* or 'other world,' and are characterized by insatiable hunger and thirst as well as being subject to immoderate heat and cold. This is one of the six classes of rebirth, one of the "unhappy destinations" below the human but above hell beings. Mostly they dwell on the earth, in remote desert and waste places, and thus may be counted as a "near-earth" realm, though they are normally invisible to humans, except in certain moods or mental states. They may appear during the day or the night, and may be recognized by their relatives. We, however, are visible to them. Generally human in appearance, the pretas are rather cadaverous, much like the traditional image of the zombie, although they can also appear as smoke or fire. The character of the smoke monster in the tv series *Lost*, which incorporates many Buddhist motifs, has the appearance of a preta. They have huge appetites but are unable to satisfy themselves, and feed on offal, including corpses and feces. Some pretas prey on human blood, like the vampire. Rebirth as a preta is the result of karma, like all rebirths, specifically falseness, corruption, compulsiveness, deceit, jealousy, greed, and addiction. Mostly they are pitiable creatures, and people often leave food offerings to them in the temples and elsewhere. However, an offering directly given cannot benefit a preta – the merit of the offering must be transferred too. This is an interesting detail that shows that the concept of dedicating merit (*punyaparinamana*) was established by the time that the Petavatthu ('Stories of the Departed') in the Minor Anthologies (Khuddaka Nikaya) of the Pali Canon, was composed, perhaps 150 years or so after the death (*parinirvana*) of the Buddha (Law, *History of Pali Literature*, p. 36). Thus, the view that the practice of transferring merit is (a) a Mahayana practice exclusively, and (b) late (5th to 7th centuries CE) is definitely disproved.

9
Buddhism and the UFO
Phenomenon

I

IN HIS YOUTUBE video, "Buddhism and Alien Abductions," the nonconformist Buddhist monk Ajahn Brahm, who has also stirred the pot on the topic of female ordination in Thailand, broached the topic of the so-called UFO contact experience, declaring that while he has never seen a UFO he has seen *garudas* and nagas! *Garudas* are enormous predatory birds with intelligence and social organization. Nagas are snakes or dragons that live in lakes or underground streams and are said to guard treasures. A famous naga even petitioned the Buddha to become a monastic! Several Buddhist saints including Gotama himself have been identified with *nagas,* which can take human form at will (Brahm's naga was an impossibly huge snake that he saw in the Asian rainforest). The Buddha says that the naga is a symbol of the arhant (MN 23).

No less impeccable an authority than A.K. Warder says that the statement of no less impeccable a Buddhist king than the great Ashoka himself that by the king's conversion to the dharma the gods are "mixing" with humanity refers to an ancient UFO flap! Of course, Warder does not use this language but the implication is clear to anyone who is familiar with the UFO phenomenon. Perhaps surprisingly, it is also supported by the Pali *suttas*! Warder writes,

The most likely reference would appear to be to divine portents seen by men, indicating the presence of gods, such as the light and radiance said to precede an appearance of Brahma. ... Perhaps Asoka was watching hopefully for the 'wheel gem,' ... to appear in the sky, and he may have been encouraged by celestial phenomena, such as the appearance of a comet, a nova, or an exceptional display of meteors, to believe that his change of heart and of imperial policy had begun to make itself felt in the universe. That gods might appear to men was widely believed in India in this period.[85]

Nor is this the only UFO account associated with Buddhism. The great Buddhist reformer Nichiren avoided execution due to the appearance of a UFO that appeared in the sky like the full moon. In the nineteenth century, the great Chinese Zen Buddhist master Xu Yun Da Shi climbed Da Luo Peak, where he witnessed numerous UFOs, which he called "wisdom lamps." Doubtless, other examples could be found.

Human beings have described contact experiences with all sorts of mythological beings all through history. We know these as faires, elves, pixies, gnomes, and other special terms for demigods and quasi-supernatural beings that appear infrequently and interact with humans in various ways. In ancient times, such experiences seem to have been far more prevalent than they are today, but as we shall see this may not be the case. Dr. W.Y. Evans-Wentz made a special study of the "fairy faith" in Ireland,[86] and concluded, based on analyzing numerous credible firsthand accounts, that such experiences are less easily dismissed than many might like to believe and that they exhibit their own internal coherence. Evans-Wentz went on to discover similar experiences among native Americans. Native Americans, East Indians, Asians, and indeed all of the indigenous peoples of the world describe similar beings, which are often said to interact with human beings, abducting people and children and leaving physical signs behind. There are even accounts of sexual relationships, both voluntary and involuntary, with such beings!

---

85. Warder, *Indian Buddhism*, p. 239f.
86. Evans-Wentz, *The Fairy Faith in Celtic Countries*.

Interestingly, Buddhism also refers to such beings. In Buddhist vertical cosmology the realm, plane, world, or dimension – I will use these terms more or less interchangeably – next above our own world, and separated from us by the thinnest of veils, is the realm called the Four Great Kings. The Four Great Kings are devas or spiritual beings, described as luminous aerial beings, attributed to the four directions and to the four elements that we know as fire, water, air, and earth – a universal archetype. Thus, the realm of the Four Great Kings is an elemental nature realm. The denizens of this realm resemble the aforementioned fairies, which are also said to be luminous and aerial, including references to deva cities and extensive interactions with humans. The devas are even said to travel in "cars fit for the gods" (DN 32:7).

In addition to the realm of the Four Great Kings, the Buddhist texts also refer to "earthbound devas" that coexist with people. These are described as socially organized; invisible, although they can make themselves visible if they choose; telepathic and able to influence people and even governments at will; and preferring to live in ancient cities or remote wilderness areas. Earthbound devas are a distinct class of being and should not be confused with either ghosts or hell beings.

Finally, the Buddhist texts refer to the asuras, another class of deva which were expelled from the higher spiritual realms and which inhabit the earth, especially the water or where earth and water meet. These are very advanced and intelligent spiritual beings but their spirituality is oriented toward self-love, power, hedonistic enjoyment, and competition – what we in the West might term "pagan." They are very ambitious; barbaric despite their spiritual development; and jealous of the higher spiritual beings; many hate people, though the texts also make a point that some asuras honour the Buddha and may even be Buddhists! Although in appearance and behaviour they are similar to the Judaeo-Christian notion of demons, in Buddhism asuras and hell-beings or demons are distinct classes of being. The Buddhist hells – really, purgatories – and their inhabitants occupy four levels below the human and three below the asuras, below the ghosts and the animals. The asuras are one plane, level, or dimension "below" the human realm, though they interact with human beings as well as the inhabitants of the realm of the Four Great Kings.

Even the inhabitants of the realm of the Thirty-Three Gods, next above the Four Great Kings, interact with human beings from time to time. Asuras are higher than the ghosts and the animals. One of the roles of the inhabitants of the realm of the Four Great Kings, and the Four Great Kings themselves, is to report to the Council of the Thirty-Three Gods on the progress of humanity, in a sort of cosmic hierarchy. This is all canonical.

Similarly, UFO contactees report encounters with a wide variety of different sorts of beings, some of which resemble the inhabitants of the Four Great Kings (e.g., smallish, gnome-like beings), asuras (e.g., the so-called reptilians), and even Brahmas (divine humanoid type beings). All of these beings seem to be associated with the UFO in a kind of cosmic hierarchy. Thus, UFOs themselves do not appear to represent a singular phenomenon but rather a plurality of mutually interrelated but also distinct phenomena.

All of this may be dismissed as mythology in our age of fasco-corporatism and scientistic nihilism were it not for one singular fact, which has been extensively documented by Jacques Vallee in his magnum opus, *Passport to Magonia*, and this is the detailed and extensive similarity of the experiences associated with these beings, including descriptions of the beings themselves, with the modern UFO phenomenon, including the contact experience, as well as clear descriptions of the distinctive traits of the UFO phenomenon in the early Buddhist texts themselves. The latter confirm Vallee's thesis, which *Passport to Magonia* elaborates, that the UFO phenomenon, whatever else it may be, is an archaic and probably primordial human phenomenon that has been experienced and described all through human history and that has psychological *and physical* aspects that clearly identify the UFO phenomenon as a real, distinct phenomenon that cannot be entirely reduced to conventional causes, including error, hoax, optical illusion, hallucination, and mental confusion or disease, as is widely claimed by skeptics who have not bothered to study the data deeply or objectively.

Unfortunately, the whole field of UFO studies has become sensationalized and popularized to the point where it is almost impossible to see it clearly. It has become the tool of an incredible variety of agendas, some of which are based on outright lies and deceptions. Even governments have become involved. Because of this confusion, the majority of the population does not take this phenomenon seriously. However, anyone who takes the trouble to study the available information objectively will quickly discover that this is a mistake. One must, however, select one's authorities carefully, since there is so much disinformation, especially on the Internet.

I certainly do not claim to be an expert in this field or to have exhausted the available resources, but the researchers that I have personally found to be most credible include astronomer and computer scientist Dr. Jacques Vallee; astronomer Dr. J. Allen Hynek; nuclear physicist Stanton Friedman; psychologist Dr. Carl Gustav Jung; Harvard professor and psychiatrist Dr. John Mack; Professor Karla Turner; journalist John Keel; anthropologist Dr. W.Y. Evans-Wentz; and novelist Whitley Strieber. I would also mention string theorist Dr. Michio Kaku in this regard, who has hinted quite broadly that he knows something about this topic. Colin Wilson's book, *Alien Dawn,* is a noteworthy popular summary of the evidence based on the research carried out by these and other individuals. Vallee himself claims to represent an "invisible college" of about a hundred scientists who are privately researching the UFO phenomenon in all of its aspects but do not seek publicity for obvious reasons. The main thing that you will notice about these experts is that, while their conclusions are indeed revolutionary, none of them subscribe to any of the prevailing popular theories about UFOs, including that they are extra-terrestrial in origin, with the notable exception of Stanton Friedman.

Vallee in particular has argued that if these objects turn out to be extra-terrestrial, he will be disappointed. His own view seems to be that they are intelligent higher-dimensional beings with a long association with humans and the earth, possibly originating beyond the space-time continuum as we understand it. Even if they originated in our universe their civilization is potentially millions or billions of years old, compared to a mere ten thousand years for human civilization. Vallee speculates that they may have mastered both space and time, in which case the question of their "origin" may be factually meaningless. Since civilization grows exponentially, the qualitative difference between these beings and us is clearly on the order of millions of times. Such a civilization will have harnessed the zero point energy and therefore be trans-galactic, even trans-universal or extra-dimensional in nature and not merely extra-terrestrial. It seems almost axiomatic that such a civilization would be universal in scope and practically incomprehensible to us.

However, it is not my purpose here to argue about the ultimate nature of the UFO phenomenon, which is clearly very complex, but only to indicate that the phenomenon is real and exhibits real similarities to the Buddhist world-view, confirming Vallee's hypothesis that UFOs have appeared all through human history. If we accept that UFOs are real, then Buddhism, along with many other religions, appears to be one of the effects of this phenomenon, at least partly, since the Buddha himself is depicted as interacting and communicating with devas or spiritual beings, to which he attributes at least some of his insights, and even appears as a UFO himself! The question that arises, therefore, and is of greatest interest to us is what the Buddhist texts themselves have to say about this phenomenon, and how this relates to the phenomenon that we experience today. Is there, in fact, a Buddhist theory of the UFO phenomenon?

II

UFO references are not incidental to the Pali Canon. One of the most extensive descriptions in the Pali Canon is the Mahasudas-sana Sutta (DN 17). Interestingly, most of the UFO references in the Pali *suttas* appear in the Digha Nikaya, which according to Buddhist scholar A.K. Warder consists of the oldest and most authentic Buddhist texts. This *sutta* immediately follows the Mahaparinibbana Sutta, which describes the death of the Buddha. *Mahasudassana* consists of *maha*, 'great,' plus *sudassa-*

na, 'easily seen,' 'having a good appearance,' the proper name of the gods of the plane of the Beautiful Devas, the third Pure Abode of the Rupaloka or world of form. Walshe translates it as 'The Great Splendour.' Rhys Davids has 'The Great King of Glory.' The language is more than suggestive.

This *sutta* was spoken in the Mallas' sal grove at Kusinara, Kosala, shortly before the Buddha's death in the same place, and is therefore one of the last talks of the Buddha. The occasion is that Ananda is unhappy that the Buddha is going to die here, "in this miserable little town of wattle and daub, right in the jungle in the back of beyond,"[87] rather than in a great city where the Buddha's funeral can be arranged by his rich followers in proper style. In response, the Buddha tells Ananda the story of King Mahasudassana, who dominated the region; Kusinara, called at that time Kusavati, was his capital. The Buddha compares Kusavati to the deva city of Alakamanda, thus asserting that devas live in cities and introducing the topic of devas into the discourse.

The king was clearly devout, as he went up to the verandah on the roof of his palace after washing his head on the day of the full moon, with the intention of fasting. It is, of course, well known that fasting sensitizes the consciousness to spiritual matters, which is why it is practised at such times. At that time a "divine Wheel Treasure appeared to him, thousand spoked, complete with felloe, hub and all appurtences."[88] A.K. Warder clearly accepts Rhys-Davids's contention that this refers to the disk of the sun. It is also a classic description of a UFO. The description is striking, and is clearly similar to the well-known vision of Ezekiel in the Bible.

The king realizes that the appearance of such an object – there is no suggestion that the wheel is anything else – is a sign that he will become a World Ruler, and he formulates the intention to become a World Ruler as an Act of Truth. Sprinkling the wheel with water, so it must have been quite small and close, the wheel then moves in the four directions, plunging in and out of the sea, and wherever the wheel goes the king travels with his army and

87. DN 17:1.2.
88. Ibid, 1.7.

conquers the land without bloodshed, whereupon the king establishes a peaceful dharma empire for himself based on the fundamental legal principles of pansil – do not kill, do not steal, do not commit adultery, do not lie, do not drink alcohol, plus moderation in eating. Thus, he conquers all of the lands from sea to sea, i.e., the whole Indian subcontinent called Jambudvipa. Finally the wheel returns to Kusavati and hovers above the king's palace, which also doubles as a court of justice. The solar wheel treasure (or 'gem' in Warder's translation) became a kind of omen or totem of a righteous World Ruler based on the rule of dharma.

The Sakkapanha Sutta (DN 21) describes another luminous aerial display in which the devas instantaneously transport themselves from the realm of the Thirty-Three Gods to Mount Vediya, where the Buddha is: "Then a tremendous light shone over Mount Vediya, illuminating the village of Amasanda – so great was the power of the devas – so that in the surrounding villages they were saying: 'Look, Mount Vediya is on fire today – it's burning! It's in flames. What is the matter, that Mount Vediya and Ambasanda are lit up like this?' and they were so terrified that their hair stood on end."[89]

The *suttas* also refer to how the devas experience time at a slower rate than human beings, suggestive of Einstein's time dilation paradox. The devas also occupy space in a peculiar way, in that a vast number of devas can manifest in a very small space. We have already mentioned how the devas prefer wilderness areas, a characteristic shared with UFOs. UFOs also appear to have a telepathic rapport with the people who observe them, like the devas. Brahma appears as an unpredictable luminous aerial display, and the Buddha himself is described as a flying UFO casting off beams of light!

The great and still unresolved question of course is what are these objects? Vallee suggests that the UFO phenomenon acts like a control system, and that UFOs appear more frequently when the fundamental ideological paradigm of human civilization shifts toward rationalism and materialism, as it did during the Greco-Roman period. Vallee also associates the appearance of

---

89. Ibid, 21:1.3.

UFOs with apocalyptic images and the end of civilizations. Vallee suggests that UFOs seem to be interested in convincing human beings that higher dimensional beings exist, but do so in such a way that the human social order is not completely disrupted. That is to say, they seem to have regard for the limitations of human cognition. Since Buddhism is at least in part a result of UFO influence, and is ancient, untainted by modern influences, its explanation is of interest with the caveat that it is well known that at some UFOs also lie, or combine truth and falsehood in various ways designed to disrupt the same expectations that they create (disinformation). This suggests that they have a sophisticated agenda insofar as human beings are concerned, which is far from understood.

As I have already mentioned, Jacques Vallee hypothesized that UFOs have a long-standing historical relationship with the earth and with humanity. This alone explains the historical frequency of UFO sightings and contact experiences, their apparent interest in people, their apparent function as a control system, their ability to communicate with us at all, and the quasi-humanoid appearance of their inhabitants. Interestingly, the Aganna Sutta (the Primordial Sutta, DN 27) supports just this view. Walshe translates the title of this *sutta* as 'On Knowledge of Beginnings' Rhys Davids has 'A Book of Genesis.' Here the Buddha says that periodically at long intervals the world contracts. We know of course that the classical view of modern scientific cosmology is that the universe originates in a singularity, expands, and after a long period gravity forces it to contract back into the original singularity, repeating forever. According to the Buddha, when the world contracts beings are mostly reborn in the Abhassara Brahma world. The name of this world literally means 'radiant' or 'shining.' This is the seventeenth plane of Buddhist cosmology, the sixth realm from the bottom of the Rupaloka, next above the Brahma realms, and twelve planes above the human realm. It is also associated with the second jhana of "thoughtless bliss."

So, the Buddha says, "there they dwell, mind-made, feeding on delight, self-luminous, moving through the air, glorious – and they stay like that for a very long time. Eventually, after a very long time, this world begins to expand again. At a time of expansion, the beings from the Abhassara Brahma world, having passed away from there, are mostly reborn in this world. Here they dwell, mind-made, feeding on delight, self-luminous, moving through the air, glorious – and they stay like that for a very long time."[90]

This passage clearly indicates the operation of karma. As the universe contracts, suffering increases, and beings degenerate, thus expiating much of their negative karma.[91] As a result, human beings are reborn in the realm of the radiant devas as luminous aerial beings. After a long period, their good karma is exhausted and they are reborn when our universe begins to expand again, retaining their energetic appearance. Thus, the Big Bang may be regarded as a tunnel or conduit from a higher dimensional world, through which these luminous aerial beings entered into our universe approximately fourteen billion years ago. These are the spiritual ancestors of humanity, the original human beings, and therefore also our true nature, "the clear light." Plato has a precisely similar notion when he describes human beings' original nature as bisexual flying spheres. The Buddha also specifically states that these beings are neither male nor female.

According to the Platonic world-view,

in primal times people had double bodies, with faces and limbs turned away from one another. As spherical creatures who wheeled around like clowns doing cartwheels (190a), these original people were very powerful. There were three sexes: the all male, the all female, and the 'androgynous,' who was half male, half female. The males were said to have descended from the sun, the females from the earth and the androgynous couples from the moon. These creatures tried to scale the heights of Olympus and planned to set upon the gods (190b-c). Zeus thought about blasting them with thunderbolts, but did not want to deprive himself of their devotions and offerings, so he decided to cripple them by chopping them in half, in effect separating the two bodies. (Wikipedia)

---

90. Ibid, 27:10.

91. This is the only explanation of why beings from a lower world would be reborn in a higher world.

Plato's description seems to associate humans with the same war in heaven that led to the expulsion of the asuras. The fact that we find this explanation of humanity in Buddhism and in Plato's *Symposium* suggests that this is one of those archetypal ideas that characterize the primordial philosophy. Certainly, there are other examples too.

So brilliant were these beings, says that Buddha, that the sun, moon, and stars were invisible. This might also allude to the early expansion of the universe, before the stars appeared (about two hundred million years after the Big Bang). However, as the universe cooled these beings' bodies became more and more material, and as it cooled the worlds evolved. Over vast eons of time, the luminous beings ingested increasingly coarse and more material matter, and as a result, their bodies became more and more physical, finally developing the sexual characteristics of male and female. Out of this came all of the institutions and the vices of human society, including lust, territoriality, lying, stealing, killing, the development of the authoritarian state, social divisions, warfare, etc.

A variant of this story is repeated in *sutta* 26 of the Digha Nikaya. Clearly, the Buddhist symbol of the precious Wheel Treasure, the first possession of the righteous World Ruler, representing the Power of Truth and the dharma itself, is a UFO!

The Pali *suttas* also attest to the reality of psychic powers. Although scientism discounts the possibility of such abilities, the psychic powers attested to by Buddhism, including telepathic communication, astronomical visions, communication with devas, time dilation, teleportation, invisibility, the ability to pass through matter, and levitation are all attested to in the UFO literature as well as in the early Pali Buddhist *suttas*. Credible modern cases suggest that many of these experiences, perhaps most or even all of them, are not merely psychological, but leave physical signs and are therefore at least partly physical in nature. Many UFO experiencers, especially contactees, have reported spontaneously developing many of these abilities after their UFO experiences. Clearly, reality is far more multifaceted and complex than the conventional view allows.

According to the oldest Buddhist texts, human beings originated in the Abhassara Brahma world. Literally meaning 'radiant,' the Abhassara world corresponds to the second jhana, characterized by the experience of delight and joy. The Abhassara devas are given to exclamations of joy, and their bodies emit flashing rays of light like lightning. The Abhassara devas look very much alike, but have individuality. The Abhassara world transcends the periodic destruction by fire that characterizes the lower worlds at the end of each age. The Abhassara world is, however, subject to periodic destruction by water. The lifespan of these devas is two or eight *mahakalpas*, perhaps three or ten trillion years according to one estimate.

When the universe is destroyed, beings are reborn in the Abhassara realm and when the universe reappears, beings from the Abhassara realm are the first to be reborn in our universe.

The texts describe the Abhassara devas as luminous aerial objects. According to our hypothesis, they enter into our universe at the "big bang," which an increasing number of theorists are hypothesizing might be a "white hole," the positive polarity of a quantum tunnel that leads to a black hole in another universe. The Buddhist texts state that these beings appeared in the universe prior to the appearance of stars and galaxies, which refers to the first two hundred million years of our fourteen billion year old universe.

Over time, with the gradual cooling of the cosmic inflation (*papanca*), the Abhassara devas become increasingly coarse and material, losing their luminous appearance as the stars and galaxies appear. This is attributed to their increasing infatuation with sensual pleasure. Ultimately, they appear as gendered human beings, who till the soil for food and develop territoriality, private property, the state, and all the vices associated with human beings – lust, greed, malice, warfare, etc.

Clearly, however, not all of the devas have lost all of their deva characteristics, and these coexist with us and interact with human beings, especially spiritually advanced human beings. The Buddhist texts refer to different kinds of such beings, especially the inhabitants of the Thirty-Three Gods, which appear as angelic beings; the inhabitants of the realm of the Four Great Kings, which appear as the nature spirits described by all human societies, and asuras, which are spiritually advanced beings that pursue a spirituality based on pride, arrogance, competitiveness, love of power and violence, etc. and are divided into tribes or clans. Nevertheless, at least some asuras, as well as other devas, are receptive to the dharma and venerate the Buddha, and thus may be said to be Buddhists.

Although most devas are generally described as aerial and mobile, some devas are earthbound and live on the earth, mostly invisibly, especially in ancient human cities and remote wilderness areas. Sometimes these devas appear to human beings and even communicate with them. As higher dimensional beings, the human mind is an open book to them. They communicate telepathically and can influence human beings, including governments, on a subconscious level. These include the nagas, reptilian beings that can also take on a human appearance at will. Nagas are regarded as relatively advanced spiritual beings in Buddhism. Many advanced Buddhist practitioners have been claimed to be nagas (perhaps, reborn in human form), including the Buddha himself, and at least one naga sought to be ordained as a monastic (a request that the Buddha rejected, which is why candidates for Buddhist ordination are still asked if they are human).

This description is strikingly similar to the UFO phenomenon, including the manifestation of UFOs as luminous aerial phenomena, their apparent intentionality suggestive of intelligence, their ability to manifest physically and communicate with human beings telepathically, and the physical appearance of their inhabitants, which include similar beings of great nobility and beauty; smaller, gnome-like beings; and reptilian type entities. UFO inhabitants also manifest a great range of behaviours, from helpful and healing to malevolent and hostile, corresponding exactly to the deva-asura polarity.

In addition to the foregoing, the Buddhist texts also describe a specific UFO-type manifestation called the Precious Wheel Treasure. The Precious Wheel Treasure symbolizes the power of truth and is associated with dharma. The manifestation of this phenomenon has all the characteristics typical of the UFO phenomenon, including luminosity, unpredictability, apparent intelligence, spiritual communications, and the classic "psychic powers" described in the Buddhist texts, including bilocation, invisibility, the ability to pass through matter, and levitation or flying behaviour, as well as inducing astronomical visions and powers of healing and time dilation or "lost time." People who have close encounters with UFOs often report developing psychic abilities themselves, and often experience personal transformations characterized by enhanced creativity, compassion, and spiritual and environmental concerns, as well as clairvoyance, clairaudience, astral travel, teleportation, and telepathy, also reported in the Buddhist literature, and dramatic physical healings.

The coincidences between the UFO phenomenon and similar descriptions in the Buddhist *suttas* are striking and extensive. It stretches credulity to believe that these similarities are accidental. These similarities further support Jacques Vallee's hypothesis that the UFO phenomenon is ancient, perhaps even primordial, and has been part of the human experience for thousands and probably tens of thousands of years at least.

10

The Wisdom of Laozi

There are those who will conquer the world
And make of it what they conceive or desire.
I see that they will not succeed.
– Laozi, Tao Te Ching

Now is the time...to destroy those who destroy the earth.
– Revelation of John

LAOZI'S TAO TE Ching is the chief book of the Tao-tsang, the canon of the Taoist school or sect, made up of 1,476 books in 5,486 volumes. The title may be rendered as 'The Book of the Way [Tao] and Its Power [Te].' The oldest extant copy is dated to between 195 and 206 BCE, but it is surely older. Western scholars judge it to have been written by 400 BCE. In Chinese custom it was written by Laozi five or six hundred years before the common era, but the teachings of the Tao Te Ching are surely much older than the text itself, which is a digest of old teachings going back to the primal proto-Asian pan-wisdom centre (see "Sacred and Profane Time," below).

Laozi means 'Old Child' and was likely given to Laozi after his death. Legend states that he was born with white hair, but it may also refer to his simple nature. He is also known as Lao Tan or Li Erh. In Chinese custom Laozi was born in 604 BCE, and thus was an elder coëval of K'ung-fu-tzu (Confucius), born in 551 BCE. He was born in Hu-hsien in the state of Chu, now known as Honan Province in southeast central China. During his life, he was employed by the king of Chou as his record-keeper. At that time, that job involved the keeping of sacred books such as the I Ching and was linked with fortune telling and star-lore (astrology). Laozi tired of court politics and retired at an advanced age. Laozi went west to the border, where Yin Hsi, also known as Kuan-yin-tzu, the Warden of the Mountain Pass of Hsien-ku, saw him. That he was seen and stopped shows that Laozi was well known. Yin Hsi would not allow Laozi to pass till he had set down his wisdom in a book, lest it be lost. Impressed by the warden's faith, Laozi paused for two days to write down the five thousand signs of the Tao Te Ching, also known as the Text of the Five Thousand Signs, although in fact the number of signs is between five and six thousand. In Lin Yutang's English version, this works out to about eight thousand words.

Right after this Laozi departs from any formal annals. Some say he went to India where he taught the Buddha, whose teachings as set down in the Pali Canon look like the teachings of the Tao Te Ching. Others say he became a recluse living on the sacred mountain range called K'un-lun on the eastern border of Tibet. In Tibetan custom, the pre-Buddhist Bon faith of Shenrab Miwo comes from Laozi. Some Western scholars doubt that Laozi was a real person, but there is nothing far-fetched in the basic story, and the point of view of the work itself is both novel and unique. Most scholars believe that Laozi was a real person, perhaps the founder of a school the teachings of which were handed down and gathered in the Tao Te Ching by those who came after. Perhaps in fairness this is the truest view, since someone clearly wrote or compiled the Tao Te Ching.

The Tao Te Ching is made up of eighty-one chapters in two parts: The first thirty-seven chapters make up the Book of the Tao ('Way'), whereas chapters 38 to 81 make up the Book of the Te ('Power' or 'Virtue'). Lin Yutang in his version has broken the book down into smaller units: Book I: The Character of Tao (Chapters 1–6), Book II: The Lessons of Tao (Chapters 7–13), Book III: The Imitation of Tao (Chapters 14–25), Book IV: The Source of Power (Chapters 26–40), Book V: The Conduct of Life (Chapters

41–56), Book VI: The Theory of Government (Chapters 57–75), and Book VII: Aphorisms (Chapters 76–81).

The Tao Te Ching presents a subtle and complex system of thought with many aspects. Six major skeins of meaning can be seen in its complex, linked maxims. The major concerns of Laozi fall into two groups of three topics. The first group refers to the world: being, cosmos, and what might be called "cosmic" or "sacred" time; the second group refers to people: ethics, the state, and the life of the spirit. What these topics mean for Laozi will be discussed here. These skeins of meaning combine to form a profound world-view that still allures and puzzles people. Many English versions of the Tao Te Ching have been written. According to Mircea Eliade, the Tao Te Ching is "the most profound and most enigmatic text in all Chinese literature."[92] The chapters of the Tao Te Ching may be studied together, given the scheme just discussed, to grasp their linked meanings better.

The Truth of Being

The famous first line of the Tao Te Ching, "The Tao that can be told of is not the Absolute Tao; the Names that can be given are not Absolute Names" (1), abstracts the vital message of the book itself. Surely, the central notion of the Tao Te Ching is the Tao. Best rendered as 'way,' for Laozi the Tao is, quite simply, the Real. Why this word and not some other best names the Real is the main subject of the Tao Te Ching, and will become clearer as we progress. Given the insight that the Tao is the Real, we can restate Lin Yutang's version of the first line of the Tao Te Ching as follows: "The real that can be talked about [i.e., the world of the senses] is not the True Real." That is to say, the main premise of the Tao Te Ching is that the Thought of the Spirit is the Real. Laozi does not believe that the Real is just matter. For Laozi, the world of the senses and mental knowledge, the world of names and forms, is not the Real, but part of the Real. The Tao is the ground, essence, and truth of the world, but not only what is known. The dyad of the Tao and the world also poses a problem,

---

92. Eliade, *A History of Religious Ideas,* Vol. 2, p. 26.

which the Tao Te Ching seeks to explain: How is it that the world and the Tao are not just the same?

First, the Tao cannot be thought about. The Tao cannot be described ("told of") using words or language ("the Names"). On the other hand, the Tao is the model of what can be described, since "that [which] can be told of" is also the Tao, and "the Names that can be given" have as their models the "Absolute Names." The mention of "Absolute Names" suggests Plato's teaching of Forms: abstract thoughts that alone make up the Real and which create the mirage of things, like shadows cast by objects on the walls of a cave in the light of a central fire.

Because the Tao cannot be thought about, it cannot be known. Why this must be true will be discussed later on. Because the Tao cannot be sensed, it cannot be studied. On the other hand, since the Tao is the ground of reason and the senses, it is known and studied all of the time, but none of that reveals the essence of the Tao. Since the Tao is the essence of all things, it is also the essence of the self. Therefore, it seems that the self can know the Tao in itself. That in the self that knows the Tao is the mind. Although the Tao itself cannot be known or studied, how the Tao appears to one who knows it can be hinted at by means of symbols, which bypass logic and words to appeal straight to the mind. Thus, Laozi uses many symbols and lyric turns of phrase to help describe what the Tao is like: the Mother of All Things, the Secret of Life, the Cosmic Mystery, the Mystery, the Deeper Mystery, the Gate to the Secret of All Life, a hollow vessel, the fountain head of all things, deep water, a bellows, the core, the Spirit of the Valley, the Mystic Female, the Door of the Mystic Female, the root of Heaven and Earth, water, the One, vital force, a newborn babe, Mystic vision, the Gate of Heaven, the Mystic Virtue, the nave of the wheel, not-being, empty space, non-existence, the belly, the Invisible, the Inaudible, the Intangible, the Form of the Formless, the Image of Nothingness, the Elusive, the Primeval Beginnings, a piece of uncarved wood, murky water, the basis of Quietude, the root (soil), the Eternal Law, Enlightenment, Nature, original nature, awakening, a fool, the Mother, Character, the life-force, the Father of All Things, the model of the world, Great, the original point, the Solid, the Quiescent, the Centre, the Light, the subtle secret, the mysterious secret of the universe, the ravine of the world, the eternal power, the Primordial Nothingness, God's own Vessel, a flood, the Great Symbol, the Subtle Light, the Nameless pristine simplicity, the fruit, the life-giving power, the ennobling power, Non-being, truth, fulfilment, harmony, that-which-is-without-form, the teaching without words, no action, the highest perfection, the greatest abundance, contentment, Heaven, a harbour, the Mother of the Universe, the Absolute, Austere Knowledge, the Main Path, the Mystic Unity, the Normal, the Female of the world, the treasure of the world, the Grand Harmony, jade, and the Way of the Sage.

The utter darkness of the Tao – "Invisible," "Inaudible," and "Intangible" (14; cf. 35) – leads to the main symbol of a primal and fecund void, empty space, or nothing. It would be a mistake, though, to posit the void as somehow above or before the world. To posit the Tao in this way leads to the absurd query: Why is there something and not nothing? Laozi makes it very clear that the Tao is not other than the world. The Tao is, rather, the truth of the world, seen in and through the world of the senses, but that which is known through the senses is not all there is to know. Knowing what is known through the senses using the mind leads to the view that there is something else. Thus, the Tao and the world do not just negate each other, as in early Buddhism, but the world and the Tao are more like part (the world) and whole (the Tao), or seeming (the world) and essence (the Tao). Therefore, the Tao Te Ching avoids the view that the essence of the world is twofold.

In addition, there is no hint of theism in the Tao Te Ching. Although in later Taoist books the Tao is often described as a person, Laozi does not address or refer to the Tao as having any kind of ego, despite his use of male and, more often, female symbols: "I do not know whose Son it is, an image of what existed before God" (4); "Before the Heaven and Earth existed there was something nebulous: silent, isolated, standing alone, changing not, eternally revolving without fail, worthy to be the Mother of All Things" (25). The Tao itself is not a person: "Nature is unkind: it treats the creation like sacrificial straw-dogs" (5). On the other hand, to model oneself after the Tao is the touchstone of human ethics and the essence of our human nature, as of all else. Only in this sense can the Tao be said to be any sort of person. Truly, human nature is the self-conscious knowledge of the Tao: "Tao is Great, the Heaven is great, the Earth is great, the King is also great. These are the Great Four in the universe, and the King is one of them" (25). Yet when we search for that knowledge, there is nothing there, or at least nothing that can be put in words!

It is a maxim of thinking about the nature of being that only mind and matter can be known. Since it is not certain that mind and matter are the same, to avoid the view that the essence of the world is twofold one must reduce one to the other, or say that the Real transcends and combines the aspects of both. In addition, if one tries to reduce one to the other one must explain how it is that they come to differ. Since neither mind nor matter implies the other as a matter of logic, the Real must come first: "These two (the Secret and its manifestations) are (in their nature) the same; they are given different names when they become manifest" (1). The sameness of mind and matter implies that the essence of mind is matter, but that the essence of matter is also mind. The latter teaching has profound results. The view that mind and matter are both real is not the view that only matter is real, which holds that mind is only matter. The belief that the Real transcends both mind and matter implies that mind and matter change into each other, and is one possible view of the belief that the Thought of the Spirit is the Real; the other view is that matter does not exist as such and is only mind, "matter" being like a shadow of the senses cast upon the mind. The former is the view of the nature of being of the Tao Te Ching; the latter is the view of the nature of being of early Buddhism.

Cosmos

In the section above, we discussed the notion of the Absolute Tao, which we linked with zero ("the Primordial Nothingness"). In the Tao Te Ching, the flux of the Tao is the primal cosmic process (as in modern physics, force and not matter comes first). The contrast between the Absolute Tao and "the Tao that can be told of" implies a different view of the Tao, i.e., the being in the world of the Absolute Tao. The being in the world of the Tao, linked with the number one, is called Te. Number symbols are plain in the Tao Te Ching: "Out of Tao, One is born; out of One, Two; out of Two, Three; out of Three, the created universe" (42). The Tao Te Ching's use of cosmic numbers predates but is very like the Hebrew Zohar, 1,600 years later, with its notion of ten *sephiroth* or 'numbers' that evolve in strict series out of a primal 'nothing,' the Ain, through one (*kether*) and a primal dyad (*chokhmah* or *chokhmah/binah*)! Te is widely rendered as 'power, virtue, or character.' It is the same as the 'life-force,' which is therefore the truth of the world, given in and through matter. Therefore, the Tao Te Ching accounts for the riddle of life and the coming into being of living matter in a way that the Buddhist view of the nature of being fails to do, except perhaps in its tantric forms, yet even the Tantric Buddhist is mainly concerned with giving up and going beyond the world of the senses. Next after the number one comes the dyad of yin and yang: "The created universe carries the yin at its back and the yang in front" (42). The two poles of yin and yang are the primal pair, which create and sustain all things. The yin is widely linked with darkness, the passive, and the female symbol. The yang is widely linked with light, the active, and the male symbol. Thus, in the Tao Te Ching, sex is a primal force that runs through all things. According to Schuhmacher and Woerner,

> Originally the word yin designated the northern slope of a mountain, i.e., the side facing away from the sun – and was further associated with cold, turgid water and a cloud-covered sky. Yang denoted the mountain slope facing the sun and was associated with brightness and warmth. ...yin is the feminine, the passive, the receptive, the dark, the soft. Symbols of yin are the moon, water, clouds, the tiger, the turtle, the colour black, the north, lead, and all even numbers. Yang corresponds to what is masculine, active, creative, bright, and hard. Sym-

bols of yang are the sun, fire, the dragon, the colour red, the south, mercury, and all odd numbers.[93]

In the Tao Te Ching, the primal dyads only seem to be set against each other. This teaching is shown in a famous picture, called the T'ai-chi-t'u. In this picture, the light half of the circle represents the yin pole, the dark half the yang. However, in the light half there is a dark dot; in the dark half, there is a light dot. The dark dot is a symbol for the secret yang pole hidden in yin. The light dot represents the secret yin pole hidden in yang. The T'ai-chi-t'u is a symbol of the two poles changing into each other, which, more than two thousand years before Hegel, is a major teaching of the Tao Te Ching:

> When the people of the Earth all know beauty as beauty,
> There arises (the recognition of) ugliness.
> When the people of the Earth all know the good as good,
> There arises (the recognition of) evil.
> Therefore:
> Being and non-being interdepend in growth;
> Difficult and easy interdepend in completion;
> Long and short interdepend in contrast;
> High and low interdepend in position;
> Tones and voice interdepend in harmony;
> Front and behind interdepend in company. (2)

In addition, the whole yin-yang symbol is itself a dot, which implies an endless series, like a fractal! The ceaseless ebb and flow of yin and yang, in which each changes into the other when it reaches its furthest limit, is called "enantiodromia."

In the last section, we said that reason cannot go beyond the primal pair. Since the Real, viz., the oneness of Tao (0) and Te (1), lies beyond the poles of yin and yang, reason cannot know it. This limit is implied by the basic nature of thinking, which is based on Aristotle's law that A and not-A cannot be the same (the "law of non-contradiction"). Since the Real unites and goes beyond the

---

93. Schuhmacher and Woerner, *The Encyclopedia of Eastern Philosophy and Religion*, p. 428.

dyad, thinking cannot reach it. This teaching leads to a unique view, discussed below in the section on "Ethics." Since the Tao is the essence of the self, it also implies that there is a higher function of the self than reason or sensing.

The congress of the primal pair, impelled by the guiding power of the Te and the Real, leads to the flux of things that is the story of the world. The congress of the primal pair results in ever-greater flux, which, still working out the basic law of yin and yang, appears as the two poles of "heaven" and "earth." The main theory of the cosmos today, the teaching of science concerning the "big bang," describes a world that begins in a tiny "singularity" (one-ness, monad), to which the laws of physics do not seem to apply, of great power and mass, and over time coming out of its primal power ever more and more complex and dense beings linked with the loss of power in which, after billions of years, living beings just seem to appear out of nothing. It comes as a surprise, perhaps, to learn that the modern theory of the first cause in all of its basic details is like Laozi's view of the cosmos! One must guard against the mistake of taking the symbol for the real (called "hypostatiza-tion"). The symbol of "heaven" refers to the sky, with its clock-work, rhythmic cycles and fixed laws. Today we would call "heav-en" the "laws of physics." The "earth" refers to the world of living beings, including people, with their pell-mell conduct in which one can still see the basic exchange of yin and yang, but out of sync with any higher law, implying some sort of freedom.

Out of the ebb and flow of all things the primal and fecund Tao becomes ever more and more obscured by change, so that slowly, over billions of years, all things become more and more dense and at odds (today we would call this "entropy"). Finally, the Tao is no longer seen, and perfect cosmos becomes perfect chaos, followed by death and, in accord with the notion of enantiodromia, rebirth ("negentropy"). This cyclic change between life, death, and rebirth is cosmic, endless, and works on many levels. On the largest level, it alludes to the increase and decrease of the world, a teaching that is also basic to the point of view of science today. On the so-cial level, it alludes to the rise and fall of cultures. In addition, on the level of the person, it alludes to life, death, and rebirth after the law of karma.

Sacred and Profane Time

In the last section, we described the flux of the Tao as a process of growing darkness. It follows from this teaching that time itself is debased. This was surely the view of Laozi, who says that the rise of manners (linked with the Confucian cult, which he opposed, but which today we might call "secular humanism") with "the decline of the great Tao" (18; cf. 32). Thus, the Tao Te Ching is mainly concerned with how to return to the primal human state, which is, ipso facto, perfect. Once again, we must guard against hypostatizing this teaching into a theory of a perfect earthly state (the legend of Shambhala comes to mind) or a theory of a primal divine "soft-boned" human race of the North,[94] for neither of which is there any clear historical basis. The basic teaching here is that the perfect primal human state occurs outside time. The Australian blacks have a like notion in their teaching of the "dreamtime," a primal state of oneness with nature, livened by primal forces and symbols, from which people have devolved and to which they should seek to return (and will, when the flux of time has reached its furthest limit). According to Laozi, this primal state of oneness with the Tao has many useful values, including order, goodness, wealth, and wise rule, whereas the flux of the Tao all through time results in their reverse: chaos, greed, lack, sickness, and bad rule, all increasing:

There were those in ancient times possessed of the One:
Through possession of the One, the Heaven was clarified,
Through possession of the One, the Earth was stabilized,
Through possession of the One, the gods were spiritualized,
Through possession of the One, the valleys were made full,
Through possession of the One, all things lived and grew,
Through possession of the One, the princes and dukes became ennobled of the people.

---

94. See, e.g., Julius Evola, *Taoism: The Magic, the Mysticism.*

– That was how each became so.
Without clarity, the Heavens would shake,
Without stability, the Earth would quake,
Without spiritual power, the gods would crumble,
Without being filled, the valleys would crack,
Without life-giving power, all things would perish,
Without the ennobling power, the princes and dukes would stumble.
(39)

Laozi also refers to how "the wise ones of old" look from the point of view of the modern, base epoch:

The wise ones of old had subtle wisdom and depth of understanding,
So profound that they could not be understood.
And because they could not be understood,
Perforce must they be so described:
Cautious, like crossing a wintry stream,
Irresolute, like one fearing danger all around,
Grave, like one acting as guest,
Self-effacing, like ice beginning to melt,
Genuine, like a piece of undressed wood,
Open-minded, like a valley,
And mixing freely, like murky water. (15)

It does not follow from our caution above that a primal human culture did not flourish. The standard protest against the presence of such a centre is that there are no facts. However, by Laozi's own account, such a culture enjoyed a state of perfect oneness with nature and may have left little or no trace, or may be so old that all of its traces have been lost. This is even truer if it is hundreds of thousands or millions of years old (current knowledge says that fire was discovered about six hundred thousand years ago, so we know human beings have been sentient for at least that long), instead of tens of thousands of years, or small and local, or it may represent an astral, non-earthly culture which was reborn on this planet (in a recent talk the Dalai Lama said that to see Shambhala one must be able to move faster than the speed of light!). Absence of proof is not proof of absence. What do we really know of the inner state of the first people? In fact, science has found the remains of a primal global shamans' culture that is at least tens of thousands of years old, scattered in remnants across the world: in the native cultures of North and South America, among the Australian blacks, in early African and European tribes, in the cults of the Middle East, and in Far Eastern Hindu, Buddhist, Taoist, and Shinto beliefs, most evolved in Tantra, and mainly in Tibet, all of which seem to share a strange likeness of teaching and practice, joined about the central notion of a return to a primal blissful state of being, and set against the Confucian/Semitic cult of moral law, which appears later. If the shamans' culture were indeed primal, this would explain both its wide extent and its debased state.

Ethics

In the section above on "Cosmos" we discussed the oneness of the Tao and the Te, and compared that oneness with the primal polar pair, which comes after it. For Laozi, ethics consists in copying the highest (the Tao). Therefore, good and evil are not always set against each other, nor are ethics alone enough to be saved: "Between 'Ah!' and 'Ough!' how much difference is there? Between 'good and evil,' how much difference is there? That which men fear is indeed to be feared; but, alas, distant yet is the dawn (of awakening)!" (20); "the good man is the Teacher of the bad, and the bad man is the lesson of the good" (27); "Tao is the mysterious secret of the universe, the good man's treasure, and the bad man's refuge. ... Though there be bad people, why reject them?" (62); "The good ones I declare good; the bad ones I also declare good" (49). It follows that the Tao is beyond good and evil, and can appear to the world to be "good" or "evil" after the point of view of the subject. Since most of the world is no longer aligned with the Tao, it brands as "evil" what it does not know. Thus, there are no moral laws or rules that are always true. The sheer genius of such a teaching needs only to be pointed out. That it does not follow that evil is always really good is clear from a close reading of the Tao Te Ching, which contains accounts of Taoist ethics after a second notion, which follows from the cosmic teaching of the oneness of the poles: that the world responds to one as one responds to the world. From this Laozi creates a doubtless set of Taoist virtues, strangely based on the disproof of good and evil: not craving, no conflict, and the practice of meekness, shame, mildness, fairness, mercy, thrift, quiet, content, goodness, cunning, a grave nature, fineness, and modest speech. The practice of these virtues will prepare the seeker for the knowledge of the Tao, and are thus the first step in the return of the world to the Tao, but do not themselves equal the Way of the Tao itself. Who has known the Tao can appear any way they choose, i.e., they are above good and evil, but it does not at all follow that evil persons know the Tao. Such a teaching really is only for those who know the Tao! Therefore, it is the highest moral teaching.

The State

The Tao Te Ching talks about the art of good rule. All primal beliefs have moral meanings and therefore meanings for the state, but the meanings for the state are often inferred from ethics later on or eschewed as not proper to the life of the spirit: in the Tao Te Ching the meanings for the state are plain. Laozi wants to return people back to their basic perfect state through turning away from the trappings of time and going back to the primal Tao: "Banish wisdom, discard knowledge, and the people shall profit a hundredfold; banish 'humanity,' discard 'justice,' and the people shall recover love of their kin; banish cunning, discard 'utility,' and the thieves and brigands shall disappear" (19); "When the world lives in accord with Tao, racing horses are turned back to haul refuse carts" (46). Laozi foresees a time when the flux of time will have reached its furthest limit, at which point it shall change: an enantiodromia: "There are those who will conquer the world and make of it (what they conceive or desire). I see that they will not succeed. (For) the world is God's own vessel. It cannot be made (by human interference). He who makes it spoils it. He who holds it loses it" (29). This is called the return to the Tao, and it seems to follow from the view of being and time of the Tao Te Ching.

The Tao Te Ching clearly sees that the people and the rulers complete each other, and therefore posits the need for a ruling class, with the same kinship between the people and the rulers as between yin and yang: "the nobility depend upon the common man for support, and the exalted ones depend upon the lowly for their base" (39). The ruling class shall aspire to know the Tao, and their leaders should be those who have reached this knowledge: "If princes and dukes can keep the Tao, the world will of its own accord be reformed" (37). They shall rule by means of Taoist ethics, subtly, behind the scenes, with low taxes and with great cunning and mildness, almost hidden away. The people shall be the makers of the wealth of the land, simple, scattered, untaught, and free. Complex machines are given up:

> (Let there be) a small country with a small population,
> Where the supply of goods are tenfold or hundredfold, more than they can use. Let the people value their lives and not migrate far.
> Though there be boats and carriages,
> None be there to ride them.
> Though there be armour and weapons,
> No occasion to display them.
> Let the people again tie ropes for reckoning,
> Let them enjoy their food,
> Beautify their clothing,
> Be satisfied with their homes,
> Delight in their customs.
> The neighbouring settlements overlook one another
> So that they can hear the barking of dogs and crowing of cocks of their neighbours,
> And the people till the end of their days shall never have been outside their own country. (80)

The Tao Te Ching's view of the state speaks strongly to the problem of modern Western people, slaves to machines, oppressed by chaos, awash in their own poisons, dazzled by glamour, controlled and used for their labour, and ever more subject to the total rule of money as the whole system declines. Now, perhaps 2,500 years after the time of Laozi, it appears that Laozi's warning is coming true – the growth of work and machines – what Buckminster Fuller calls the "acceleration of ephemeralization" – is about to reach its furthest limit. The question must be asked, then, how do the teachings of the Tao Te Ching help us to get

through the rough waters ahead? Using Laozi as a guide, it seems
that a Taoist plan for the present day would have to include this
list:

- give up machines;
- return to the land;
- revive hand crafts and the arts;
- make the laws simple;
- give up urban life;
- scatter the people;
- reduce the number of people;
- each locale should produce for itself;
- give up "higher" teaching for all;
- reduce work;
- make the rulers account to the people;
- give up putting law breakers to death;
- relax legal quid pro quo;
- keep taxes low;
- reduce the armed forces;
- prescribe working together;
- maintain closed borders.

In his basic notion of an ideal culture based on giving up all
forms of falseness, ruled by noble sages who are bound to the
people, in a closed culture of the land, Laozi is close to Plato's *Republic*.

The Science of the Spirit

Of the six topics described in this paper, the largest part of the
Tao Te Ching by far (about 40%) is about the science of the spirit,
called "soteriology." For Laozi, the science of the spirit is about
going back to the Tao. Ethics alone are not enough to find the Tao
within oneself, though they are the basis. To truly know the Tao in
oneself involves a basic change of the whole self, which is
achieved by very few. For those who do achieve it, Laozi says that
one will enjoy nothing less than the knowledge of the Real, health,
long life, and the deathless state after the death of the body.
About the nature of the deathless state itself, Laozi is silent. The

deathless state is only for those who have achieved "at-one-ment" with the Tao. As to what one is in one's essence, that will become one's fate when one dies: "He who follows the Tao is identified with the Tao. He who follows Character (Teh) is identified with Character. He who abandons (Tao) is identified with abandonment (of Tao). He who is identified with Tao – Tao is also glad to welcome him. He who is identified with Character – Character is also glad to welcome him. He who is identified with abandonment – abandonment is also glad to welcome him" (23).

To achieve "at-one-ment" with the Tao, Laozi prescribes a number of tasks, very like our talk above of "Ethics," but applied inside rather than outside. Of these, the first and foremost is "doing nothing": "The student of knowledge (aims at) learning day by day; the student of Tao (aims at) losing day by day. By continual losing one reaches doing nothing (laissez-faire). By doing nothing everything is done" (48). "Doing nothing" does not mean stasis, but rather no conflict, even while living in the world (one cannot give up the world, since it is also Tao!). Allow life to move in accord with its own nature, and all things achieve the nature proper to them, and all things, oneself and the world (to the extent that one is part of it) become perfect. "Doing nothing" is like the yin pole, which is closer to the Tao than the yang and therefore the pole through which one transcends the dyad and achieves "at-one-ment" (cf. nirvana and samsara). "At-one-ment" is a real state in which all of one's knots are untied, and all things achieve perfect concord. "Doing nothing" includes being without desire, giving up the self, leading a simple life, thinking about profound things, self-control, and quiet: "Attain the utmost in Passivity, hold firm to the basis of Quietude" (16).

Those who have achieved oneness with the Tao are the proper rulers of the people. Today, they are scattered and few. No one can transmit the knowledge of the Tao to anyone else, and only one who knows the Tao can see it in others. Therefore, oneness with the Tao is very hard to attain. Many people have never heard of it.

11

The Status of Women in Ancient India and the Pali Tradition

The Traditional Indian View of Women in the Early and Late Vedic Period

Indus Valley Civilization (3500–1300 BCE)

ANCIENT INDIAN CIVILIZATION originated in the fourth millennium BCE. It extended from northeast Afghanistan in the west to Pakistan and northwest India in the east. It flourished until about 2000 BCE. At its peak, it included about five million people and is considered one of the three great civilizations of antiquity and the largest in extent (1.6 million km²). Indus Valley seals have been discovered as far west as Sumer. This was a Bronze Age civilization that developed new techniques of handicraft and metallurgy, including copper, bronze, lead, and tin. It was a highly organized, mercantile society that included urban planning, baked brick houses, elaborate drainage systems, water supply systems, and large, non-residential building complexes. The Indus Valley civilization is also referred to as Harappan civilization, named after Harappa, the first site to be excavated in the 1920s. Over 2,600 archeological sites have been identified. Although the Indus script has yet to be deciphered, many scholars consider it to be related to Dravidian, an Indo-Aryan language the descendants of which are still spoken in southern India and elsewhere.

Not much is known about Harappan culture. It appears to have been a class-based society consisting of religious, merchant, and worker classes. The recent discovery that men moved into their bride's homes suggests a matrilineal influence and that women were powerful and perhaps even equal to men. This is in striking contrast to other ancient civilizations, which were generally patriarchal and oppressed women. Clay figurines of goddesses have been discovered. "The women portrayed on the seals are shown with elaborate coiffures, sporting heavy jewelry, suggesting that the Indus Valley people were an urbane people with cultivated tastes and a refined aesthetic sensibility."[95] Gupta says,

> One of the most known figurines is perhaps the `dancing girl' (in bronze) naked but for a necklace and a series of bangles almost covering one arm, her hair dressed in a complicated coiffure, standing in a provocative posture, with one arm on her hip and one lanky leg half bent. This face has an air of lively pertness quite unlike anything in the work of other ancient civilizations. Her thin boyish figure and those of the mother goddesses found here, indicate incidentally, that the ideas of female beauty among the Harappan people were very different from those of later India. ... The Harappan people also made rough terracotta statuettes of women, usually naked, but with elaborate headdresses. These are certainly icons of the mother goddess and are so numerous that they seem to have been kept in nearly every home. They are crudely fashioned so historians assume that the Goddess was not favoured by the upper classes who commanded the services of the best craftsmen, but that her effigies were mass-produced by humble potters to meet popular demand.[96]

The Indus Valley civilization is generally regarded as having been relatively pacific.

---

95. Vinay Lal, "Indus Valley Civilization."
96. Deep Raj Gupta, "Harappan Civilization: An Analysis in Modern Context."

Aryan Migration (1500–1200 BCE)

The indigenous Indian society was disrupted after a period of internal decline, possibly related to environmental factors and resulting economic decline, due to a series of conflicts with patriarchal, militaristic tribes originating near the Black Sea, the so-called Aryans. This "invasion" is referred to in the Rigveda. The Dravidians were then pushed down into Southern India. It seems that these conflicts resulted in the progressive assimilation of the local Harappan culture, reviving the Indus Valley civilization that led to the Vedic period that became the basis of historical Indian civilization to the present day. The Aryans introduced the consumption of soma, possibly ephedrine, a kind of amphetamine, possibly mixed with poppy and cannabis, to Indian religion. The inspiration of the Vedas themselves was attributed to the god Soma.[97]

Rigvedic Period (1500–1000 BCE)

The view that ancient Harappan culture conferred a special status on women is consistent with the scholarly consensus that the women of ancient India enjoyed a unique status very different from the misogyny that we find in India today. Gurholt suggests that "sexism and patriarchy are contrary to the fundamental teachings and beliefs of ancient Vedic and Buddhist philosophies."[98] Although she recognizes that Indus Valley civilization was probably also patriarchal, she specifically associates the qualities of patrilinealism, patrilocalism, and patriarchy with the Aryan incursion that promoted the institution of Brahmanism. She concludes, "The Indo-European Aryans contributed to and heightened the hierarchical, patriarchal, social structure of ancient India."[99] Nevertheless, during the early Vedic period women enjoyed

---

97. Other candidates for ingredients of soma include honey, Amanita muscaria (fly agaric), ephedra, poppy seeds or pollen, cannabis, psilocybin (Psilocybe cubensis), a fermented alcoholic drink, Syrian rue (Peganum harmala), rhubarb, ginseng, opium, wild chicory, and even ayahuasca!

98. Anya Gurholt, "The Androgyny of Enlightenment: Questioning Women's Status in Ancient Indian Religions."

99. Ibid.

many rights and privileges, including participation in society, including tribal assembles and religious ceremonies; education; choosing one's own husband; marrying more than one husband; voluntary remarriage of widows; divorce; and the pursuit of spiritual development, including the practice of asceticism. In addition, the practice of child marriage was unknown. Many of these rights and privileges are attested in the Vedic texts themselves, despite the fact that they were written by and for men. Even the rishis, the reputed divine seers (lit. 'hearers') who authored the Vedas, included women. "The Rig Veda mentions Romasha, Lopamudra, Apala, Kadru, Visvavara, Ghosha, Juhu, Vagambhrini, Paulomi, Yami, Indrani, Savitri, and Devajami. The Sama Veda adds Nodha, Akrishtabhasha, Sikatanivavari, and Gaupayana. In Mahabharata 12, on the other hand, there is the post-Vedic list of Marici, Atri, Angiras, Pulaha, Kratu, Pulastya and Vashista" (Wikipedia). In addition, Gurholt also cites Sulabha (*Mahabharata*), Maitreyi (Rigveda), and Gargi (Brihadaranyaka Upanishad).

Later Vedic Period (1000 BCE–500 BCE)

During the later Vedic period, the dominance of Brahmanism led to increasing patriarchy. Interestingly, the rise of Brahmanism corresponded to the replacement of the consumption of soma by symbolic ritual enactment (the "fire sacrifice"), and finally the formula for soma itself was forgotten. Female divinities were relegated to second-class status, and women progressively lost the rights and privileges they had previously enjoyed. An increasingly rigid gender hierarchy was enforced. Women were secluded and became less able to participate in society. Their role was confined to the household, where their exclusive duty was seen to be obedience to their husbands. Education and participation in the tribal assemblies was forbidden to them. They were not encouraged or allowed to pursue the spiritual life. This included studying the Vedas. Vedic study became the exclusive prerogative of male brahman priests. Arranged marriages and child marriages were instituted. Women were not allowed to divorce their husbands or inherit their property; widows were not allowed to remarry. Female chastity came to be viewed as a valuable commodity, conferring social status on the family. Women were regarded as chattel, and they could be given away or loaned like any other property. The practice of *sati*, in which the widow immolates herself on her husband's funeral pyre, was celebrated as the supreme act of filial piety, and veiling (*purdah*) was required. Women were equated with the sudra, the lowest caste of slaves or servants in the Brahmanic four-caste system.

These developments appear to correspond to a schism that occurred in Vedic society during this period. This schism was associated with two classes of Vedic deity, the asuras and the devas (a.k.a. *suras*). Originally the *asuras* (lit. 'lord') were a class of superior devas who inhabited the realm of the Thirty-Three Gods (*trayastrimsa*) on top of Mount Meru. The names of many asuras refer to natural abstractions, rather as in Native American spiritualism, Indus Valley civilization, etc. A new cult of deva worship emerged during the late Vedic period that declared the asuras demonic and began to persecute the older group of asura worshippers. The new deva worshippers were authoritarian. They supported the superiority of the brahmans, the caste system, and they were misogynistic. The conflict between the asura and deva worshippers was mythologized. In the eastern part of the Indian subcontinent the deva worshippers achieved pre-eminence, whereas in the west the asura worshippers maintained their prestige, demonizing the devas in return. The latter became the foundation of Zoroastrianism in Iran, with the supreme god Ahura (*Asura*) Mazda, the god of Wisdom, at its head.

Developments in 5th–6th Century BCE India

By the time of the Buddha,[100] the traditional Brahmanic culture had become completely ossified and decadent. The Vedic beliefs were no longer relevant to the new iron-age society. Prosperity, money, and trading were increasing, greatly enhancing the social status of the merchant and worker classes, but social relativism

---

100. Although the conventional Western dates of the Buddha are still given as 563–483 BCE, an increasing number of scholars now believe that the Buddha was born in the first half of the fifth century BCE. Hajime Nakamura puts his death as recently as 383 BCE.

was causing widespread social and spiritual questioning and discontent. This resulted in new philosophical movements and religious sects in the Middle Gangetic Plain. Interestingly, this is the same area where the Indus Valley civilization had flourished two millennia before. The more mystical teachings of the Upanishads were being popularized and becoming increasingly influential; criticism of the Brahman orthodoxy was growing. In northeast India, where the Buddha lived and brahmanic influence was weakest, corrupt autocratic kingdoms and despotic autocracies vied for power with nascent quasi-republics and constitutional oligarchies. These were the sixteen great realms, the *mahajanapadas*, which flourished from 600 to 300 BCE, ranging from Kamboja in the north and west to Assaka in the south and Anga in the east. Wars and political assassinations were frequent occurrences. The Buddha lived to see the genocide of his own clan, the Sakyans, by the Kosalan king, Virudhaka. The people were oppressed, subject to brigands who haunted the roads and the vast forests. They were often over-taxed by the state, which was desperate to maintain its control in relation to the emerging mercantile class. On the other hand, workers were organizing themselves into trade guilds, arts and crafts were flourishing, work was becoming increasingly specialized, and knowledge was expanding. Others, essentially small farmers, became wealthy through land ownership. This turned the traditional caste system upside down. The position of women, especially widows, was untenable, and many women turned to prostitution in order to survive, since they were forbidden from inheriting the estates of their husbands. For this reason the Buddhists tolerated prostitution, rejected by the brahmans.

This period corresponds to a worldwide phenomenon that German philosopher Karl Jaspers has called the Axial Age (*Achsenzeit*), which he identifies with the period from 800 to 200 BCE. Revolutionary new ways of thinking developed more or less simultaneously in Persia, India, China, Greece, and Judea during this period, including the birth of rational philosophy itself. Eric Voegelin has called this period the Great Leap of Being. Interestingly, the midpoint of the Axial Age (500 BCE) is exactly the same distance from the advent of the Kali Yuga (3102 BCE) as 2100 CE.

The nineteenth century began a period of science, exploration, invention, discovery, technology, and the beginning of industrialization and globalization. The year 2400, three hundred years hence, corresponds to the full manifestation of Shambhala (2424 CE) according to the Kalachakra. One might argue that this latter period (1800–2400) represents the advent of a new Axial Age, and will be looked upon as such by humans of the future. Futurist and inventor Ray Kurzweil has suggested that the crucial transformational moment of the new age will occur in 2045. This is the year of the Singularity. This event will transform human society in qualitatively unpredictable ways because of the convergence of biology and technology. This is also fairly close to the end of the Mayan epoch in 2012 CE, which began in 3113 or 3114 BCE, only eleven or twelve years after the advent of the Kali Yuga. The Buddha himself was born very close to the midpoint of the Axial Age (500 BCE). The great tantric adept, Padmasambhava, who is credited with the conversion of Tibet to Vajrayana Buddhism, flourished during the late eighth century CE, at the midpoint of the interval from the advent of the Buddhist epoch (c 400 BCE) to our own time (c 2000 CE).

The View of Women in the Shakti, Samana, and Shaivite Countercultures

Shaktism

A famous motif found on a seal in the Mohenjo-Daro excavation of the Indus Valley civilization is a horned figure sitting cross-legged and surrounded by animals. This figure, called Pashupati ('Lord of the Animals'), has been identified with a precursor of the Indian god Shiva. Phallic symbols have also been found and identified as precursors of the Shivalingam. The significance of the possible evidence for a Shiva cult in the Indus Valley civilization, which also practised fertility rituals, is the association of Shiva, the male creative principle that dies and is reborn (phallic tumescence/detumescence) with Shakti, the universal goddess principle without which Shiva is literally impotent. The word Shakti literally means 'power' or 'energy.' Shakti is, therefore, the dynamic, creative aspect of existence. In the human being, this energy is equated with intelligence, compassion, and divine love.

Regardless of whether one accepts the identification of the horned figure of Mohenjo-Daro with Shiva and, by implication, Shiva's consort, Shakti – although in view of the apparently female-positive character of the Indus Valley civilization, such an association is tempting – Shakti is mentioned a dozen times in the Rigveda, and goddess figures, many of whom are cognate with Shakti, another forty times. Although modern Shaktism did not fully flower until about 400 CE, its precursors clearly originate during the Vedic period and extend far back, even into the Late Stone Age (c 20,000 BCE).

S(h)amanism

As we have already discussed, by the fifth and sixth centuries BCE the established Vedic Brahman orthodoxy of India was no longer able to satisfy the religious and spiritual needs of many people. There were widespread skepticism, longing, and discontent. In response to this social, political, and spiritual ferment new religious and philosophical movements appeared and defined and organized themselves. They gained the respect and adherence of many people. By the time of the Buddha, this *samana* counterculture was already well established, especially in northeast India, where the Brahmanic orthodoxy was weakest. Materialist, hedonist, deterministic, and agnostic philosophies competed with Upanishadic Brahmanism and religious renunciants. It was this last group that the Buddha joined when he chose to renounce the worldly life at the age of 29, shaving his head and adopting the ochre robe, entirely without reference to joining any particular organization or monastic institution (which did not yet exist).

The Pali word *samana* is very interesting. It is derived from the Sanskrit *sram*. *Sram* is a verb meaning 'to heat, cook, ripen, mature, seethe, boil, subdue, make weary, overcome, and conquer.' The origin of the word is also conflated with *sam*, 'to gather together' or 'integrate.' *Sram* is the root of the English word 'shaman,' a spiritual practitioner who cultivates a state of transcendent

ecstasy in which he experiences visions of other worlds, com-
municates with spiritual beings, and acquires psychic powers. *Sam* is the root of *samadhi,* 'one-pointed concentration' or
'meditation.' The PED says merely that a *samana* is a religious
wanderer or recluse, but heat and light symbolism pervade the
Pali Canon as well as clear references to altered states of consciousness and psychic powers or iddhis. The *samana* counterculture rejected the authority of Brahmanism and the Vedas, although many of the spiritual and religious concepts of the *samanas*
were also prefigured in the Upanishads. It is important to note
that the *samana* movement specifically rejected the authority of
both the brahman caste and the Vedic textual traditions, despite
these similarities. Thus, the philosophy of the Buddha must be
decisively distinguished from the so-called *astika* schools, which
accepted Vedic authority. The latter became the well-known Samkhya, Yoga, and Vedanta philosophical schools of orthodox Hinduism, among others. This is an important point to remember in
the context of the late Vedic attitude toward and treatment of
women.

The *samanas* set out to discover the truth for themselves experientially. To this end, they adopted three fundamental practices:
austerity, to purify karma; meditation, to cultivate mental concentration; and "view" or philosophy, to cultivate wisdom or understanding – the same threefold division that we find in the Pali
Canon. Jainism was already old when the Buddha appeared. It appears to have been founded in the seventh to ninth centuries BCE
by Parsva. Thus, it was probably at least four hundred years old at
the time of the Buddha. Jainism may have been a non-Aryan remnant of the Indus Valley civilization, though scholars dispute this.
There are many similarities between Buddhism and Jainism. Nevertheless, the Buddha also criticized Mahavira, the leader of Jainism about the same time as the Buddha, and distinguished himself
from it as well.

After his renunciation the Buddha studied with two philosophical teachers of the time, Alara Kalama and Uddaka Ramaputta.
Alara Kalama was a proto-Samkhya meditation master in
the *astika* tradition, under whom the Buddha achieved the reali-

zation of the realm of "Nothingness." Uddaka Ramaputta was a Jain meditation master (in the *nastika* tradition, therefore) under whom the Buddha achieved the realization of the realm of "Nei-ther-perception nor-non-perception." He also appears to have been something of a charlatan![101] Finally, the Buddha fell in with the Group of Five, led by Kondanna, the brahman ascetic who had predicted at his birth that Gotama would become a World Teach-er. The group of five had renounced the worldly life about the same time as the Buddha and practised extreme austerities, in-cluding mortification of the body, breath control, mind control, and extreme fasting, practising in cemeteries and elsewhere, simi-lar to the Shaivites (see below). After failing to find what he sought with Kalama and Ramaputta, Gotama joined them in these practices, until he was on the verge of dying. Although many sources imply that Gotama practised with the group of five for six years, this is unlikely since he must have studied with Kalama and Ramaputta for at least some time first. If one assumes that he spent a year with each of these, then perhaps the Buddha prac-tised with the group of five for three years, followed by a year alone. The Buddha's practice of these austerities is vividly de-scribed in the Pali Canon. About the age of thirty-five, on the very verge of death, Gotama accepted some rice pudding from a pass-ing village girl, Sujata, at which point the Group of Five aban-doned him as having reverted to the effeminate life of his youth. Gotama was on his own and had still not found what he sought.

Shaivism

Shaivism developed out of the Shvetashvetara Upanishad. This Upanishad is the earliest textual source for Shaivism, and may have been written down about 400 BCE, the year of the Bud-dha's *parinirvana*. However, its origins are certainly significantly older. The practices of Shaivism included extreme asceticism, self-purification, a cemetery cult of human bones, the practice of yoga based on the cross-legged posture, disrespect for caste, asso-ciation with untouchables, renunciation of the householder life

---

101. See SN 35:103.

and procreation, a northern Indian provenance, rejection of brahman superiority, and reverence for the female principle. Shaivism is based on the worship of the original divine principle in Indian mythology, Pashupati, which is widely regarded as a proto- type of Shiva. Similarly, during his *samana* period Gotama prac- tised extreme self-mortification; fasting; yoga, including breath control and mind control; and lived and slept in cemeteries. In his later philosophy the Buddha rejects the caste system, admits women to the sangha in defiance of social norms, and references a return to a primordial tradition of which the Brahmanic cult and even the Vedas themselves are degenerations. Richard Gombrich ("Who Was Angulimala?")[102] has suggested that Angulimala (An- gulimala Sutta, MN 86) was a practitioner of just this type. This makes the Buddha's acceptance of Angulimala as his personal at- tendant especially interesting.

Evaluating the Buddha's View Toward and Treatment of Women

The Sex Life of the Buddha

Unlike Yeshua, the Galilean bodhisattva of the Jews, who is por- trayed in the canonical texts of Christianity as virtually sexless, the Buddha is portrayed, in the words of the title of the book by John Powers, as *A Bull of Man.* This is consistent with the Indian tradi- tion of karma, in which a great man must have a great body! Thus, the Buddha was identified as a great man at his birth, by the ap- pearance of certain physical signs, including long, slender fingers; soft, smooth, golden-coloured skin; a handsome, well- proportioned body, including beautiful thighs, strong torso, and erect posture; closely spaced, even white teeth; a strong jaw; long- eyelashes; black, curly hair; deep blue eyes; a large cranium; and a deep, resonant voice. These are among the thirty-two signs of a great man. This is the basis of the prediction made at the Bud-

---

102. Gombrich, *How Buddhism Began,* Chap. V.

dha's birth that he would become either a world ruler or a world teacher.[103]

Chief Suddhodana, anxious that his son should succeed him as the leader of the Shakyan clan, a small republic located between Kosala and Vajji, pampered him and plied him with every sort of pleasure. Gotama was so attracted to women that he actually lived in the women's quarters in his teens and 20s, and was doubtless acquainted with sex. He married the princess Yasodhara at the age of 16, and had a son, Rahula, by her, purportedly at the age of 29. According to one story, Gotama renounced the world in reaction to the aftermath of a party in which the musicians, all female, were lying sleeping about the palace, in ungainly poses, snoring and exposing their breasts. It does not take much imagination to realize that Gotama was a rich playboy and probably sexually promiscuous as well, which may explain in part the severity of the renunciation that followed. For example, in the Magandiya Sutta (MN 75) the Buddha says,

> Magandiya, formerly when I lived the home life, I enjoyed myself, provided and endowed with the five cords of sensual pleasure; with forms cognizable by the eye ... sounds cognizable by the ear ... odours cognizable by the nose ... flavours cognizable by the tongue ... tangible cognisable by the body that are wished for, desired, agreeable, and likable, connected with sensual desire and provocative of lust. I had three palaces, one for the rainy season, one for the winter, and one for the summer. I lived in the rains' palace for the four months of the rainy season, enjoying myself with musicians who were all female, and I did not go down to the lower palace.

Thus, as a suitable basis for his final renunciation and Enlightenment, it was necessary for the Buddha to fulfil the life of the world completely. Remember that at this stage of his spiritual career Gotama was a bodhisattva in his last birth, mere years away from full Enlightenment. This self-description does not sound like the ruminations of a misogynist or a neurotic prude either.

---

103. How they were able to discern some of these signs in an infant, including erect posture, even white teeth, black curly hair, and a deep resonant voice, is not explained.

Negative Views of Women in the Pali Canon

The Pali *suttas* include many negative views of women, including the statement that a woman is incapable of attaining Buddhahood; that the female birth is karmically inferior because a woman is subject to five types of suffering to which a man is not subject, viz., being separated from her family, menstruation, pregnancy, childbirth, and being subservient to a man; that a wife is inferior to her husband and should be willing to obey him and even die rather than displease him in the slightest particular; and that a Buddhist nun (bhikkuni), no matter what her attainment or seniority, should be inferior to a monk (bhikku) of even a single day's seniority. The Buddha describes sexual intercourse as "Dhamma's opposite ... the low, vulgar ideal that is impure and ends in ablution, that is done in secrecy by couples," and states that it is better to insert one's penis into the mouth of a "hideous venomous viper or cobra [or bed of red hot coals] than that it should enter a woman" (Suttavibhanga). With reference to woman's capacity to elicit lust, the Buddha says that the female form is more seductive than any other object of sense and refers to women as "sharks" and "snares of Mara." The female form is so irresistible, in fact, that the Buddha says mothers and sons will commit incest and a man might even commit acts of necrophilia, given the chance, for which reason a monk may not approach a woman even if she is dead (Anguttara Nikaya). The Vinaya also includes cases of Buddhist monks engaging in these and other perverse erotic behaviours.[104] The Buddha says that women are reborn with three qualities: miserliness, envy, and sensuality and lust, because of which most women are reborn in worlds of hellish suffering (Anguttara Nikaya). Elsewhere he says that women are angry, envious, miserly, and unintelligent, and therefore incapable of participating in government, engaging in business, or travel away from home (Anguttara Nikaya). He says that the ways of women are secretive, like brahmans and heretics (those of perverse views). Like black snakes, women are impure, foul-smelling, frightening, dangerous, and disloyal (Angttara Nikaya). They are

---

104. See esp. I.B. Horner, trans., *The Book of the Discipline*, Vol. I, pp. 349–72.

insatiable in respect of sexual intercourse and childbirth, even on their deathbed (Anguttara Nikaya). The Buddha made it clear to Ananda that a monk should neither associate nor communicate with women if he can possibly avoid it, and that a monk who has sex with a woman will be subject to rebirth in a hellish world of suffering. The Pali Canon portrays women as cunning liars, secretive, fond of intrigue, and unfaithful.

According to the Pali Canon, the original sangha of the Buddha was a sangha of men only. After the death of the his father, King Suddhodana, about seven or eight years following the Buddha's Enlightenment and the establishment of the sangha (perhaps c 440 BCE) the Buddha's aunt and foster-mother, Maha Pajapti Gotami, resolves to be ordained, along with five hundred women of the court. She approaches the Buddha when he is visiting Kapilavastu, for permission to join the sangha, but he refuses her request. Distraught, the women shave their heads and put on robes anyway, and follow the Buddha to Vesali, a distance of about 300 kms (186 miles). This must have taken them about two months, perhaps longer. Distraught and physically exhausted, she approaches Ananda, who is portrayed in the *suttas* as quite sympathetic to women in general, to intercede with the Buddha. Ananda approaches the Buddha on her behalf. Once again, the Buddha refuses. Ananda's subsequent discussion with the Buddha is famous. He asks the Buddha whether, therefore, women are capable of attainment. The Buddha admits that, like men, they are capable of attaining arhantship. The self-contradiction in the Buddha's position thus exposed, the Buddha finally relents, acceding to Ananda's request, but he declares that because of the ordination of women the longevity of the sangha will be halved, from one thousand to only five hundred years (a situation subsequently resolved by imposing special limitations on female monastics).[105] He imposes eight special rules on the *bhikkhunisangha* that permanently subordinates them to the *bhikkhusangha*. These are called the eight *Garudhammas*, viz.:

---

105. See AN VIII:51(8) and Bodhi, *The Numerical Discourses of the Buddha* and n. 1747, p. 1805.

1) A nun who has been ordained even for a hundred years must greet respectfully, rise up from her seat, salute with joined palms, and do proper homage to a monk ordained but that day.

2) A nun must not spend the rains in a residence where there are no monks.

3) Every half month a nun should desire two things from the Order of Monks: the asking as to the date of the Observance (*uposatha*) day, and the coming for the exhortation (*bhikkhunovada*).

4) After the three-month rainy season retreat, a nun must "invite" (*pavarana*) before both orders in respect of three matters, namely what was seen, what was heard, what was suspected.

5) A nun, offending against an important rule, must undergo *manatta* (discipline or penance) for half a month before both orders.

6) When, as a probationer, she has trained in the six rules (*cha dhamma*) for two years, she should seek higher ordination from both orders.

7) A monk must not be abused or reviled in any way by a nun.

8) Admonition of monks by nuns is forbidden.

Over the course of time, these eight additional rules expanded to 311 rules for nuns, compared to 227 for monks. According to another computation, there are 110 extra rules for nuns. After a thousand years, the *bhikkhunisangha* died out in India and most other places. In Thailand, which follows the conservative Theravada tradition inherited from Sri Lanka, it is actually illegal for a woman to "impersonate" a monastic by putting on robes.[106]

There are many rules in the Buddhist Vinaya, the monastic rules applicable to monks, concerning women and nuns. A monk may not have sexual intercourse or lustful bodily contact with a woman, nor may he make lustful remarks to a woman, including ask-

---

106. Banning Ajahn Brahm's speech on *bhikkuni* ordination from the 11th United Nations Day of Vesak 2014 is merely the most recent confirmation of the misogyny of Theravada Buddhists. See Dipananda, "Banning Ajahn Brahm's speech on nuns was a spectacular own-goal." Note that restoring *bhikkuni* ordination does not restore gender equity between men and women, since the Buddhist formula of ordination for *bhikkunis* is inherently and intentionally discriminatory.

ing her for sexual favours. He may not arrange for a date, affair, or marriage with a woman on behalf of another person. An unrelated nun may not wash a monk's robes or give him robes as a gift. A nun may not wash, dye, or card raw wool for a monk. A monk may not lie down in the same building as a woman. He may not teach a woman more than five or six lines of dharma, unless another knowledgeable man is present. He may not exhort the nuns in the nuns' quarters unless she is ill. He may not exhort the nuns for worldly gain in any case. He may not give an unrelated nun cloth for a robe, or sew it or have it sewn, unless it is given in exchange. A monk may not travel on the road with a nun, even between villages, unless it is by caravan and the road is unsafe, or travel with a nun by boat in any direction upstream or downstream other than directly crossing a river. He may not travel on a road with a woman in any case. He may not eat alms food obtained by the prompting of a nun. He may not sit alone with a nun. He may not accept food from an unrelated nun. The punishment for violating any of these rules ranges from expulsion from the order to verbal acknowledgement, depending on the severity of the offence. The fact that these rules exist proves that all of these actions occurred in the sangha.

Positive Views of Women in the Pali Canon

Despite the views summarized above, the Buddha also expresses many positive views concerning women in various places. Women figure prominently in both the *suttas* and the post-canonical commentaries (see Hellmuth Hecker, "Great Women Disciples of the Buddha," chapter 7 of Nyanaponika and Hecker, *Great Disciples of the Buddha*). I have already mentioned the Buddha's acknowledgement that women are capable of attaining arhantship. This is elaborated at great length in other *suttas,* where the Buddha describes all the levels of attainment from faith follower to arhant, and emphasizes that many members of the sangha, including both men and women, have attained all of the various stages of spiritual development. Indeed, the Buddha implies that women must exist at all levels of spiritual development for the sangha to be complete. The Buddha criticizes the brahman practice of arranged marriage and defends the right of women to marry freely for love. He explicitly identifies women's rights as the fifth principle of a healthy and stable society, referring specifically to the Vajjians. When the married Bhagga householders Nakulapita and Nakulmata approach the Buddha and declare their love for each other, asking him whether they can ensure that they would be reborn together, rather than criticize them the Buddha praises the couple and declares that they can be reborn together as deva beings, a destination reserved for the most pious, if they observe the same faith, morality, generosity, and wisdom.[107] The evidence of the Pali Canon, especially the Songs of the Wise Women (Therigatha), clearly shows that the early sangha included many women, both monastic and lay, many of whom were highly esteemed and spiritually advanced practitioners, even arhants, just as was the case during the early Vedic period. Some great women disciples of the Buddha included Visakha, the Buddha's chief patroness; Mallika; Khema of great wisdom; Bhadda Kundalakesa, the debating ascetic; Kisagotami; Sona; Nanda, the Buddha's half-sister; Queen Samavati, the embodiment of loving kindness; Patacara, preserver of the Vinaya; Ambapali, the generous courtesan; Sirima; Uttara; and Isidasi. This is perhaps the best evidence of all for the view that the Buddha made no distinction between women and men.[108]

---

107. See AN IV:55.

108. Although most *suttas* are addressed to bhikkus, there are also *suttas* spoken by or to bhikkunis, and the Therigatha is composed entirely of verses of early bhikkunis. The first *sutta* attributed to a bhikkuni is the Culavedalla Sutta (MN 44), attributed to Dhammadinna, declared by the Buddha to be the nun foremost in expounding the dharma. In this *sutta,* she expounds the dharma concerning personality, personality view, the Noble Eightfold Path, concentration, formations, the attainment of cessation, feeling, underlying tendencies, and counterparts. In the Dakkhinavibhanga Sutta (MN 142), his aunt, Mahapajapati Gotami, presents the Buddha with robes that she made for him herself. And in the Nadakovada Sutta (MN 146), Mahapajapati Gotami asks the Buddha to teach the bhikkunis. The small number of "bhikkuni *suttas*" contrasted with the frequent references to the bhikkunis all through the Pali Canon suggests a deliberate suppression of *suttas* in which bhikkunis were featured prominently, presumably due to the obvious gender bias of the First Buddhist Council. The insights of these "wise women" have been lost forever.

Analysis

In the introduction to his translation of the Numerical Discourses of the Buddha (Anguttara Nikaya), Bhikku Bodhi acknowledges that the positive and negative statements concerning women found all through the Pali Canon are mutually self-contradictory. It is impossible to believe that the Buddha held all these views simultaneously. Bodhi also doubts the historicity of the famous dialogue in which Ananda convinces the Buddha to admit women to the sangha, citing "anachronisms hard to reconcile with other chronological information in the canon and commentaries."[109] Scholars also doubt the antiquity of the *garudhammas,* one of which refers to probationary nuns, a category that did not exist when Mahapajapati was ordained. Consequently, it cannot be original. There is also reason to disbelieve the account of the admission of Mahapajapati to the sangha, since the Exposition of Offerings (Dakkhinavibhangha Sutta, MN 142) presents the *bhikkhunisangha* as already existing when Mahapajapati goes for refuge to the Buddha, the Dharma, and the Sangha, without any suggestion that the Buddha opposed her admission. It appears, then, that this whole complex was invented to justify the *garudhammas.*

In defence of the Buddha's purported reluctance to ordain women, apologists have cited possible concerns about social prejudice, including the Buddha's realization that the sangha could not survive without popular support, and the safety of the nuns, who would be subjected not only to social scorn and even abuse, but also by the ravages of the environment at a time when the sangha had not yet established itself with parks and monasteries. By accepting women into the sangha, the Buddha was setting himself against the entire late Vedic tradition of the deva worshippers that was now universally accepted by the society of his time. It was unheard of for women to leave the household life and follow the path of a *samana,* much as it was in Hindu India until very recently. Although he was criticized for breaking up the family unit, and the sangha was not welcomed everywhere, it is a tes-

---

109. Bodhi, *The Numerical Discourses of the Buddha,* p. 62.

tament to the Buddha's charisma and the respect in which he was held that there is not more indication of dissension in the Pali Canon than there is.

Thus, the Pali Canon itself forces us to make a judgment. Either we accept that the Buddha reluctantly admitted women to the sangha on what amounts to a technicality, but instituted rules to curtail and limit the damage resulting from this concession, or we take the view that the misogynistic passages are later additions that reflect the social prejudices of fifth century BCE India, especially male monastics, that we have seen began to supplant the older, more tolerant view of women during the late Vedic period. The latter view is consistent with the Buddha's declaration that he considered the Brahmanism of his time to be a degenerate remnant of a primordial tradition that he sought to restore. With respect to the latter, it is interesting to note that the Buddha clearly opposed the caste system, arranged marriage, and authoritarianism, all things that appeared during the late Vedic period with the rise of the newer deva worshippers who cast down the asuras to the foot of Mount Meru. This makes one wonder if the older tradition to which the Buddha alludes was in fact that of the older system of asura worship, which also, like the Buddha, opposed the gods (devas), despite the reversal of terms that clearly predominates in the Pali Canon itself.

The View of Women in the Early Buddhist Councils

The First Buddhist Council

The First Buddhist Council was convened in the year following the Buddha's passing on (*parinirvana*) about 400 BCE according to modern scholarship by King Ajatashatru, the king of Magadha in Rajgir, the capital, according to tradition. Although in his final instructions the Buddha had said that the sangha should have no leader after him, but should be led by the dharma alone, Mahakassapa, the Buddha's foremost disciple in ascetic practices, assumed the leadership of the sangha after the Buddha's death, and called the First Buddhist Council together in response to suggestions by the monk Subhadda that with the Buddha's death the Vi-

naya rules of the order might be relaxed. Although this is presented in the Theravadin literature as a criticism, in fact according to
the Great Passing (Mahaparinibbana Sutta, DN 16), the Buddha
had indicated that after his death the lesser and minor rules of the
Vinaya might be abolished. Thus, Mahakassapa convened five
hundred arhants to consolidate the tradition of the dharma, including Ananda, who conveniently attained arhantship during the
night before the council began to meet from July to the following
January. Upali, the foremost disciple in keeping the precepts, began by reciting the rules of the Vinaya in their entirety, especially
the *parajika* – the rules that entail mandatory and automatic expulsion from the sangha – i.e., sex, stealing, killing, and lying
about one's spiritual attainment. Ananda then recited the *suttas*.

Ananda had a hard time of it, however. Mahakassapa attacked
him, presumably for "convincing" the Buddha to ordain women.
Many male arhants were extremely opposed to this, despite the
clear fact that the Buddha had approved it. There was also the
question of the minor and lesser rules of the Vinaya that the Buddha had said in his final instructions to Ananda might be abolished. Since it had not occurred to Ananda to ask the Buddha
which rules he was referring to, the conservative Council decided
to keep them all. The Council also decided to allow the ordination
of women, subject to the eight *garudhammas* and expanded the
rules to include an additional 110 rules for nuns, despite the fact
that the Buddha had also declared that no new rules were to be
made. It seems likely that the eight *garudhammas* were codified at
this time, perhaps as a compromise between two competing fac-
tions.

The foregoing account creates serious "theological" issues for
the Hinayana in general and the Theravada in particular, since all
of the members of the First Buddhist Council are regarded as arhants. This problem came to a head a hundred years later during
the Second Buddhist Council, during which the fallibility and imperfection of arhants became a bone of contention between two
nascent Buddhist schools, the Mahasamghikas, who took the view
that arhants are fallible, and the Sthaviras, who took the view that
arhants are infallible. These differences were summarized in the

Five Points of Mahadeva. The Mahasamghikas represented the majority view, and subsequently developed into the Mahayana, whereas the minority, the Sthaviras, subsequently developed into the Theravada. With respect to the present topic, it is clear that the First Buddhist Council endorsed a view of women and nuns that is fundamentally misogynistic, and the Pali Canon, which is the record of Buddhist teachings accepted by the Theravada, is explicitly so. As I have also shown, the First Buddhist Council overruled the Buddha's own injunctions to not appoint a leader, to abolish the lesser and minor rules, and subsequent councils clearly also added rules and in particular rules designed to subordinate the nuns to the monks. That the attainments of arhantship and Buddhahood are different also seems to be supported by the canonical assertion, if we accept it, that women can become arhants but not buddhas. The ten powers of an arhant also differ qualitatively from the ten powers of a Buddha according to the Pali texts. On the other hand, if we accept the Hinayana/Theravada view that arhants are infallible, then we must accept Buddhist misogyny as a view. If we are not willing to accept the inferiority of women, we cannot in good conscience accept the lineage derived from the minority Sthavira position. Therefore, we cannot accept Hinayana or Theravada as the final dharma. Since the Buddha indicated that in the absence of consensus we must accept majority rule, we are compelled to the alternative view as the correct dharmic view.

The View of Women in Buddhism Today

After the Buddha's death about 400 BCE, Indian society continued to suppress women. Beginning in the fifth century CE, by the eleventh century the practice of *sati,* or widow burning, became the model of how a pious wife should respond to the death of her husband. The Muslim incursion into India (12th–16th centuries), which virtually wiped Buddhism out of India, including the *bhikkunisangha,* followed by the British conquest of India, beginning in the seventeenth century, further intensified the already deeply-rooted Indian misogyny. Meanwhile, the *bhikkhunisangha* had virtually disappeared from India and Sri Lanka by the eleventh century. Widely disparaged in Buddhist countries, and discriminated against where it did exist, the *bhikkhunisangha* only survived continuously in Eastern (Chinese) Buddhism, ironically in view of Confucian ideas of the subordination of women. Today efforts are underway in several countries to restore the *bhikkunisangha,* but based on the old model; the Dalai Lama has made similar efforts in northeast India. As a result, there are about 130,000 Buddhist nuns in the world today.

Socially, Buddhist women have fared better than Indian women have. In general, Buddhist societies respect single women, including unmarried women, divorced women, and widows. Laws concerning divorce and the division of property and children are fairly equal between husband and wife. Outside China, where Confucian notions predominate, women are fairly free, including in business, trade, and agriculture. Even in Eastern Buddhism, however, Zen/Chan Buddhism emphasizes sexual equality. Women may also be found exercising the professions of law and medicine, and have been politically influential. Many Buddhist women enjoy sexual freedom, property rights, and self-determination. Women may also be influential in religious institutions. Mahayana tends to view men and women as equal whereas Theravada still sees the bodhisattva path as suited only for rare and heroic men. Female spiritual figures are most widespread in Vajrayana (Tantra).

Conclusion

Indian culture differs from the other great originating cultures of humanity in that most cultures began with the patriarchal suppression of women, followed by their progressive emancipation, whereas Indian civilization began with women holding a position of unique power and privilege, followed by their progressive suppression commencing about 1100 BCE. This "transvaluation of all values" appears to have coincided with a social schism in which an original cult of asura worship, great cosmological abstractions associated with the powers of nature, was displaced by a new, aggressive cult of deva worship based on notions of patriarchal authority, the status quo, brahmanic dominance, caste, and misogyny derived from the Aryan incursion. By the time of the Buddha, Vedic society was breaking down and a counterculture of wandering "shamans," suggestive of the later Shakti and Shaiva cults that eventually developed into Tantra, had emerged. After studying meditative or cognitive (jhana) yoga with Brahman and Jain teachers in succession, the Buddha joined the *samanas* and became an extreme ascetic for a number of years, almost dying in the process, followed by his Enlightenment experience. It is noteworthy that both the Shakti and Shaivite cults were not misogynistic in their attitudes to the female principle.

The conflicting attitudes toward men and women in Indian society appear in the Pali Canon in the conflicting attitudes to women attributed to the Buddha. However, it appears that the Buddha did not make a fundamental distinction between men and women, asserting that both men and women are equally capable of attainment, and freely teaching women and admitting them to the sangha on an equal basis, rather like Yeshua, the founder of Christianity, for which the latter was also severely criticized by the Jewish establishment in Jerusalem. If the Buddha did make a distinction between the orders of monks and nuns, it was to protect the nuns and appease social prejudice. This unpopularly tolerant attitude must have created a great deal of consternation among the more conservative male followers of the Buddha, but they appear to have largely avoided criticism out of respect for the Buddha. This changed after the Buddha's death, when a major rift seems to have occurred during the First Buddhist Council, when the male monastics attacked Ananda for supporting the ordination of women. That they were not the only side of this debate is suggested by the fact that a compromise appears to have been reached in which the order of nuns was subordinated to the order of monks but allowed to exist. Otherwise, it seems likely that the nuns would have been suppressed altogether. The pious forgeries concerning Mahapajapati, Ananda's subsequent debate with the Buddha, and the *garudhamma* were created to explain the final decision of the First Buddhist Council, which led ultimately to the disappearance of the *bhikkunisangha*. Moreover, the addition of numerous special rules for nuns, all with the purpose of subordinating the nuns to the monks, clearly violates the Buddha's instructions not to add extra rules to the Vinaya. Over the following three centuries numerous misogynistic passages were introduced into the *suttas*, while the more favourable statements of the Buddha concerning women were also allowed to stand because they were too well-established to be refuted, thus creating the somewhat bizarre self-contradictions that we find in the Pali texts today. Very likely, over the course of three hundred years there were diverse currents and sub-currents of thought among the anonymous redactors of the Pali Canon itself, of which we know little or nothing. Meanwhile, Indian society continued in its misogynistic course, exacerbated by Muslim and British colonial influences. Thus, in contemporary Nepal, for example, we find a significantly more liberal society than India proper, since Nepal was never subjugated to Muslim and British influences. Buddhism itself split into two large movements, one aligned with the dominant conservative social attitude and one aligned with the more liberal attitude that, it appears, was actually advocated by the Buddha. Fortunately, for those of us who do not believe in the inferiority of women, the latter has become the majority view in the Buddhist world today.

Abbreviations

V   Vinaya
DN   Digha Nikaya
MN   Majjhima Nikaya
SN   Samyutta Nikaya
AN   Anguttara Nikaya

References

Unsourced References

Buddhacarita
Dhammapada
Dipavamsa
Great Commentary of the Abhidhamma
I-Ching
Infinite Life Sutra
Itivuttaka
Jataka
Mahabharata
Maharatnakuta Sutra
Mahavastu
Pali Canon
Plato's Republic
Prajnaparamita
Q
Quran
Rigveda
Samayabhedoparacanacakra
Sariputraparipriccha
Tattvasiddhi Sastra
Theragatha
Therigatha
Torah
Udana
Upanishads
Veda
Yoga Sutras of Patanjali
Zohar

Bibliographic References

Allen, C. *The Buddha and Dr. Führer.* London: Haus Publishing, 2008.

Baipai, Omesh, et al. "Phenological Study of Two Dominant Tree Species in Tropical Moist Deciduous Forest from the Northern India." *International Journal of Botany,* 8: 66-72. July 11, 2012. http://scialert.net/fulltext/?doi=ijb.2012.66.72&org=11.

Bertolucci, Bernardo, dir. *Little Buddha* (movie). 1993. Recorded Picture Company. 140 min.

Bodhi, trans. *The Connected Discourses of the Buddha: A New Translation of the Samyutta Nikaya.* Boston: Wisdom Publications, 2000.

———. "Dharma and Non-duality" Access to Insight (Legacy Edition). April 4, 2011. http://www.accesstoinsight.org/lib/authors/bodhi/bps-essay_27.html.

———, trans. *The Numerical Discourses of the Buddha: A Translation of the Anguttara Nikaya.* Boston: Wisdom Publications, 2012. http://www.accesstoinsight.org/lib/authors/bodhi/bps-essay_27.html.

———. "Sutta-Nipata: The Oldest Discourses in the Pali Canon." http://bodhimonastery.org/sutta-nipata.html.

Brahm, Ajahn. "Buddhism and Alien Abductions" (video). April 26, 2015. https://www.youtube.com/watch?v=eLvNFS1VCNU.

Chapman, David. "Theravada Reinvents Meditation." https://meaningness.wordpress.com/2011/07/07/theravada-reinvents-meditation.

Cowell, E.B., F. Max Muller, and J. Takakusu, trans. *Buddhist Mahayana Texts.* Sacred Books of the East. Vol. XLIX. Oxford, 1894; rpt. New York, Dover, 1969.

Dhammika. "Footprints in the Dust: A Study of the Buddha's Travels." http://www.bhantedhammika.net/essays/footprints-in-the-dust-a-study-of-the-buddhas-travels.

Dipananda, B.D. "Banning Ajan Brahm's Speech on Nuns Was a Spectacular Own-Goal." May 30, 2014. https://www.buddhistdoor.net/features/banning-ajahn-brahms-speech-on-nuns-was-a-spectacular-own-goal.

Duncan, Alexander (Tseten Thokmey). "Beyond Good and Evil: The Story of Angulimala" (blog post). August 11, 2012. https://palisuttas.wordpress.com/2012/08/11/beyond-good-and-evil-the-story-of-angulimala.

———, trans. *The Book of the Right Way (Tao Te Ching).* Unpublished.

———. *Conversations with the Buddha: A Reader's Guide to the Digha Nikaya.* 2nd ed. Toronto: Chroniker Press, 2015.

———. *Fundamental View: Ten Talks on the Pali Canon.* Rev. 1st ed. Toronto: Chroniker Press, 2015.

Eliade, Mircea. *A History of Religious Ideas.* Trans. Willard R. Trask. Vol. 2. 1982; rpt. Chicago: University of Chicago Press, 1984.

Evans-Wentz, W.Y. *The Fairy Faith in Celtic Countries.* 1911; rpt. New York: Citadel Press, 1994.

Evola, Julius. *Taoism: The Magic, the Mysticism.* Trans. Guido Stucco. Edmonds, WA: Oriental Classics—Holmes Publishing Group, 1995.

Fausböll, V., trans. *The Sutta-Nipata: A Collection of Discourses, Being One of the Canonical Books of the Buddhists.* Oxford: Clarendon Press, 1881.

Gethin, Rupert. Review of Richard F. Gombrich, *What the Buddha Thought.* H-Buddhism, H-Net Reviews. January, 2012. http://www.h-net.org/reviews/showrev.php?id=31586.

Gombrich, Richard. *How Buddhism Began: The Conditioned Genesis of the Early Teachings.* 2nd ed. London: Routledge Taylor & Francis Group, 2006. http://www.watflorida.org/documents/How%20Buddhism%20Began_Gombrich.pdf.

Gupta, Deep Raj. "Harappan Civilization: An Analysis in Modern Context." *IGNCA Newsletter.* Vol. 5. Sept.-Oct. 2002. http://ignca.nic.in/nl002308.htm.

Gurholt, Anya. "The Androgyny of Enlightenment: Questioning Women's Status in Ancient Indian Religions." Westminster College. McNair Scholars Program. 2004. http://people.westminstercollege.edu/staff/mjhinsdale/Research_Journal_1/anya_paper.pdf.

Horner, I.B., trans. *The Book of the Discipline (Vinaya-Pitaka).* Vol. I: 1938; rpt. Bristol: Pali Text Society, 2014. Vol. II: 1940; rpt. Bristol: Pali Text Society, 2012. Vol. III: 1942; rpt. Bristol: Pali Text Society, 2012. Vol. IV: 1951; rpt. Lancaster: Pali Text Society, 2007.

———, trans. *The Minor Anthologies of the Pali Canon.* Sacred Books of the Buddhists. Vol. VII. Part III. 1975; rpt. Lancaster: Pali Text Society, 2007.

Horner, I.B., N.A. Jayawickrama, and H.S. Gehman, trans. *The Minor Anthologies of the Pali Canon.* Sacred Books of the Buddhists. Vol. XXX. Part IV. 1942; rpt. Oxford: Pali Text Society, 2005.

Kabilsingh, Chatsumarn. "The History of the Bhikkhuni Sang-
    ha." http://archive.thubtenchodron.org/BuddhistNunsMonastic
    Life/LifeAsAWesternBuddhistNun/the_history_of_the_bhikkhu
    ni_sangha.html.
Kirby, Peter. Early Christian Writings. Feb. 1. 2014.
    http://www.earlychristianwritings.com.
Lal, Vinay. "Indus Valley Civilza-
    tion." http://www.sscnet.ucla.edu/southasia/History/Ancient/In
    dus2.html.
Law, Bimala Churn. "Chronology of the Pali Can-
    on." http://www.budsas.org/ebud/ebsuto53.htm.
———. A History of Pali Literature. London: Kegan Paul, Trench, Trub-
    ner, 1933.
Lebkowicz, L.F., T. Ditrich, and P. Pecenko, trans. The Way Things Really
    Are: A Translation of Book IV of the Sutta-Nipata. N.p.: Buddha
    Dharma Education Association,
    n.d. http://www.buddhanet.net/pdf_file/Sutta-nipataBM6.pdf.
Levman, Bryan. "Sakaya Niruttiya Revisit-
    ed." http://www.sareligionuoft.ca/wp-
    content/uploads/2013/01/Levman-sakāya-niruttiyā.pdf.
Lin Yutang, trans. The Wisdom of Laotse. New York: Modern Library –
    Random House, 1948.
Masefield, Peter. Divine Revelation in Pali Buddhism. London: George
    Allen & Unwin, 1986.
Mettanando. "How the Buddha Died." Bangkok Post. May 15, 2001. Also
    published as "Did the Buddha Die of Mesenteric Infarction?"
    May 17, 2000.
    http://www.lankalibrary.com/Bud/buddha_death.htm.
    http://www.budsas.org/ebud/ebdha192.htm.
    http://www.ananda-travel.com/FR/b_death1.htm.
Miller, Robert J., ed. The Complete Gospels.: Annotated Scholars Version.
    3rd ed. San Francisco: Harper Collins–Polebridge Press, 1994.
Mills, L.K., trans. Sutta Nipata. N.p.: Sutta Central,
    2015. https://suttacentral.net/files/snp.pdf.
Nakamura, Hajime. Gotama Buddha: A Biography Based on the Most Re-
    liable Texts. Vol. 1. Tokyo: Kosei Publishing Co., 2000.
Nanamoli and Bodhi, trans. The Middle Length Discourses of the Buddha:
    A New Translation of the Majjhima Nikaya. Boston: Wisdom
    Publications, 1995.

New World Encyclopedia. "Theravada Buddhism." http://www.newworldencyclopedia.org/entry/Theravada_Buddhism.

Norman, K.R., trans. *The Group of Discourses (Sutta Nipata).* 2nd ed. Pali Text Society Translation Series No. 45. Oxford: Pali text Society, 2001.

Nyanaponika and Hellmuth Hecker. *Great Disciples of the Buddha: Their Lives, Their Works, their Legacy.* Ed. Bodhi. Boston: Wisdom Publications, 1997.

Pande, G.C. *Studies in the Origins of Buddhism.* 4th. ed. Motilal Banarsidass, 1995. http://www.ahandfulofleaves.org/documents/Studies%20in%20the%20Origins%20of%20Buddhism_Pande.pdf.

Pannobhasa, trans. *The Atthakavagga.* N.p.: Path Press Publications, 2012.

Powers, John. *A Bull of a Man: Images of Masculinity, Sex, and the Body in Indian Buddhism.* Cambridge, MA: Harvard University Press, 2012.

Rhys Davids, trans. and ed. *The Minor Anthologies of the Pali Canon.* Sacred Books of the Buddhists. Vol. XXXI. Part I. 1931; rpt. Oxford: Pali Text Society, 1996.

Rhys Davids, T.W., and Wm. Stede, eds. (1921–1925). *Pali-English Dictionary.* Rpt. London: Pali Text Society.

Saddhatissa, H.R., trans. *The Sutta-Nipata.* 1985; rpt. Abbingdon: Curzon Press, 1998.

Schuhmacher, Stephan and Gert Woerner, eds. *The Encyclopedia of Eastern Philosophy and Religion: Buddhism, Hinduism, Taoism, Zen.* Boston: Shambhala, 1989.

Spiro, Melford E. *Buddhism and Society: A Great Tradition and Its Burmese Vicissitudes.* Rev. ed. Oakland, CA: University of California Press, 1982.

Sucitto, Ajahn. "What is Theravada?" 21012. http://ajahnsucitto.org/articles/what-is-theravada-2012.

Sujato. "On the 32 Marks" (blog post). April 6, 2011. https://sujato.wordpress.com/2011/04/06/on-the-32-marks.

Sujato and Brahmali. "The Authenticity of the Early Buddhist Texts." http://ocbs.org/wp-content/uploads/2015/09/authenticity.pdf.

Vallee, Jacques. *Passport to Magonia.* 1969; rpt. Daily Grail Publishing, 2014.

Vasu-Mitra. *Origin and Doctrines of Early Indian Buddhist Schools: A Translation of the Hsuan-Chwang Version of Vasumitra's Treatise.* Trans. Jiryo Masuda.
https://www2.ihp.sinica.edu.tw/file/1143INtSgsf.pdf.

Walshe, Maurice, trans. *The Long Discourses of the Buddha: A Translation of the Digha Nikaya.* 1987; rpt. Boston: Wisdom Publications, 1995.

Warder, A.K. *Indian Buddhism.* 3rd rev. ed. Delhi: Motilal Banarsidass, 2000.

Whitehead, Alfred North. *Process and Reality: An Essay in Cosmology.* Corrected Edition. Ed. David Ray Griffin and Donald W. Sherburne. 1929; rpt. New York: Free Press, 1978.

Wilson, Colin. *Alien Dawn: An Investigation into the Contact Experience.* London: Virgin Publishing, 1998.

Woodward, F.L., trans. *The Minor Anthologies of the Pali Canon.* Sacred Books of the Buddhists. Vol. VIII. Part II. 1935; rpt. Oxford: Pali Text Society, 2003.

Wynne, A. "How Old Is the Suttapitaka?" 2003.
http://www.budsas.org/ebud/ebsuto56.htm.